Beneath the
Equator

Beneath the
Equator

CULTURES OF DESIRE,

MALE HOMOSEXUALITY,

AND

EMERGING GAY COMMUNITIES

IN BRAZIL

Richard Parker

Routledge

New York and London

Published in 1999 by
Routledge
29 West 35th Street
New York, NY 10001

Published in Great Britain in 1999 by
Routledge
11 New Fetter Lane
London EC4P 4EE

Printed in the United States of America on acid-free paper
Design: Jack Donner

Library of Congress Cataloging-in-Publication Data

Parker, Richard G. (Richard Guy), 1956–
  Beneath the equator : cultures of desire, male homosexuality, and emerging
gay communities in Brazil / Richard G. Parker.
    p.   cm.
  Includes bibliographical references and index.
  ISBN 0–415–91619–4. — ISBN 0–415–91620–8 (pbk.: alk. paper)
  1. Gays—Brazil. I. Title.
HQ76.2.B6P37 1998
305.9'0664'0981—dc21   98–17428
                                                            CIP

For Vagner, again . . .

There is a mode of vital experience—experience of space and time, of self and others, of life's possibilities and perils—that is shared by men and women all over the world today. I will call this body of experience "modernity." To be modern is to find ourselves in an environment that promises adventure, power, joy, growth, transformation of ourselves and the world—and, at the same time, that threatens to destroy everything we have, everything we know, everything we are. Modern environments and experiences cut across all boundaries of geography and ethnicity, of class and nationality, of religion and ideology; in this sense, modernity can be said to unite all mankind. But it is a paradoxical unity, a unity of disunity; it pours us all into a maelstrom of perpetual disintegration and renewal, of struggle and contradiction, of ambiguity and anguish. To be modern is to be part of a universe in which, as Marx said, "all that is solid melts into air."

Marshall Berman

Contents

Acknowledgments

As in any project that is developed over a period of many years, the individual and institutional debts that one acquires along the way are unavoidably extensive.

Initial field research in Brazil was conducted in 1982, from 1983 to 1984, and in 1986, and was made possible by grants from the Tinker Foundation and the Center for Latin American Studies, a Robert H. Lowie Scholarship from the Department of Anthropology, a Traveling Fellowship in International Relations, and a Graduate Humanities Research Grant from the Graduate Division, all at the University of California, Berkeley; as well as a Fulbright Full Grant and a Grant-in-Aid from the Wenner-Gren Foundation for Anthropological Research. From 1988 through 1989, further fieldwork on the social dimensions of AIDS in Brazil was made possible by grants from the Wenner-Gren Foundation for Anthropological Research as well as the Joint Committee on Latin American Studies of the Social Science Research Council and the American Council of Learned Societies, with funds provided by the National Endowment for the Humanities and the Ford Foundation. From 1989 to 1990, an initial study of the behavioral changes among gay and bisexual men in response to HIV/AIDS was made possible through support from the Social and Behavioural Research Unit of the Global Program on AIDS at the World Health Organization. And from 1990 to 1992, this work was extended through funding provided by the Foundation for the Support of Research in the State of Rio de Janeiro (FAPERJ) as part of its program of cooperation with the State University of Rio de Janeiro, which made it possible for me initially to join the faculty of the Institute of Social Medicine.

In the ensuing years, from 1992 to 1997, at least two lines of funding were central in providing ongoing support for the work that is presented here. Support provided by the Ford Foundation, and later by the John D. and Catherine T. MacArthur Foundation, for the Program on Gender, Sexuality, and Health in the Center for Research and Study of Collective Health (CEPESC) at the Institute of Social Medicine made possible both repeated waves of data collection on sexual behavior and behavior changes as well as a comparative ethnographic study carried out in Rio de Janeiro, São Paulo, and Fortaleza. For the most part simultaneously, from 1993 to 1997, support provided to the Brazilian Interdisciplinary AIDS Association (ABIA) by the USAID/FHI/AIDSCAP Project in Brazil, together with additional funding from the National AIDS Program of the Brazilian Ministry of Health, enabled the development of an extensive program of community mobilization and HIV/AIDS prevention in both Rio de Janeiro and São Paulo, carried out in close collaboration with the Grupo Pela Vidda-Rio de Janeiro (from 1993 to 1995) and the Grupo Pela Vidda-São Paulo (1993 to 1996), as well as with the cooperation of a range of diverse gay rights advocacy organizations in both of these cities.

Over this period, the list of individuals who have contributed in one way or another to the work presented here is even more extensive, and the emotional and intellectual debts can only begin to be enumerated. Special thanks are due, early on in the process, to Joe Carrier, Gil Herdt, Paul Kutsche, and Clark Taylor, all of whom encouraged my work on what at the time seemed to be a relatively risky topic of research in academic anthropology. Roberto Da Matta and Gilberto Velho provided initial institutional affiliations with the Postgraduate Program in Social Anthropology of the Federal University of Rio de Janeiro at the National Museum in Rio de Janeiro. Edward MacRae, Néstor Perlongher, and, especially, Peter Fry, introduced me to the already extensive body of work on homosexuality carried out primarily by anthropologists and sociologists based in Brazil. Joan Dassin helped to facilitate my return to Brazil in order to study the social impact of HIV/AIDS at a time when few people or institutions wanted to assist AIDS research, while Brad Smith, José Barzelatto, Sarah Costa, Stuart Burden, Carmen Barroso, and Maria Eugênia Lemos Fernandes all provided ongoing support and encouragement. John Gagnon influenced my thinking in more ways that he probably realizes, Rosemary Messick provided friendship and support throughout, and Vera Paiva became not only an ally but a trusted friend and confidant.

At the Institute of Social Medicine, thanks are due to Jurandir Freire Costa, Kenneth Camargo Jr., and Claudio J. Struchiner, as well as to Benilton Bezerra Jr., Joel Birman, Sérgio Carrara, Luiz Antonio de Castro Santos, Hésio Cordeiro, Mario Dal Poz, Reinaldo Guimarães, Maria Andrea Loyola, Madel Luz, José Noronha, Tania Salem, Ricardo Tavares, and Renato Veras.

Special thanks are due, as well, to Regina Maria Barbosa, who worked together with me to develop the Program in Gender, Sexuality, and Health and who has been a constant source of support both as a friend and as a colleague. At ABIA, Herbert de Souza helped shape my understanding of AIDS; Claudio Mesquita and Herbert Daniel will never know how much they taught me nor how central their friendship was to me; and Jane Galvão will probably never realize how much her unwavering friendship and all that we have gone through together have meant to me. Finally, in my new home in the HIV Center for Clinical and Behavioral Studies at the New York State Psychiatric Institute and Columbia University, Anke A. Ehrhardt and Zena Stein, as well as Delia Easton, Roberta Leftenant, Barbara Muller, Pat Warne, and Chris White all contributed in different ways to make it possible to complete work on the manuscript.

Neither the research itself nor the crafting of the text would have been possible without extensive help from diverse quarters. I owe special thanks to Rogério Gondim, Telma Martins, and Lígia Kerr Pontes for their help (and friendship) in Fortaleza; to Bia Salgueiro and her colleagues at A 4 Mãos graphics in Rio de Janeiro for putting up with my maddening demands in making and remaking the maps (and for the *companheirismo* of many years of trusted collaboration); and to Eliane Nonato da Silva for such true friendship and for caring for us so well for so many years.

Special thanks are due to my friends and colleagues Dennis Altman, Peter Aggleton, and Roger Lancaster for ongoing conversations, for their time and patience in reading and commenting on various installments of the manuscript over a number of years, and for their prompt willingness to help on a moment's notice as deadlines approached and the author's anxieties increased. While they are in no way responsible for whatever failings remain in the text, they have all contributed centrally to whatever is of value.

Very, very special thanks are due, as well, to Veriano Terto Jr. and Juan Carlos de la Concepción Raxach, who have been partners in the entire enterprise, participating in the research, commenting on rough drafts, tracking down obscure references, preparing feasts of Cuban food, and laughing and joking along the way. They have contributed not only to the making of this text but also to the conditions that have made it possible to carry on.

Finally, thanks are not enough for Vagner de Almeida, who has been an unwavering partner in work and in life, and has taught me through his constant example what it means to live with dignity, solidarity, and love. This book is dedicated to him.

Figures and Tables

Tables

1

Introduction

Beneath the Equator

"Beneath the equator, sin does not exist," the Dutch historian, Gaspar von Barlaeus wrote in 1660, upon his return from travel to Brazil (see Barlaeus 1980; Parker 1991). For nearly four centuries—since the earliest European encounter with what was believed to be the New World—similar images of a world divided, separated into distinct moral universes, north and south of the equator, have become among the most familiar tropes of the western imagination. And within this wider moral vision, sexuality has become a kind of quintessential test case—a fundamental marker of difference within a global system of symbolic exchanges. Much like race, sexuality (above and below the equator) has been neatly packaged as an especially important figure in the range of images used to distinguish North from South, the First World from the Third World, the developed nations from the developing countries.[1] Perhaps the central argument of this book is that such sets of oppositions are largely untenable, and probably always have been. Whatever might have been the case in the past, within the complex global system of the late twentieth century, notions of sexual difference, linked to broader configurations of cultural difference, can no longer be understood along such static and bounded lines. Sexualities, like cultures, can no longer be thought of as neatly unified, internally coherent systems that can somehow be set off and studied, interpreted and understood, compared and contrasted, and held up individually as examples of diversity and difference. On the contrary, sexuality, as much as any other aspect of human life, has increasingly become subject to a range of rapidly accelerating, and often highly disjunctive, processes of change, taking place within the context of the exceptionally complex globalization that has marked the closing decades of the twentieth century (see Appadurai 1996; more generally, see also Harvey 1990). And it is only by seeking to interpret the specificities of local sexual cultures as they are caught up within the cross-currents of these global processes of change that we can begin to move past a largely superficial reading of sexual similarities and differences in order to build up a more complex understanding of the vicissitudes of sexual experience in the contemporary world (see Parker and Gagnon 1995).

This is not to say that all sexual cultures are somehow the same; on the contrary, they quite clearly are not. But it is to say that we can only begin to approach an understanding of their differences to the extent that we are able to situate them within broader processes of history and political economy, developing what might be described as a necessary analytic tension between an emphasis on local meanings and an understanding of global processes (see, for example, Lancaster and di Leonardo 1997; Manderson and Jolly 1997; Parker and Gagnon 1995). And if the need for such a tension is true in seeking to approach sexuality more generally, nowhere is it more evident than in the specific case of homosexuality. Precisely because homosexuality has served, over the course of at least the last century, as the key marker of difference in relation to normative heterosexuality—and hence as one of the central elements in the production and reproduction of the dominant regime of sexual life in contemporary western society (see, in particular, the discussion in Sedgwick 1990)—it has been especially well-suited to the task of distinguishing the western (sexual) self from a nonwestern other.[2] Much of the most important research carried out on homosexuality outside of western Europe and the United States has thus focused on the significant differences that set off the construction of nonwestern homosexualities from the organization of gay and lesbian life in the Anglo-European world (see, for example, Blackwood 1986). Yet, ironically, over the course of the past ten to fifteen years, a number of significant changes have been taking place in the organization of homosexuality both north and south of the equator that have begun to call into question such stark contrasts—what Dennis Altman has recently described as a process of "global queering" (see Altman 1997b)—in which the experience of homosexuality in nonwestern societies would appear to increasingly intersect with gay and lesbian life in the industrialized West, while the once apparent uniformity of the gay and lesbian communities in the western world has increasingly seemed to melt into a more complex diversity that is itself sometimes reminiscent of the cacophonous homosexualities thought to characterize the nonwestern world.

Drawing on research carried out in Brazil over the course of more than fifteen years now, this book is perhaps above all an attempt to illuminate at least some small part of the complex changes that seem to be taking place in the social organization of homosexuality in the late twentieth century. While it focuses in a highly specific way on the contours and changes taking place in contemporary Brazilian society, it simultaneously seeks to offer insight (precisely by attending to the details of the Brazilian case) into a set of processes that I suspect may ultimately prove to be far more wide-ranging in terms of both their extension and impact. By seeking to work at the intersection between the local meanings through which Brazilian homosexualities are lived and experienced, and the global processes that increasingly impinge upon local contexts and meanings, my intention is that the extended interpretation of what I describe as the diverse homosexual subcultures and the emerging gay communities in contemporary Brazilian life may ultimately make some contribution to a fuller understanding of a range of changes taking place in the organization and articulation of diverse sexualities in the late-modern/postmodern world. Ultimately, I would hope that it might also help us to think more broadly not only about the disjunctures that set off distinct realms of experience (sexual, as well as others), but also about the shifting social, cultural, economic, and political flows that today shape this experience in increasingly interconnected ways.[3]

With these concerns in mind, in this brief introduction I want to situate the project and a number of the different currents and concerns that it seeks to respond to. First, I look more closely at some of the dominant ways in which cross-cultural differences in the construction of (almost always male) homosexuality have been interpreted and understood, particularly in social sciences such as anthropology, over the course of the 1980s and 1990s. Then I turn briefly to the emergence, roughly over the same period of time, of what has come to be known as gay and lesbian studies and, more recently, queer theory, and to look at some of the interpretive possibilities that these recent developments may open up, as well as some of the limitations that, thus far at least, have in large part characterized this rapidly expanding body of work. With these issues in mind, I will then describe the ways in which my own work has evolved in Brazil over more than fifteen years now—the broader collective project within which it has been developed, the limitations that necessarily characterize it, and so on. Finally, I will briefly outline the structure of the book, give the reader a sense of the major sources of data that it will draw on and the terrain that it will seek to cover, and define at least some of its key goals.

Homosexuality, North and South

For nearly twenty years now, the vast majority of social science research on homosexuality has been dominated (both explicitly as well as implicitly) by an increasingly tired debate between notions of essentialism and constructionism (see, for example, Stein 1992). Theoretical arguments as well as professional animosities have in large part revolved around the extent to which a given reading falls on one side or another of the essentialist/constructionist divide—the extent to which homosexuality is interpreted, on the one hand, as everywhere a universal part of our biological or psychological nature or, on the other, as the construct of specific social, cultural, political, and economic systems. The limitations of such polarized theoretical formulations have been discussed at length elsewhere (see, for example, Altman et al. 1989; Plummer 1992; Vance 1991; Weeks 1985). What is perhaps most striking, however, at least within the present context, is the extent to which this theoretical polarization has led, ironically on both sides of the essentialist/constructionist divide, to an almost exclusive emphasis on the juxtaposition of radical difference in cross-cultural analysis—as opposed to attempts to situate and interpret such difference within broader interacting systems.

Both essentialist and social constructionist traditions have placed the focus on the apparent differences between us and them—which cross-culturally have translated into the repeated oppositions between civilized and primitive, developed and underdeveloped, North and South, and so on. In both the essentialist as well as the constructionist frameworks, homosexuality in the industrialized West has thus been contrasted with radically different manifestations of homosexuality in nonwestern societies in order to illustrate the workings of a particular theoretical paradigm. In the case of more blatantly essentialist readings, the goal has been to build up a portrait of sexual diversity in order to ultimately unmask such differences as striking, yet in actual fact superficial, manifestations of a deeper underlying, and ultimately unifying, reality; arcane ethnographic accounts of same-sex interactions in exotic cultures have thus been mined in order to compile a record of gay and lesbian people as a kind of universal expression of human sexuality independent of time or place. In the case of more constructionist readings, however, the goal has been to emphasize sexual difference in order to radically oppose the ontological constitution of apparently similar behavioral phenomena in distinct social settings—to describe and document exotic homosexualities as perhaps the key example of the ways in which distinct social and cultural traditions construct and constitute unique (and consequently not reducible) sexual worlds. Yet in both cases, in spite of their very different premises and goals, one of the key outcomes of such debates has thus generally been to draw research attention and theoretical reflection to focus on sharply opposed contrasts between *our* homosexuality and *theirs*— between the gay and lesbian communities of the Anglo-European world and the contrasting organization of gay (or homosexual) life, identities, and the like, in diverse nonwestern settings.

Over the course of recent decades, attention and debate have of course evolved—indeed, fashions have changed as much in the analysis of homosexuality as in any other area of scholarly debate (see Plummer 1992). But attention has been called recurrently to images of radical difference as the point of departure for debate. In the late 1970s and early 1980s, for example, forms of ritualized homosexuality described in great detail by Gilbert Herdt among the Sambia (see Herdt 1981, 1987; Herdt and Stoller 1990), and in less detail but equally vivid terms by a range of other researchers working throughout highland New Guinea and Melanesia (see, for example, Herdt 1984; Kelly 1976; Schiefflin 1976; see also Blackwood 1986), captured the anthropological imagination and were rapidly transformed into perhaps the quintessential expression of cross-cultural homosexual difference in a range of comparative analyses over the course of the next decade (see, for example, Gilmore 1990; Greenberg 1988; Lindenbaum 1989). Shortly thereafter, renewed interest in the Native American berdache (and parallel, indigenous, South American figures) became increasingly fashionable, providing yet another standard character in debates focusing on sexuality, gender, and the diversity of homoerotic practice (see, for example, Roscoe 1991; Whitehead 1981; Williams 1986; see also Blackwood 1986; Gregor 1985). Indeed, over the course of the 1980s, a range of "primitive" homosexualities were thus documented and debated, in some cases interpreted with great sophistication and nuance as the constructs of complex sociocultural systems, and in others as the superficial manifestation of our underlying human diversity—yet, intentionally or not, consistently reinforcing notions of (homo)sexual difference as among the key characteristics used to distinguish the West from the Rest.

By the late 1980s and early 1990s, particularly in the wake of the global AIDS pandemic, the collection of homoerotic exotica became all the more intense, driven now not merely by academic interests but also by practical exigencies in responding to the epidemic. Within this context, the construction of contrasting homosexual types took on added force— debates about whether or not homosexuality (both behaviors and identities) even exists in Africa came to be the focus of significant attention (both in Africa as well as abroad [see Aina 1991; Cohen and Trussell 1996; Lindenbaum 1989; Sheperd 1987; Standing and Kisekka 1989]). Such debates, in turn, were quickly juxtaposed to the altogether new intellectual configuration of "men who have sex with men" in Asia and Latin America (and, later, in even more complicated fashion, among a range of ethnic minorities in the industrialized West), as opposed to gay men (and lesbians) in the Anglo-European world (see, for example, the discussions in Aggleton 1996; Daniel and Parker 1993; Dowsett 1993; Parker and Gagnon 1995; Tan 1994, 1995).

The ironic underside of this process has been that at the same time that a notion of homosexual diversity in the nonwestern world has taken shape as a kind of loosely organized encyclopedia of exotica, we have also seen the simplification of gay and lesbian experience in the industrialized West. Particularly in the wake of HIV/AIDS, a notion of "the gay community" has been consolidated as a kind of Weberian ideal type and has been configured in common sense as well as in much of the research literature, as though it were somehow unified and unitary—often taken for granted as white, male, middle class, and Anglo-Saxon, in spite of the incredibly limited view that such an understanding implies (on the problematic notion of gay community, see, for example, Murray 1996; Plummer 1992; Whittle 1994). Yet as questionable as such a vision obviously is, it is in many ways the image that has been constructed in opposition to the radical difference of the Rest. If the Sambia in highland New Guinea (or perhaps the Native American berdache) has thus become a kind of quintessential homosexual other, then festive crowds of largely middle-class, white men from the Castro in San Francisco (or Greenwich Village in New York) have thus become the key image of the western (gay) self.

It is important to remember that such arguments and analyses are not simply naive or wrong-headed. On the contrary, they have often been rooted in carefully conducted, long-term research (such as Herdt's work on the Sambia). Similarly, they have often been strategically useful as a way of deconstructing ultimately problematic biomedical notions of a kind of universal sexual naturalism—as in the use of "men who have sex with men" in order to problematize the unreflexive application of western epidemiological models and HIV/AIDS prevention interventions in potentially inappropriate social settings and cultural contexts. But they are also problematic representations in a late-modern or postmodern world that is no longer clearly organized (if indeed it ever was even in the first place) in terms of such extremes. Although notions of North and South, the developed as opposed to the developing world, center and periphery, the First World and the Third World, and so on, are obviously still powerful symbolic configurations, with a profound impact on the way in which the global system functions (see, for example, Buell 1994; Smart 1993; Waters 1995), they in large part fail to describe the ways in which the world is in fact experienced today—and this is as true, I would argue, for the experience of homosexuality as it is for any other aspect of contemporary life.

In short, to be able to move toward a fuller understanding of same-sex relations and experience in different social and cultural settings, we must also seek to move past the theoretical configurations that operate in large part through relatively simplistic comparison and contrast. Whether in the search for essential sameness or in the affirmation of radical differ-ence, we are pushed in the direction of superficial extremes, which ulti-mately fail to grasp the often messy reality of life in the contemporary, globalized or globalizing, late-modern or postmodern world—a world in which things often fail to fit neatly or hold coherently together, but in which a set of complex relationships does in fact exist and is marked by processes of social, cultural, economic, and political change that ulti-mately link both the West and the Rest as part of an interacting system. Although these processes and inter-relationships have in general been more carefully examined with regard to what are perceived to be less per-sonal or intimate concerns, they are no less important in relation to the intimacies of sexual experience—and perhaps of homosexuality and gay life in particular. It is ultimately only by turning our attention to them more fully that we may be able gradually to build more complete under-standings of the forces that most powerfully shape such experience, whether North or South, in late twentieth-century life.

Gay Studies and Queer Theory

In seeking to break down, at least in part, the most blatant forms of over-simplification built up around notions of sexual difference, the gradual emergence, first, of gay and lesbian studies and, more recently, of what has been described as queer theory, would seem to offer a growing range of theoretical and methodological possibilities. Although a detailed discus-sion of the development of lesbian and gay research over the course of roughly the past two decades is beyond the scope of the present study—and has already been ably developed elsewhere by writers such as Jeffrey Escoffier and Ken Plummer (see Escoffier 1992; Plummer 1992; see also Abelove, Barale, and Halperin 1993)—it is nonetheless important to call attention to the extent to which these emerging fields offer new concep-tual insights and interpretive tools capable of contributing to a fuller understanding of the complex processes of change that, I am convinced, currently impact upon the organization and experience of diverse homo-sexualities both inside and outside of the Anglo-European world. Drawing on recent developments across a variety of different disciplinary tradi-tions, increasingly sophisticated theoretical and methodological approaches have made it possible to move beyond many of the limitations that have characterized the interpretation of sexual difference in the past, and have offered examples of how to begin to recoup exotic readings of homosexuality in nonwestern settings and to situate them in more useful interpretive frameworks.

This is perhaps especially true with regard to recent gay and lesbian historiography. For a time, historical studies of homosexuality tended to produce the same kinds of oppositions that characterized many early anthropological studies—oscillating between largely worn-out poles of essentialism and constructionism, between what might be described as a search for gays throughout history as opposed to the detailed description of radical ruptures that would seem to separate modern homosexuality from the very different organization of same-sex relations in different chronological periods. Increasingly, however, more nuanced readings of historical data (influenced both by ethnographic approaches as well as by contemporary literary theory) have begun to emerge and to open the way for a fuller understanding of different modes of organization in the structure of same-sex social milieus and networks, which nonetheless maintain a sensitivity to broader, and more long-term, social, cultural, economic and political processes (see, for example, Duberman, Vicinus, and Chauncey 1989; Weeks 1991). In a range of recent studies, for example, careful attention to the details of real lives as well as the structuring conditions of broader social and historical forces has helped to open the way for a reconfiguration and reappropriation of lesbian and gay history that has increasingly succeeded in reframing questions of sexual and cultural difference in relation to more nuanced understandings of social process (see, for example, Chauncey 1994; Kennedy and Davis 1993; Plummer 1992).

Like lesbian and gay history (though perhaps more timidly), lesbian and gay studies in anthropology have also expanded rapidly in recent years (see Herdt 1997; Weston 1993), offering at least some hope of an increasingly sophisticated interpretation of changing homosexualities not only through time but also across space (and hence, at least, the possibility of building the basis for a more complex form of cross-cultural comparison). Much important research has been carried out on the variability of the cultural categories and classifications that map out same-sex experience in distinct social contexts, making possible more nuanced readings of the constitution of sexual subcultures in different settings (see, for example, Herdt 1992; Lancaster 1992; Parker 1991). Increasingly, historical concerns have also been incorporated in cross-cultural anthropological investigation, providing new insight into the ways in which same-sex networks and communities take shape differentially over time within distinct social and cultural milieus (see, for example, Newton 1993). And in many recent studies, a careful focus on the contours of specific, contextualized, life histories has made it possible to more fully apprehend the ways in which different milieus, in turn, shape and structure the personal experience of women and men involved in same-sex relations (see, for example, Carrier 1995; Herdt and Boxer 1993; Lancaster 1992; Lewin 1993; Weston 1991).

These advances in fields such as history and anthropology have been important, but it is perhaps above all in literary criticism and cultural studies that a veritable boom industry in feminist interpretive practice and postmodern readings of both elite and popular cultures has also spilled over into gay and lesbian studies, offering more specific analyses of the structures of thought, knowledge, and perception that have shaped our understandings of homosexuality (and heterosexuality) in western culture (see, for example, Bleys 1996; Edelman 1994; Fuss 1991; Sedgwick 1990). The development of feminist and antiheterosexist literary criticism and cultural studies has been extended, in turn, in the recent development of queer theory, leading to especially creative possibilities for the juxtaposition of questions related to identity, intersubjectivity, and textualities, on the one hand, to issues such as gender performance, racial and ethnic diversity, and socioeconomic class, on the other (see, in particular, de Lauretis 1991).

These recent developments have offered important new insights that have helped us to rethink the kind of oversimplistic oppositions that have traditionally characterized the cross-cultural analysis of homosexuality and gay life. In particular, they have moved us forward by breaking down earlier, monolithic, notions of "gay (and lesbian) community" in the Anglo-European world. By focusing on questions of internal difference, gender power, race and ethnicity, social class, and so on, such approaches have thus pushed in the direction of more dialectical understandings of the relationship between local contexts and cultures, on the one hand, and broader social and historical processes, on the other (see Plummer 1992).

For the most part, however, these advances in our understandings of Anglo-European gay cultures and communities have only to a very limited extent been applied in research on nonwestern homosexualities. In spite of a gradually growing body of work focusing on homosexuality outside of North America and Western Europe, relatively few studies have been able to build up more complex understandings of same-sex experience in specific settings outside of the Anglo-European world. And even to the extent that a small number of studies have been able to develop more sophisticated analyses of the interface between local sexual cultures and broader social processes,[4] the fact remains that, with relatively few exceptions, the impact on same-sex experience of the massive social, cultural, and economic changes currently taking place on a global level, and within a global system, has in large part been ignored. A concern with building a more nuanced understanding of alternative sexualities, queer identities, and diverse lesbian and gay communities in the Anglo-European world has for the most part not been accompanied by more systematic or concerted efforts to understand the complex and rapid changes taking place in both the conceptualization and the social organization of homosexual experience in the societies and cultures of the non-Anglo-European world—in short, among the Rest in the societies of Asia, Africa, and Latin America that make up the vast majority of the human population in the contemporary world.

It is really only in the past few years, stimulated perhaps more than anything else by the international AIDS pandemic, and by the social and cultural responses to HIV/AIDS around the world, that a growing sense of the interconnectedness of late twentieth century life has led at least a few of us to begin to think more directly about the ways in which changes taking place at the global level impact upon the lived experience of sexuality at the local level—about the ways in which recent changes in the global system have influenced all aspects of daily life, including sexual life, in what is still understood (rather inappropriately) as the developing world.[5] Dennis Altman was one of the first to call attention to the ways in which such global processes have begun to impact upon the lived realities of diverse homosexualities in countries around the world.[6] In a series of seminal exploratory articles, Altman has suggested that forces of global change now play a fundamental role in the configuration and reconfiguration of local sexualities (both North and South)—and, in particular, in the formation of gay identities and communities in many developing-country settings that, until quite recently, would seem to have organized the experience of same-sex relations and homosexual lives in very different ways (see Altman 1995a, 1995b, 1995c, 1996, 1997a, 1997b; for a number of similar arguments, see also Herdt 1997: 150–52).

While Altman's provocative ideas have drawn, as usual, a good deal of polemic (see Altman 1997b), and are clearly only in the very initial stages of elaboration, Altman has nonetheless called attention to the urgent need for a return, particularly within the context of lesbian and gay studies, from the current preoccupation with literary theory and cultural studies (as crucial as their contributions have been) to a renewed emphasis on social and political theory. He has suggested that this emphasis should focus, perhaps above all else, on the key processes of change shaping life on a truly global scale in the late twentieth century, and has argued for a renewed focus on the empirical detail of homosexual lives as they are lived in specific settings of the so-called developing world. He has called our attention to the need to move beyond superficial stereotypes (that often take shape as either a romantic longing for a world that in large part no longer exists, or a premature celebration of freedoms that have yet to be constructed), and to try to look, on the ground, at what in fact seems to be going on in real people's lives (see Altman 1995b, 1995c, 1996, 1997a, 1997b).

However limited it may be by the boundaries of my own training and the horizons of my own situation, this book is in many ways my own attempt to take up this challenge, to build upon the analytic space that has been opened up in recent years through lesbian and gay studies, queer theory, HIV/AIDS research, and related efforts, and to try to offer some insight—based on work carried out for more than fifteen years now in one specific setting—into the complex processes of change that seem to be taking place in the organization and experience of homosexuality and gay life in an unavoidably interconnected world. Before going any further, then, it is important to at least briefly describe the development of the work leading up to this current study, and to highlight just how much my own work—like my understanding of the world and, ultimately, even the shape of my life—has been conditioned and molded by the very processes of change that this book seeks to highlight.

Anthropology (Through the Looking Glass? Over the Rainbow?)

For better or worse, the bulk of my experience over the last fifteen years would hardly have been possible were it not for the very processes that this book seeks to explore—in particular, the impact upon the local organization of homosexual life (in this specific case, within Brazilian society) of the accelerating pace of globalization, the rapid spread of and response to HIV/AIDS internationally, and the continuing changes that have been brought about in a remarkable range of areas by the evolving gay and lesbian movement. When I first went to Brazil in the early 1980s as part of my doctoral training in social and cultural anthropology, I could hardly have imagined the ways in which these different forces would change my life (and anything that I might have expected for it) over the course of the next decade and a half.

I traveled to Brazil in 1982 to initiate research on the politics of popular culture for my doctoral dissertation in social and cultural anthropology at the University of California, Berkeley. At the time, the notion of focusing on sexuality, let alone homosexuality, as an object of study seemed incredibly remote—an almost suicidal move in terms of the contracting job market in my field and the long-standing marginalization of things sexual as legitimate issues within the hierarchy of academic values.

Yet in spite of such concerns (real enough, of course, but also easily forgotten in the excitement of one's first experience in the field), as time passed much of my intellectual attention increasingly came to focus on sexuality, as I sought to make some sense of the new sexual universe that I had suddenly parachuted into—patterns in both behavior and meaning that were at once partially recognizable yet strangely distorted or different from what I was familiar with, a bit like the reflection of one's own image in a house of mirrors. While the analogy seems a bit worn to me now, I remember at the time commenting to friends that I felt a bit like Alice passing through the looking glass—ultimately finding my feet, of course, even if in a somewhat unfamiliar terrain, but continuing to feel more than a little unsettled by the series of odd events and perplexing meanings everywhere around me.

This relatively abstract intellectual curiosity in the construction of sexual meanings in Brazil was quickly transformed into an intensely personal affair, however, when early on in my fieldwork I met Vagner de Almeida, a Brazilian playwright and actor who would become my partner in both work and life for more than fifteen years now. Bridging cultural gaps, making sense out of one another's understandings of the world, finding a way to mediate differences without ignoring or disrespecting them, all became crucial issues in seeking to make my way in day-to-day life. Other concerns (academic respectability, professional future, etc.) rapidly receded from view as I sought to work through my own personal immersion in the dilemma of sexuality and cultural difference by making this dilemma the central focus of my work.

By chance, historical accident, or what have you, by the time I had finished my first extended period of fieldwork in Brazil, and Vagner and I had returned to the United States in mid-1984, both the early precursors of gay and lesbian studies as a new area of intellectual concern, as well as the initial impact of HIV/AIDS (ominously announcing what was to lie ahead, both in the United States as well as in Brazil) had already begun. While I continued to develop a detailed study of what I described, in quite general terms, as Brazilian sexual culture (see, in particular, Parker 1991), I also became increasingly convinced of the need to work in a more focused way on HIV/AIDS, and on the impact of the epidemic not only on Brazilian society as a whole, but in particular on the lives of men who have sex with men. Ultimately, it was this set of concerns that would lead me back to Brazil, and to the research that has become the focus of the current volume.

By the time I finished my doctoral dissertation at Berkeley in early 1988, Vagner and I had already decided to return to Brazil. When faced with the dilemma of how to manage two careers, the possibilities of combining his work in theater with my own work in anthropology seemed less realistic in the United States than in Brazil, where he would be able to work in his field again while I tried to develop a new study that would examine the social impact of AIDS—an issue that was still almost altogether unexplored by Brazilian researchers in spite of the size that the epidemic had rapidly assumed (see Parker 1987; Daniel and Parker 1991, 1993). By the time we arrived in Brazil in 1988, however, I had already begun to revise my analogy from Alice falling through the looking glass to Dorothy confiding in Toto that they probably weren't in Kansas anymore—a fairly frequent (humorous/sarcastic) take on migrating from the Midwest in order to be part of gay life in California or New York (especially in the Castro or Greenwich Village), which struck me as actually far more appropriate to the often fantastic/surrealistic world that I now became part of south of the equator.

Over the course of the next ten years, I had the opportunity to work in a range of different settings, and with a truly remarkable group of colleagues. Through mid-1997 (when I returned to the United States to take up a new position in the HIV Center for Clinical and Behavioral Studies at Columbia University and the New York State Psychiatric Institute in New York City), I was based at the Institute of Social Medicine at the State University of Rio de Janeiro, where I joined the staff as a visiting professor from 1989 through 1991 and became a regular tenured professor in 1992. Beginning in 1989, together with a number of colleagues and students at the Institute, I was able to build upon earlier ethnographic work and to initiate a long-term study of the response to HIV/AIDS on the part of homosexual and bisexual men in urban Brazil that would ultimately become the basis for the current examination of the changing organization of gay life in Brazil.

Over much the same period, I also worked closely with ABIA, the Brazilian Interdisciplinary AIDS Association, one of the first nongovernmental AIDS-service and advocacy organizations formed in response to the HIV/AIDS epidemic in Brazil, where I continue to serve as a member of the board of directors even today. Shortly after my return to Brazil in 1988, I had formed a deep friendship and intellectual partnership with Herbert Daniel, a writer as well as a gay and AIDS activist who founded the first organization of people living with AIDS in Brazil, and who served as executive director of ABIA until his death in March of 1992. Daniel and I worked together intensely for a number of years, publishing two collections of essays on sexuality, politics, and AIDS in Brazil (one in Portuguese and the other in English [see Daniel and Parker 1991, 1993]). I ultimately joined ABIA as executive director at Daniel's request when he became seriously ill in late 1991. From then on, much of my time and energy would focus on AIDS advocacy work, as well as on the need to build effective coalitions involving AIDS activists, the growing Brazilian feminist movement, and the more nascent, but nonetheless important, gay and lesbian movement. Together with colleagues at ABIA (many of whom have also been students at the Institute of Social Medicine) and in conjunction with my ongoing research activities, from 1992 through 1997 I also participated actively in the development of AIDS prevention activities, and helped to design and develop the first large-scale intervention for men who have sex with men in Rio de Janeiro and São Paulo (see Parker 1994; Parker et al. 1995; Parker and Terto 1998; Terto 1994).

The details of the work carried out within these settings over the past decade could of course be extended at length—and would perhaps even be of some interest were the focus here on the process of anthropological fieldwork, the kinds of issues involved in developing long-term cross-cultural research and collaboration, or the remarkable dilemmas involved in becoming not exactly a native, but at least an actor accepted on more or less equal terms within a given (native) sphere of work.[7] In the present context, however, I must be clear about ways in which the material presented here is conditioned by the context in which my work has evolved—indeed, the ways in which my own perspective, and the interpretations that I make, are necessarily situated within and contingent upon this context. With this in mind, at least three important caveats should be made explicit.

First, for better or worse, my own life is implicated in the work that is presented here in ways that are impossible to ignore. Far more than may be the case in much anthropological research, the personal and the professional intertwine. Were it not for an intense personal relationship with a Brazilian partner, it is possible that neither sexuality nor homosexuality would have been the focus for much of my work. Were it not for this relationship, it is unlikely that I ever would have had the kind of access that I had to a whole network of friends and informants who shaped my understanding of Brazilian life.[8] Were it not for the long-term evolution of this relationship, it is unlikely that I ever would have returned to live and work in Brazil for an extended period. And were it not for the tragic ways in which the AIDS epidemic (linked as it has been to sexuality and homosexuality) would enter our personal life, our network of friends, the communities that we identified with, it is equally unlikely that the kind of work I developed would look at all (for better or worse) like what it in fact turned out to be. While underlying personal concerns are probably always present in relation to any body of work, they are surely especially present in relation to my work on homosexuality and AIDS in Brazil, and they are inextricably linked to the issues that I try to explore here.

The second caveat, in some ways linked to the first but also extending beyond it, is the extent to which the analysis developed here emerges from an intersection between academic research and activism. In part, this intersection has grown out of the very decision to return to Brazil, since the space for an exclusively academic career, in Brazil as in many other developing countries (and in sharp opposition to the dominant patterns at least in North America), is exceptionally limited. The immense social problems facing Brazilian society are simply too pressing, and the consequent pressure for scientists and intellectuals to confront these issues in more socially and politically engaged ways is a constant part of daily life. There is little room for disengaged reflection. And the stakes are only all the higher, of course, in the midst of an epidemic. Again, for better or worse, just as my understanding of the questions explored in this book has been unavoidably conditioned (perhaps simultaneously limited and expanded) by my own personal life and trajectory, it has also been shaped by what Brazilians would describe as my *dupla militância* (double militancy) as both academic and activist—and hence by my own engagement as an actor in many of the processes that are described and analyzed here. There is no privileged vantage point from which to offer an objective interpretation free from the biases of my position in a given hermeneutic circle, and the best that I can do in this regard is simply to try to make my own situated reading as explicit as possible and to use this situatedness, in a sense, as an advantage offering me the possibility of at least some insights that would be impossible were it not for my particular perspective.

Finally, the third caveat, which in no ways cancels out the first and second but perhaps decenters them in a number of important ways: given the peculiar ways in which my work has evolved, perhaps far more than is normally the case (or at least assumed), it is anything but an individual project developed by a single researcher. On the contrary, while I must of course assume responsibility for errors of analysis and interpretation, it is fundamentally important to stress how much the arguments developed here are part of a much broader collective project, involving a range of partially overlapping communities. At the most general level, this work would be unimaginable were it not for the broader development, touched on above, of lesbian and gay studies in social and cultural anthropology more generally—and of a growing community of researchers working on sexuality and homosexuality in Latin/o America more specifically. Although my own arguments are often at odds with those of at least some researchers and writers working in this field (see, for example, Murray 1995), the possibility of the work that I have carried out, the kinds of issues that I have been able to address, and the conclusions that I have reached have all nonetheless been shaped and nurtured along the way by this community. Whatever impact this study may have will in large part depend upon the ways in which it intersects with the broader concerns of this community and contributes in some way to pushing our (collective) work forward.

For a number of different reasons, the study of homosexuality in Latin America seems to have drawn special attention over the course of the past twenty years—to have been an unusually rich part of the cross-cultural investigation of sexuality and, in particular, of homosexuality. When I was a student in the late 1970s, groundbreaking work had already been initiated in a range of settings, principally by anthropologists like Joe Carrier (1971, 1985, 1995) and Clark Taylor (1978, 1985) working in Mexico. By the early to mid-1980s, a kind of second wave of research had begun to emerge in the work of researchers such as Roger Lancaster (1988, 1992, 1995, 1997) and Barry Adam (1993) in Nicaragua; and Paul Kutsche (1983, 1995; see also Kutsche and Page 1991) in Costa Rica. And by the mid- to late 1980s, in the wake of the emerging HIV/AIDS pandemic, yet another wave of research virtually exploded across Latin America, and even north of the border, with the work of researchers such as Carlos Cáceres (1996) in Peru; M. González Block and Ana Louisa Ligouri (1992), José Antônio Izazola (1994), Hector Carrillo-Rosado (1994), Carter Wilson (1995), and Annick Prieur (1996) in Mexico; Ian Lumsden in Mexico and Cuba (1991, 1996); Jacobo Schifter and Johnny Madrigal (1992) in Costa Rica; Tim Frasca (1997) in Chile; Tim Wright in Bolivia (see Wright 1993; Wright and Wright 1997); Antonio de Moya and Rafael García (1996) in the Dominican Republic; and Ana Luisa Alonso and Maria Teresa Koreck (1989), Tomás Almoguer (1991), Alex Carballo-Diéguez (1989), and Rafael Díaz (1997) among diverse Latino populations living in the United States. As the list of names would seem to suggest, over time this expanding research community has become increasingly indigenous—comprised not only of Anglo-European anthropologists or sociologists but also of Latin American and Latino American scholars from diverse disciplines. The original dominance of social and cultural anthropologists has given way to multidimensional and multidisciplinary perspectives involving sociology, social psychology, and even epidemiology.

If a community working on issues related to homosexuality in Latin America as a whole has been central in framing the social and intellectual space for the current study, just as central has been the exceptionally large and active research community in Brazil. Indeed, probably nowhere else in Latin America has such an extensive body of work been carried out on gay (and, to a lesser extent, lesbian) issues, and my own research has been little more than an extension of this broader body of work. Again, the development of this work over the past fifteen to twenty years has taken place in a number of distinct phases. Even well before this more recent period, a ground-breaking study had been published by José Fábio Barbosa da Silva (1959). Beginning in the mid-1970s, important research began to be carried out by Alan Young (1972), Carmen Dora Guimarães (1974), Fredrick Whitam (1979), Peter Fry (1982; see also Fry and MacRae 1983), Edward MacRae (1983, 1990, 1992), Herbert Daniel and Leila Míccolis (1983), as well as by João Silvério Trevisan (1986) and Néstor Perlongher (1987). Luiz Mott has carried out significant historical and anthropological work for nearly two decades now (see, for example, Mott 1985, 1986, 1988, 1995). More recently, Jurandir Freire Costa (1992, 1995) has made an important contribution, and a range of younger researchers have become active, including Veriano Terto Jr. (1989, 1996, 1997), Carlos Alberto Messeder Pereira (1979, 1994), Rommel Mendes-Leite (1993), Hélio Silva (1993; see also Silva and Florentino 1996), Patrick Larvie (1997), Jared Braiterman (1994), Charles Klein (1996, 1998), Don Kulick (1997), Fernando Seffner (1995), Fabiano de Souza Gontijo (1995), and James N. Green (1996).[9] Interestingly, a good portion of this work has been carried out by foreigners who, like myself, have lived and worked in Brazil on a long-term basis, and a certain cosmopolitan interface between local research traditions and international or global research communities seems especially pronounced, with a degree of intellectual exchange that is probably not unique but is nonetheless significant, especially when compared with many other parts of Latin America. Again, as in relation to the broader Latin/o American research community, the arguments developed here are built upon the foundation provided by this body of work; while they seek to extend it in a variety of ways that I think are largely new, they would be impossible outside of the context provided by the broader discourse on Brazilian homosexualities and the research community that sustains this discourse.

Finally, but perhaps most significantly, it is important to emphasize just how much the current study emerges from a collective project involving a group of collaborators who are in important ways the coauthors of this text. While my work in Brazil began, in traditional anthropological fashion, as an essentially individual enterprise, it has evolved, at least since my return to Brazil in 1988, as an increasingly interdisciplinary and fundamentally collaborative undertaking that has involved a large group of collaborators at both the Institute of Social Medicine and at ABIA. As in any research group that evolves over a reasonable period of time, there have been comings and goings over the course of the past decade. Nonetheless, the work reported here counted on the ongoing participation of Vagner de Almeida, Regina Maria Barbosa, Juan Carlos de la Concepción Raxach, Jurandir Freire Costa, Jane Galvão, Katia Guimarães, Maria Luiza Heilborn, Murilo Peixoto da Mota, Veriano Terto Jr., and Anna Paula Uziel. In recent years it has extended beyond the boundaries of the institutions where I have been based in Rio de Janeiro to involve colleagues and institutions in São Paulo, where Maria Eugênia Lemos Fernandes and the FHI AIDSCAP Project/Brazil have collaborated with our work, and in Fortaleza, where Rogério Gondim of the AIDS Prevention Support Group-Ceará, Lígia Kerr Pontes of the Federal University of Ceará, and Telma Martins of State AIDS Program in Ceará have been key partners. While the conventions (and the actual process) of authorship often tend to disguise the collective nature of the text, it is thus important to emphasize the extent to which the current book has been built up as a joint venture on the part of an interdisciplinary team of investigators—as well as the fact that it is only one among a number of texts that have been prepared by members of this team in order to present findings from the work carried out on different aspects of sexuality and homosexuality in contemporary Brazilian life.[10]

What has emerged then, and what forms the basis for the analyses developed here, is in many ways a far cry from the kind of anthropology that I was originally trained in during the late 1970s and early '80s. In a sense, my perspective has probably been shaped less by the traditional demands (and expectations) of the discipline than by the unexpected contingencies of my own personal life and by the new challenges that have emerged in large part across disciplinary boundaries (in both lesbian and gay studies and HIV/AIDS research) over the course of the past decade—a kind of hybrid, in which the personal and the professional mix together in complex ways, in which analytic distance and activist engagement must be constantly juxtaposed and mediated, and in which the traditional roles of outsider and insider are perhaps unusually difficult to manage. Yet, at the same time, as I have tried to emphasize, it is also perhaps symptomatic of an increasingly interconnected world in which relations of time and space, of cultural difference and sexual diversity, have changed with unprecedented velocity—a world in which the effects of phenomena as apparently distinct as economic and cultural globalization, migration and population movement, technological innovation, and the global HIV/AIDS pandemic have combined to reinvent sexual cultures, identities, and communities in countries around the globe. This book seeks to understand more fully some of the ways in which these processes of change have taken place within this specific context—the impact that they have had in refiguring and reimagining homosexuality and the possibilities of gay life in contemporary Brazilian society.

Beneath the Equator

With these basic goals in mind, I will briefly sketch out the sources of data that I draw upon, some of the choices that I have made in seeking to define the scope of the current study, and the structure that I have adopted for the pages to follow.

At least three different (though interrelated) sets of data have been used, either directly or indirectly, in developing the current study. First, and perhaps most important, my own ethnographic fieldwork, initiated in 1982 and carried on periodically through 1988, has been extended systematically by a team of researchers working together with me in at least three distinct waves of data collection. From 1989 to 1991, this research focused primarily on the behavioral response to HIV/AIDS on the part of men who have sex with men and was carried out primarily in public venues in Rio de Janeiro. From 1992 to 1993, as we became increasingly convinced that behavioral issues related to HIV/AIDS were in fact shaped by changes taking place in the organization of sexual and friendship networks, subcultural universes, and sexual communities, the scope of this work expanded significantly and was carried out in a broader range of venues, commercial establishments, and community-based organizations, again primarily in Rio. Finally, and from 1994 through 1996, the scope of ethnographic work was broadened further still to look not only at emerging communities among men who have sex with men, but also at the shape and organization of female homosexuality and lesbian communities, as part of a broader and more complex gay world that seems to be taking shape in many urban centers, with ethnographic work carried out in a wide range of public venues, commercial establishments, and community-based organizations—not only in Rio but also in the cities of São Paulo, Fortaleza, and, to a lesser extent, Belo Horizonte and Recife (see Map 1.1).

As an extension of this ethnographic work, over the full period from 1989 through 1996, more than 200 life histories were collected with men involved in same-sex interactions—primarily in Rio de Janeiro, but also, from 1994 to 1996, in São Paulo, Fortaleza, Belo Horizonte, and Recife. Like the focus of the ethnographic work—indeed, in intentional conjunction with it—the focus of these life-history interviews also shifted over time, from an initial intent to examine the ways in which issues associated with AIDS-related behavioral change had impacted upon the lives of different individuals, to a growing concern with a broader set of changes taking place in social networks, subcultures, and communities. Again, during the most recent period of work, a number of interviews were also included with women, but largely as a pilot study for a more

Map 1.1. Brazil: Primary Field Sites

ambitious project on lesbian experience that is currently being designed by members of our research group.

Finally, a series of cross-sectional surveys were also carried out with homosexual and bisexual men, first by our team in Rio de Janeiro and then later in collaboration with local research institutions in São Paulo and Fortaleza. Three waves of data collection were carried out in Rio: (1) in 1989, when 503 men were interviewed; (2) in 1993, when an additional 300 interviews were carried out; and (3) in 1995, when a further 300 interviews were conducted. In conjunction with our work in Rio, and using the same basic question schedule that we had designed, in 1995 an additional survey of 300 men was carried out by colleagues in São Paulo and of 400 men by colleagues in Fortaleza.[11]

One of the greatest dilemmas in developing the current study has been how to sift through what is an almost overwhelming quantity of information on different issues to focus on those data that would be most relevant to the issues examined here. At least two decisions were made early on, which have been especially important in terms of delimiting the scope of the present text. First, given the primary emphasis of our research on male homosexuality (at least up until the most recent phase of our work), I decided to make this the exclusive focus here and to resist the temptation to incorporate our preliminary findings on lesbian networks and communities. While some discussion of the growing interface between emerging gay and lesbian communities enters my analysis at a number of points, it is largely to illustrate the reconfiguration of the gay world in recent years rather than to make any claim to have illuminated what would appear to be the somewhat different dynamic of lesbian subcultures and communities. Indeed, other researchers—some of them members of our own research group—are far better situated than I am to be able to make such a contribution, and as such work begins to be published it will obviously complement the discussions developed here (see, in particular, Heilborn 1992, 1996).[12]

A decision was also made to include relatively little of the behavioral data from the series of cross-sectional studies. Again, some data drawn from the surveys are occasionally included when they seem to illustrate specific issues, such as changing patterns of self-identification. But these data are largely marginal to the main lines of argument. This is not to say that it would not be of interest—on the contrary, a careful, systematic, and (to the extent possible) representative examination of the ways in which the changing social and cultural structures described here may also translate into changes in sexual behavior and practice would obviously be of great value. But it would also take us far beyond what it is possible to do in a single volume, and has thus been left as a task for other publications.[13]

With these limitations in mind, then, the pages that follow describe of the changing shape of male homosexuality and gay life in Brazil. Following this introduction, I have divided the body of the text into two major parts. In the first, "Cultures of Desire," I look primarily at what might be described as the changing cultural organization of same-sex desires and practices in Brazil, both over time as well as space. In particular, I try to examine in fairly broad strokes three quite different systems of meaning, associated with distinct historical moments, that have combined to structure the cultural field of homosexuality in Brazilian life, and that serve as a kind of backdrop for a reading of the alterations that seem to be taking place in the structure of homosexual experience in recent decades. Building on this historical discussion, I look at a number of the different sexual subcultures, organized in large part around homoerotic desire and practice, that seem to coexist in contemporary Brazilian life and that together map out what might be described as the contours of the urban gay world in contemporary Brazilian society.

In the second part, "Local Contexts/Imagined Worlds," I link this discussion of sexual cultures to a closer examination of those social, economic, and demographic factors that have increasingly tied the fate of gay life in Brazil to a set of wider contexts and forces in the late twentieth century—concentrating on how these factors have increasingly transformed not only the character of social and sexual interaction but even the imagination of possible sexual realities. In particular, I extend some of the work that has been done on the relationship between capitalism and gay sexuality in the Anglo-European world, and examine the ways in which processes of urbanization and industrialization, within the context of dependent capitalist development, have been tied to the emergence of a distinct sense of gay identity not only in the so-called developed nations but also in developing countries such as Brazil. From here, I move on to the evolving gay communities that have begun to emerge in two of the major cities where our work has been carried out—paying particular attention to Rio de Janeiro in southeastern Brazil, where our research has been most extensive, but also examining similar changes in the northeastern city of Fortaleza, where a number of parallel developments seem to be taking place in recent years. Finally, I discuss the centrality of what might be described as dislocation: in particular, the role of movement, of migration and immigration, both within Brazil and beyond Brazil, in joining such emerging gay communities together as part of an extensive social configuration, as well as in tying the emerging gay communities in Brazil to the wider gay world that has taken shape globally in the late twentieth century.

Finally, in the Epilogue, "Globalization, Sexuality, and Identity," I very briefly pull some of these pieces back together—first, in order to give at least a partial picture of how the changes described here in relation to Brazilian society respond to a set of transformations in the late modern or post modern world of the late twentieth century; and then more broadly, to question the extent to which these changes in Brazilian gay life may be symptomatic of transformations taking place more generally in a range of developing societies at the close of the twentieth century. Ultimately, I want to emphasize, yet again, what I see as the impossibility of thinking about sexuality in general, or about homosexuality more specifically, as isolated or changeless within the context of what is in fact a constantly evolving, fragmented, yet nonetheless fundamentally interconnected world—and to call attention to the need to seek new ways of thinking about social and sexual change, interconnectedness, and the impact that this has on the ways in which people live their lives in the contemporary world.

This is all a tall order, of course, and one that probably cannot be adequately filled by any single volume, no matter how thorough and complete. Indeed, the current volume is essentially the first in a series of publications, and two additional volumes are already in preparation that will examine the impact of these changes on homosexual experience by focusing in greater detail on a number of the life histories that we have collected over the past decade. Even when taken together, however, these texts make no pretense to being either a definitive or totalizing account of homosexuality in Brazil. They do not claim, for example, to offer any great insight into the experience of same-sex relations in rural Brazil or in the most traditional or conservative sectors of Brazilian society, where the processes of change described here are in many ways rejected (it might be interesting, in this regard, to look at the growth of fundamentalism and evangelism). Nor do they claim, other than almost altogether peripherally, to address the important processes of change that are also taking place in the organization of female homosexuality and lesbian experience. And even as to the experience of homosexual or bisexual men in urban settings, they do not somehow offer a totalizing view of our subject matter— a complete picture of life as it is lived in such settings.

On the contrary (in what is perhaps appropriately postmodern fashion), this book is probably best described as a collection of fragments, slices of life, bits and pieces that we have tried to capture of the slippery subject that we have sought to understand something about. In this sense, it is simply an extension of the broader project, involving a community of scholars and activists who have sought, and who continue to seek, to move forward our understanding of sexual difference, gay life, and the struggle to build, as best we can, a better world.

Part One

Cultures
of Desire

2
Brazilian Homosexualities

Like any highly complex society, Brazil is a kind of patchwork quilt of cultures and subcultures that seem to intersect and intertwine in the flow of daily life. This intricate weave of cultural systems is as characteristic of sexuality as of any other aspect of Brazilian life, and Brazilian sexual culture can be seen as built up out of an almost endless range of distinct cultural frames that overlap and interact in remarkably diverse ways—and that are ultimately central in shaping the sexual experiences and understandings of different individuals (see Parker 1991). Responding, perhaps above all else, to a complex interplay between continuity and change, between tradition and modernity, in the uncertain world of the late twentieth century, these multiple cultural frames seem often to both contradict and yet at the same time intersect one another, opening up not a single, unique sexual reality, but rather a set of multiple realities (see Parker 1991; more generally, see Parker and Gagnon 1995). And nowhere can this multiplicity be seen more clearly than in the case of male homosexuality, which, in Brazil at least, must be characterized less as a unitary phenomenon than as fundamentally diverse—a case, at the very least, of a variety of somewhat different homosexualities rather than of a single, unified homosexuality (see Fry 1982; Parker 1985, 1987, 1989; Trevisan 1986).

In this chapter, I will develop some of these ideas more fully in examining the social and cultural organization of male homosexuality. I will concentrate on a number of very distinct systems of sexual meaning that seem to structure same-sex interactions in Brazilian culture, and will examine some of the different ways in which these systems influence the experience of sexual desire and sexual identity. In particular, I will focus on what might be described as three different dimensions in the evolving history of homosexuality in Brazilian life: (1) the traditional constitution of same-sex relations within the sexual ideology of popular culture; (2) the recent impact of science, medicine, and the media in building up a more rationalized notion of homosexuality as a distinct sexual identity; and (3) the increasingly rapid emergence of distinct cultures or subcultures, organized around understandings of homoerotic desire, within the fabric of contemporary Brazilian life.

Ultimately, I will suggest that male homosexuality—like any other form of sexual expression, and in Brazil as much as anywhere else—is constantly transformed, both at the level of society and at the level of individual experience, and that an understanding of the transitory nature of sexual meanings is thus intrinsic to an understanding of sexual experience (see also Parker 1991). At the same time, if sexual experience is in fact constantly in motion, fluid, flexible, and in the process of being transformed, it is also never endlessly so (see Parker and Gagnon 1995). On the contrary, sexual experience, and homosexual experience in particular, always take shape (in Brazil as elsewhere) within limits—within a complex field of power and domination, in which the possibilities for transformation, the freedom of movement experienced by individuals or groups, the choices or options opened up by different cultural systems, are simultaneously shaped and molded by relations of force (see Foucault 1978; Lancaster 1992; Parker 1991). Indeed, culture and power are best understood as mutually implicated, and the task of seeking to make some sense out of sexual experience in any setting is in large part an exercise of unraveling the strands that weave together these two apparently disparate domains—of developing what, following Roger Lancaster, might best be described as a kind of "political economy of the body" (see Lancaster 1995; Lancaster and di Leonardo 1997) capable of offering some insight into the ways in which the subjective experience of sexual life has been constituted in specific settings.

Activity and Passivity

In seeking to develop some understanding of the experience of male homosexuality in Brazil, one must realize that the very notion of homosexuality, as a distinct sexual category, is actually a relatively recent development. While new (and rapidly changing) ideas related to homosexual behavior as well as to gay identity have begun to emerge in Brazilian culture in recent years, they have in large part been the product of a complex and ongoing cultural dialectic in which the traditions of Brazilian society have necessarily had to confront and interact with a wider set of cultural symbols and sexual meanings in an increasingly globalized world system. Making sense of the diverse and complex spectrum of meanings that organize same-sex relations in contemporary Brazilian life thus requires at least some understanding of the very different economy of sexuality in traditional culture—an economy organized less around the symbolic value of sexual desires or sexual identities than of sexual roles (see Daniel and Parker 1991, 1993; Parker 1989, 1991, 1994).

As I have argued elsewhere (see, in particular, Parker 1991), this "traditional" system of sexual meanings is hardly free-floating. Instead, it is anchored in a wider set of meanings and practices that throughout the Latin world have come to be known rather generically as "machismo" (see, for example, Brandes 1980; Lancaster 1992; Parker 1991). And in Brazil, at least, it can be further rooted in the complex social and cultural system that was gradually built up around a highly concrete mode of production—the rural plantation economy that dominated Brazilian life for nearly four centuries, and that has only very recently given way (even if only partially) to the rapid urbanization and industrialization of the past fifty years (see Freyre 1963; Parker 1991). In spite of the rapid changes that have recently taken place in the organization of Brazilian society, particularly in the most developed urban areas, the heritage of this traditional system continues to exert profound influence over the flow of daily life, constituting a kind of cultural grammar that continues to organize important aspects of experience even in settings that would otherwise seem far removed from the past (see Parker 1991).

Within this traditional cultural system, understandings about the nature of sexual interactions can hardly be separated from the social construction of gender—indeed, the body itself, particularly in its sexual performances, becomes the raw material for the construction and reconstruction of gender, just as the relations of power that traditionally circumscribe and organize the universe of gender become the basic structures organizing the sexual field. Within this model of sexual life, cultural emphasis seems to be placed not merely on sexual practices in and of themselves, but on the relationship between sexual practices and gender roles—in particular, on a distinction between perceived masculine *atividade* (activity) and feminine *passividade* (passivity) as central to the organization of sexual reality. It is in terms of this symbolic distinction between *atividade* and *passividade* that notions of *macho* (male) and *fêmea* (female), of *masculinidade* (masculinity) and *feminilidade* (femininity), and the like, have been organized in Brazil. In daily life, of course, these notions are constructed rather informally in the discourses of popular culture. They are less a product of self-conscious reflection than of the implicit values encoded in the gendered language that is commonly used to speak about the body and its practices, about the combination of gendered bodies, and about the classificatory categories that flow from such combinations (see Parker 1991).[1]

Perhaps nowhere is this distinction between *atividade* and *passividade* more evident than in the popular language used in describing sexual relations, in verbs such as *comer* (literally, to eat) and *dar* (to give). *Comer*, for example, is used to describe the male's active penetration of the female during sexual intercourse. It implies a kind of symbolic domination that is typical of Brazil's traditional culture of gender, and can be used as a synonym, in a number of different contexts, for verbs such as *possuir* (to possess) or *vencer* (to vanquish). *Dar*, on the other hand, is used to describe the female's supposedly passive submission to her male partner, her role of being penetrated during intercourse. Drawing on these categories (and any number of others that function in precisely the same way), then, the sexual universe is continually structured and restructured, in even the simplest and most common verbal exchanges, along the lines of a rigid hierarchy: a distinction between sexual *atividade* and *passividade* that is translated into relations of power and domination between *machos* and *fêmeas*, between *homens* (men) and *mulheres* (women). What is particularly important to understand, however, is not simply the structure of this hierarchy but the fact that, within the traditional context of popular culture, it has been used to organize and to conceptualize sexual relations both between members of the opposite sex and between members of the same sex. The symbolic structure of male/female interactions seems to function in many ways as a kind of model for the organization of same-sex interactions in Brazilian culture. Within the terms of this model, what is central is perhaps less the shared biological sex of the participants than the social/sexual roles that they play out—their *atividade* or *passividade* as sexual partners and social persons:

> What really matters is what you do in bed, whether you like being *ativo* or *passivo*. An *homem* fucking another *homem* isn't really that much different than if he was screwing a *mulher*. . . . As long as he's the one who is doing the fucking, who is penetrating the other guy, it doesn't really matter. He's still an *homem*—even a "*machão*" (a real macho man). (Marcos, a twenty-eight-year-old informant from the middle class, originally from Fortaleza, but currently living in Rio de Janeiro)

The *homem* who enters into a sexual relationship with another male, then, does not necessarily sacrifice his culturally constituted *masculinidade*—at least so long as he performs the culturally perceived active, masculine role during sexual intercourse and conducts himself as a male within society. The male who adopts a passive, female posture, however, whether in sexual intercourse or social interaction, almost inevitably undercuts his own *masculinidade*. By upsetting the culturally prescribed fit between biological sex and social gender, he sacrifices his appropriate categorization as *homem* and comes to be known as a *viado* (originally from the term, *veado*, which literally means "deer," but more commonly is spelled with the accentuated "i" replacing the "e") or a *bicha* (literally, worm or intestinal parasite, but also, instructively, the feminine form of *bicho* or animal, and thus a female animal) thanks to his inappropriate femininity (see also Parker 1991):

> It's different for the *bicha*. If you're a *passivona* [literally, a big, passive woman; figuratively, an effeminate (and sexually passive) homosexual man], then everyone stigmatizes you as a *bicha*. And the stigma is so strong that you wind up internalizing it, not only in bed, but all the time. You start talking differently, walking differently, using effeminate mannerisms. You actually become a *bicha* and think about yourself as a *bicha*. (Joel, a thirty-three-year-old informant from a working-class background in Rio de Janeiro)

On the basis of his/her perceived passivity and internalized femininity, then, the *bicha* or *viado* is seen as a kind of walking failure on both social and biological counts—as a being who is unable to realize his natural potential because of inappropriate social behavior, yet who is equally unable to cross the culturally constituted boundaries of gender due to the unavoidable constraints of anatomy. Not surprisingly, he is thus subject to among the most severe symbolic and often physical violence found anywhere in Brazilian society—a constant object of ridicule and shame, which serves to stigmatize and marginalize deviant gender performances while at the same time reinforcing normative patterns of masculinity and femininity (see Parker 1989, 1991).[2]

Within the framework of this relatively traditional model, then, there exists a fairly explicit cultural construction of homosexual desires and practices. What is perhaps most striking is that an individual's same-sex object choice seems to be, in some ways, rather less significant than his sexual role; less significant, in other words, than the connection between anatomical and social gender as played out in terms of the calculus of *atividade* and *passividade*. In light of this, it is hardly surprising that the central cultural emphasis has been on the problem of assuring the *atividade* of young boys as they grow and develop. Typical parents may be unlikely to reflect upon the deeper psychological processes involved in the formation of gender identities, but they nonetheless tend to view the *masculinidade* of the young sons as almost constantly threatened by too close contact with female relatives such as mothers, aunts, and sisters (see Parker 1991). Men, in particular, make a conscious effort to encourage active, aggressive, masculine behaviors on the part of young male relatives—and to reprimand and stigmatize unacceptably feminine behavior:

> I remember that my older brothers were always teasing me—because I never liked to play football (soccer), or to pick fights, or do the other things that boys are supposed to do. They would call me names—saying that if I didn't watch out I would grow up to be a *bicha*. (Reinaldo, a twenty-four-year-old informant from the lower class in Rio de Janeiro)

The consequences of this social molding of an appropriately active stance (and of the stigmatization of inappropriate passivity) become fully evident only as the child begins to take part in sexual activities. Upon entering adolescence, boys or young men who are perceived, from the perspective of the hegemonic gender hierarchy, to have successfully built up (or in whom society has successfully built up) an "active" stance in relation to their gender identity are clearly expected to demonstrate and even follow through on their desire for the opposite sex. As they progress through adolescence and on into full adulthood, however, sexual play with members of the same sex may not be uncommon, and indeed in some instances may even be used as a way of reaffirming notions of masculinity:

> Playing around sexually with your friends when you're a kid is almost universal—everyone does it, or at least they did where I grew up. The more masculine guys would compete a lot to see who was more macho—who had the biggest cock, who could jack off and come first, who could shoot the farthest. . . . It was like a constant competition. To stay macho, nobody could let themselves get fucked. But we would all screw the younger boys, who were weaker, or the more effeminate ones. Every community had at least a couple of kids who served all of the other guys—who let the older or stronger boys fuck them. (João, a thirty-nine-year-old informant from the lower-middle class in Rio de Janeiro)

For appropriately masculine boys, then, same-sex play and exploration becomes a means of reaffirming one's growing masculinity, whether through the competitions of size and force that confirm masculine virility, or through the sexual domination of younger or weaker playmates. At the same time, if such play tends to produce a sense of masculinity by reproducing the hierarchy of activity and passivity, it is not a kind of straitjacket excluding any possibility for freedom of movement. On the contrary, at least on some occasions (and particularly in private settings involving only two relatively egalitarian friends or partners), there may also be room to play with this structure of domination and submission as long as an implicit pact of equality is basically maintained. The space of sexual exploration is almost institutionalized through the culturally recognized game of *troca-troca* (literally, exchange-exchange), in which two (or more) boys take turns, each inserting the penis in their partner's anus:

> Sometimes even more macho guys would take turns with one another, playing *troca-troca*—so long as nobody else would find out. (João)

If the possibilities for sexual exploration are particularly evident in the notion of *troca-troca*,[3] however, they are equally obvious in expressions such as, "*Homem, para ser homem, tem que dar primeiro*" ("A man, to be a man, has to give [i.e., take the passive role in anal intercourse] first"), which are often used by older boys seeking to *comer* their slightly younger playmates. Such experiences seem relatively widespread and, as the very name of a game such as *troca-troca* would indicate, offer participants with at least some room to explore both active and passive roles (see Parker 1989, 1991).[4]

Assuming that the cultural system has successfully carried out its mandate, such early adolescent play is quite explicitly not expected to disrupt in any fundamental way the process of development that will ultimately transform the young "*rapaz*" (boy) into an active *homem* at the end of the day. For the *rapaz* who, for whatever reasons, has failed to acquire an appropriately active stance, however, it is in such adolescent sexual play that psychological disposition begins to be transformed into a distinct social role. For such individuals, the available role is not the positively sanctioned category of the *homem* but the negatively stigmatized categories of the *bicha*, the *viado*, or any number of other regional variations, such as the *baitola* or *boiola* in the northeast, or the *maricas* in the south— terms that can only partially, and somewhat inadequately, be translated using "queer" or "faggot" as English language equivalents (see Parker 1991). As Roger Lancaster has argued with regard to the category of the *cochón* in Nicaragua (see Lancaster 1988, 1992, 1995), the crucial point here is that the *bicha* or *viado* has a different ontological status from such English-language parallels—that they are produced in a distinct sex/ gender system, and that the circulation of stigma associated with such figures (whether in Brazil or other Latin/o societies) is simply qualitatively different from the stigma and oppression that marks out the space of the "queer" or "faggot" in English.

Independent of the specific origins or regional variants, terms such as *bicha*, *viado*, or *baitola* all call attention to the fact of sexual passivity— which in turn seems to translate into an all-pervasive emphasis on the social or performance style of the opposite sex:

> The *bicha* becomes a woman, or almost a woman—kind of an exaggerated version, rolling her hips and talking funny. (João Carlos, a twenty-one-year-old informant from the working class in Rio de Janeiro)

What is perhaps most difficult to understand in this cultural construction of the *bicha* or *baitola*, however, is the degree to which the role is simultaneously stigmatized and institutionalized in traditional popular culture:

> (Excerpt from an interview with Arnaldo, a thirty-three-year-old informant from a very poor background in the interior of Pernambuco, who migrated to Rio nearly a decade ago. Arnaldo is stereotypically effeminate, and works as a hairdresser in a women's hair salon in the Tijuca neighborhood in Rio de Janeiro. He lives in a favela in the North Zone of the city.)
>
> ARNALDO: It's just that there is a lot of prejudice in the society.
> INTERVIEWER: Tell me what you mean.
> ARNALDO: People laugh at you and make jokes. Someone is always messing with you, on the bus or in the street.
> INTERVIEWER: Because of how you look?
> ARNALDO: They call you names. It was worse in Pernambuco— that's why I came to Rio, that and to find work—but sometimes people are like that here too.

All too frequently, such stigma breaks out in outright violence, socially sanctioned and approved:

> No one gives a damn about beating up a *viado*. It's because the *viado* violates the norms of good behavior in the society. The *viado* is very exaggerated—he goes overboard, sometimes even in front of women and children, affronting families. Sometimes you don't have any choice—you have to give him a beating. (Carlos, a thirty-five-year-old informant from the working class in São Paulo)

Yet at the same time, there is also a socially constructed space for the *bicha* in popular culture, often in quite unexpected places. Any number of studies have pointed to the importance of effeminate *bichas* in the structure of Afro-Brazilian religious cults, for example (see, for example, Fry 1985; Landes 1946; Wafer 1991). Much like female prostitutes, *bichas* or *baitolas* can be found in virtually any small town or city in the interior of the country or on the frontier—often highly valued, much like the female prostitute, for (sexual) services rendered to the local male population. And in the working-class communities and *favelas* or shantytowns in all major cities, similar figures can be found, specializing in a range of otherwise feminine professions (such as hair stylists or make-up artists), and surprisingly integrated in community life:

> INTERVIEWER: But you talked a lot about how badly people treat you in the street, about the prejudice that you feel. . . . How about in your neighborhood, where you live?
>
> ARNALDO: No, it's different there. . . . Everybody treats me with respect. They ask me to cut their hair for them, and they help me with things.
>
> INTERVIEWER: Like what?
>
> ARNALDO: Like last week, when I bought the new refrigerator that I told you about, the guys from down the street carried it up the stairs and installed it for me. They're always helping me with things like that.
>
> INTERVIEWER: Do you ever have sex with them?
>
> ARNALDO: No, not really. . . . Once I went out for a time with one, but he didn't want people in the community to know, so it was very complicated. Mostly we're just friends, have a beer together on the weekend, or watch television together. They treat me with a lot of respect.

Precisely because the *bicha* violates the traditional expectations of *masculinidade* in popular culture, s/he is at one and the same time rejected and yet necessary. S/he is subjected to violent discrimination, and often to outright physical violence, particularly in the impersonal world of the street, yet also accepted as a friend and neighbor, integrated into a network of personal relationships in the traditional culture and highly personalized social relations of what in Brazil, as in other parts of Latin America, are described as the *classes populares* (the popular classes, i.e., the poor, in what is still an overwhelmingly poor country).

Ultimately, then, this traditional system of meanings and practices takes shape as a quite specific economy of the body, organizing the sex/gender system in particular ways and opening up a predetermined range of possibilities for the experience of sexual life. It defines what an *homem* is and what he is not, what he can do and what he cannot, what he should desire and what he should not. It determines how both opposite-sex and same-sex relations can be organized and the consequent practices and identities that can be produced around such relations within the flow of daily life and the structures of popular culture. Bringing meaning and power together in highly specific ways, it provides what is still today (even in social settings that are far removed from the context in which this system originally emerged) perhaps the most deeply rooted and deeply felt framework for the organization of sexual relations between men.

The Invention of Sexual Identity

While certainly subject to at least some regional variation in terminology and usage, the basic structure of the traditional or popular model of sexual reality has been central throughout Brazilian history. As a number of writers have suggested, this model seems to have dominated the sexual landscape throughout the nineteenth and early twentieth centuries, and continues to function even today both in rural areas as well as among the lower classes (many of whom are themselves migrants from the countryside) in larger, more modernized, and industrialized cities (see Fry 1982; Parker 1991; Trevisan 1986). Indeed, quite literally, all Brazilians are familiar with and implicitly understand the cultural logic of this system of sexual meanings, even if they may not necessarily use it today as the primary framework for the organization of their own sexual experience (Parker 1991).

By the latter part of the nineteenth century, however, a number of important changes had begun to take place in Brazilian society that would pave the way for the appearance of more alternatives in the social organization of same-sex relations. In particular, the rural agricultural society, where the traditional gender hierarchy and the active/passive system of sexual roles was most clearly rooted, gradually began to give way to progressive urbanization and industrialization (see part two in this volume). These developments, in turn, were linked to the emergence and the gradual consolidation, over the course of nearly a century, of a Brazilian bourgeoisie closely associated with this growing urban world.

The details of this transition are of course complex, and have been analyzed in detail in a range of historical and demographic studies (see, for example, Bacha and Klein 1986; Sahato 1968; see also Parker 1997a). For our purposes here, however, what is most critical is a sense of the extent to which these transformations simultaneously opened up a set of changes in the organization of gender and sexuality (see, in particular, Costa 1979). Situated, in a sense, between the extremes of the powerful plantation oligarchy, on the one hand, and the disenfranchised ex-slave/peasant population, on the other, the rising bourgeoisie (or perhaps falling, since it can be understood as in many ways to be a spin-off of the plantation class [see Freyre 1963]) would be linked to the appearance of a whole new urban world of increasingly specialized professionals—academics, lawyers, and doctors, educated in large part at the old-world universities of the major European centers, and responsible as well for much of what might be described as the "modernization" of Brazilian social and cultural life during the late nineteenth and early twentieth centuries. It was during this period that the developments of western science and technology began to make their way to Brazil, and that a whole new range of techniques aimed at social engineering began to emerge—disciplines such as social medicine and psychiatry began to take shape and to exercise increasing influence over the regulation of social life (see Costa 1979, 1989).

At least one of the relatively rapid consequences of all this was the increasing importation and incorporation into Brazilian reality of a whole new set of disciplines and rationalities linked to the investigation and organization of sexual life (see Carrara 1996; Costa 1979; Parker 1991). New models for the conceptualization of sexual experience also began to compete with the earlier system of sexual meanings. In particular, a new medical/scientific model of sexual classification—introduced into Brazilian culture, at least initially, through the writings of medical doctors, psychiatrists, and psychoanalysts, and translated only gradually into the wider discourse of popular culture—seems to have marked a fundamental shift in cultural attention away from a distinction between active and passive roles as the building blocks of gender hierarchy, and toward the importance, along Anglo-European lines, of sexual desire and, in particular, sexual object choice as central to the very definition of the sexual subject:

> These days, it's not so important what you do, whether you're the one fucking (*comendo*) or being fucked (*sendo comido*). . . . What matters is your sexual orientation (*orientação sexual*), who you're attracted to. (Francisco, a twenty-nine-year-old informant from the lower-middle class in Fortaleza)

In practical terms, this new emphasis on sexual attraction, on sexual orientation, resulted from the invention of a new set of classificatory categories—notions such as *homossexualidade* (homosexuality), *heterossexualidade* (heterosexuality), and *bissexualidade* (bisexuality)—for mapping out and interpreting the sexual landscape. The appearance of these categories in western medical and scientific discourse has of course been documented at some length by any number of writers (see, in particular, Foucault 1978; Halperin 1990; Katz 1995), but the exportation and importation of these categories outside of the Anglo-European world has received almost no attention. In this regard, Peter Fry's early work in Brazil was groundbreaking (see, in particular, Fry 1982; Fry and MacRae 1983; see also Parker 1991:67–97), but much still remains to be done to begin to develop a fuller understanding of the global incorporation of western medical and scientific rationalities.

By the mid-twentieth century, these new categories had become central to the medical and scientific discussion of sexual life and had been fully incorporated into the languages of law, government, and organized religion marking out a world of *normalidade* (normality) and *anormalidade* (abnormality)—of sexual *saúde* (health) as opposed to *doença* (sickness), *perversão* (perversion), and *desvio* (deviance).[5] But until perhaps the late 1960s or the early 1970s, the influence of this new system seems to have been limited almost entirely to a small, highly educated elite—the same segment of the population that has traditionally maintained contact with and been most influenced by European and North American culture (see Fry 1982; Fry and MacRae 1983; Parker 1991).

Restricted to this elite, notions such as *homossexualidade* (understood not merely as a form of sexual behavior, but also as a class of people, or even a distinct way of being in the world) had largely failed to penetrate the language of daily life or popular culture or to play a significant role in the lives and experiences of the vast majority of the population. When my own research in Brazil began in the early 1980s, for example, a remarkably large number of my informants, particularly from what in Brazil are described as the popular classes (as opposed to the elite), were altogether unaware of categories such as *homossexual* or *homossexualidade*:

> The word *homossexualidade* is almost never used outside of medical circles. If you use it when you're talking to someone from the working class, they won't even know what you're talking about. (Antônio, a twenty-eight-year-old informant from the upper-middle class in Rio de Janeiro)

If *homossexualidade* (and, by extension, *heterossexualidade*) were largely restricted for use as sexual classifications, first to medical or scientific discourses and then only gradually to more general educated circles over the course of the 1980s, it was perhaps above all else as a direct consequence of the emerging AIDS epidemic that these new categories would increasingly begin to be incorporated into daily life:

> Since about 1984 or 1985, almost all of the discussion of AIDS, particularly in the media, has been in terms of *homossexualidade* and *heterossexualidade*. Before this, these categories hardly even existed, at least not for lay-people. But today, more and more people use these terms—not so much in the popular classes, perhaps, but certainly the middle class. And even in the popular classes, men who are homosexual are becoming more and more likely to identify themselves using the term. (Excerpt from a 1989 conversation in Rio de Janeiro with Herbert Daniel, a writer and leading AIDS activist)

Precisely because AIDS took shape in Brazil (as in many parts of the world) through a complex set of cultural discourses and social representations, the shape of sexual life began to change because of AIDS even before most Brazilians had ever had any direct or intimate contact with the epidemic or the people affected by it (see Daniel and Parker 1991, 1993). Particularly through media reports, which served (often in quite distorted ways) as filters for medical and epidemiological information about the epidemic, categories such as *homossexualidade* began to become increasingly common as ways of carving up the sexual universe and organizing sexual experience. Indeed, in less than a decade following the emergence of the epidemic, even relatively sophisticated distinctions between *comportamento sexual* (sexual behavior) and *identidade sexual* (sexual identity) advanced by social scientists (such as my colleagues and myself) had become the stuff of newspaper reports and television talk shows, offering a whole new, rationalized, and at times profoundly medicalized map for the sexual landscape. It spread out, it would seem, from the clinics of medical doctors and psychoanalysts through the offices of epidemiologists, the newsrooms of journalists, the sets and studios of television talk-show hosts, and so on, into the living rooms not only of the educated elite but also of Brazilians from all walks of life.

The growing significance of this new system of classification can be seen quite vividly in the successive cross-sectional surveys that we carried out in Rio de Janeiro between 1989 and 1995. In 1989, when asked for a term to describe their sexual identity, 50 percent of the men interviewed described themselves as *homossexual*, while fully 33 percent either failed to respond at all or responded using popular categories such as *bicha* or *viado*. By 1995, the use of *homossexual* had climbed to 57 percent, while nonresponse and use of popular classifications had fallen to only 17 percent. The extent to which such highly rationalized and medicalized systems have in fact become the key organizing principles for the experience of sexual life on the part of anything more than a small minority is of course a question that is open to debate. Yet the fact remains that over the course of the past fifteen years, growing numbers of men engaging in same-sex relations have come to define themselves as either *homossexual* or *bissexual*, and the notion of sexual identity (as opposed to sexual role) has become increasingly widespread as somehow definitive of sexual experience:

> Being active or passive isn't so important now. People may still prefer one or the other, but it doesn't really matter. What is important is that you're having sex with another person of the same sex, not whether you're being active or passive. Sexual attraction, desire, excitement (*tesão*) determine sexual identity. (Chico, a thirty-five-year-old informant from the lower-middle class in São Paulo)

For better or for worse, then, the increasing rationalization of sexual life has taken place at a remarkably rapid pace, and the question of *homossexualidade* has been absolutely pivotal to this process. A new relationship between meaning and power has emerged, focused far less on the relations of oppression and domination that are implicit in the hierarchy of gender, than on what, following Foucault, might better be described as the subjectification of sexual life (see Foucault 1982).

In its relationship to sexual experience, then, it would seem that power has come to function not merely through the ideology of popular culture but through the elite discourses of science and medicine—discourses that have been incorporated into Brazilian life through a process of cross-cultural transmission that began to take place long before discussions of globalization had become fashionable. Passed from one elite to another (in what is in fact often typical of the processes of cultural globalization), and then increasingly repassed through a complex process of diffusion from elite culture to popular culture, these once highly specialized discourses have thus spread out to offer ordinary people a way of organizing and understanding their experience. And if, at one level, this process can be understood as a form of subjectivization in which medicine, psychiatry, psychoanalysis, and related disciplines have come to exercise oppressive power over the lives of more individual subjects, it has simultaneously offered many lay people a vantage point from which to critique the oppressive categories of the traditional gender hierarchy:

A sense of homosexual identity has been really important for many people. When you are growing up, prejudice and discrimination are everywhere. If you are even the least bit effeminate, people will call you a *viado*—sometimes even people in your own family. It's really easy to start believing what everyone says. But when you start to think about being homosexual, and when you realize that homosexuality is just as normal as heterosexuality is— different, but just as normal—everything changes. You begin to see how oppressive everything that you learned as a little kid really is, how oppressive the whole way that society treats sexuality is. (Jorge, a thirty-eight-year-old informant from the middle class in Rio de Janeiro)

Indeed, in Brazil, as in the Anglo-European world, the highly rationalized discourse of *homossexualidade* has at one and the same time become a point of departure for strategies of resistance aimed not only at the stigma and discrimination of the traditional gender system but also at the notions of *normalidade* and *anormalidade* that this new system itself has imposed. From this point of view, assuming the condition of *homossexual* not as a form of deviance but as a part of the natural range of sexual variation, more men and women have begun to challenge the otherwise hegemonic structures not only of gender but also of a scientific, medicalized, and ultimately oppressive sexuality that has sought to define them as deviants and to subject them to diverse forms of treatment and cure:

Homosexuality used to be seen as if it were a kind of sickness (*doença*) that needed to be cured. Psychoanalysts and therapists from the Zona Sul [the well-to-do neighborhoods of the South Zone in Rio de Janeiro] still make a fortune trying to cure people even today. But just because I'm a homosexual doesn't mean that I need to be treated as if I were sick (*doente*). I'm just as normal as anyone else is. The real sickness is to discriminate against people because of their sexual identities (*identidades sexuais*). (Jorge)

It is perhaps only within this framework, with its articulation of *identidade sexual* as a new principle for organizing the sexual universe, that the very notion of a *movimento homossexual* (homosexual movement) or, increasingly, *movimento gay* (gay movement) as a distinct framework for political action (again, modeled in important ways on Anglo-European experience) began to emerge in the late 1970s and early 1980s and to take shape more clearly over the course of the 1990s (see Daniel and Míccolis 1983; MacRae 1990; Parker 1989, 1991; Trevisan 1986).

The ways in which this new understanding of sexual identity as a framework for interpreting the sexual universe will develop over time are of course impossible to fully predict. Yet what is already clear is that it has come to offer an important new frame of reference for the organization of sexual experience and for the reorganization of the power relations that stake out the sexual field. It has opened up a new set of possibilities that have begun to be explored by both men and women as options for building up a life course, and for taking a stance in relation to the violence (both physical as well as psychological or symbolic) that so often marks normal daily life.

Cultures of Desire/Cultures of Resistance

In Brazil, as in the Anglo-European world, however, one should not read the relatively recent invention of terms of sexual identity to suggest that nothing in the way of a gay world existed prior to the 1980s or '90s. On the contrary, much as George Chauncey has recently argued with regard to New York City (see Chauncey 1994), a complex (and only partially secretive) sexual subculture organized around male same-sex desires and practices has clearly been present in urban Brazil since at least the early twentieth century, and has continued to become more diverse and complex, particularly in rapidly industrializing and modernizing cities such as Rio de Janeiro and São Paulo, over the course of the past fifty years. In recent decades, this urban subculture has rapidly become more visible and multidimensional, breaking down into any number of diverse (though overlapping) subcultures, each with its own particularities and specificities—multiple social worlds that might best be thought of as diverse cultures of desire, organized around varying forms of same-sex practice and, simultaneously, as cultures of resistance, which provide at least partial protection from the violence, stigma, and oppression encountered in the outside world.[6]

While this emerging gay world crosses constantly with both the traditional world of active versus passive gendered relations and with the more recent elaboration of a rationalized sexual identity, it is also importantly distinct from both. Again, it is rooted in a specific social and economic system, linked to the urbanization and industrialization that have transformed Brazil into a predominantly urban society in a period of less than fifty years and that have created the relatively new (at least in Brazil) social space of a rapidly expanding industrial working class, together with the relative anonymity and impersonality of urban existence. Its history thus contrasts sharply with that of the active/passive gender hierarchy inherited from the plantation past, as well as with the rationalized homosexuality/heterosexuality of the rising bourgeoisie. And yet it intersects with

these other systems constantly: the constant flow of rural migrants entering the city merge with the industrial proletariat in the living conditions
of the *favelas* and the *subúrbios* (poor, suburban areas on the outskirts of
all major Brazilian cities) or in the vicissitudes of the informal labor market, the rationalized systems of classification employed by doctors or
lawyers intersect with popular cultural systems in clinic consultation
rooms, social services, and mass media news reports.

Within this immense, often impersonal, and remarkably complex urban
system, it has generally been more through their shared sexual desires and
practices, and the complex sexual geography present within the relative
anonymity of city life, that diverse types of men who have sex with men
have nonetheless been able to find one another and to establish a shared
social world. The symbolic center of this urban subculture has thus been
less psychological than spatial—the cafés or bars, the plazas and streets
where individuals seeking such sexual contacts were known to meet:

> Every Brazilian city, or at least every large city, has always had gay
> areas. But you have to know how to find them. Some are more hid-
> den or disguised than others. The plazas and parks in the center of
> town are always a good place to look—you'll always find some-
> thing going on. Usually in the surrounding restaurants or bars as
> well, but it's harder to tell exactly which ones. Look for people
> who are cruising, then when they make eye contact you can strike
> up a conversation and ask them what the best places are. (Chico)

Protected, at least up to a point, by the increased anonymity of urban life,
a loosely organized, flexible, and constantly shifting homoerotic subculture (or set of subcultures) began to take shape in the streets of Brazil's
larger cities at the same time that a notion of *homossexualidade* as a distinct mode of sexual being was beginning to form in the salons and studies of the well-to-do and well-educated (see Parker 1989; Trevisan 1986; see
also Green 1996).

Since at least the mid-twentieth century, then, and particularly over the
course of the 1960s and '70s, yet another model for the conceptualization
and organization of same-sex desires and practices began to emerge. At
first glance, this new model, organized around homoerotic desire and
practice, would seem to contrast rather sharply both with the traditional,
gender-based model of active/passive, same-sex interactions available in
popular culture, as well as with the interrogation of sexual identity that
had begun to emerge in medical/scientific discourse and in elite culture.
Instead, it would seem to have converged largely on the eroticization of
otherwise public space while at the same time carving out at least partially

protected, safe havens in an otherwise hostile world. Within this model, virtually any public space might become a locus for homoerotic interaction. Public toilets, parks, plazas, public baths, and the like became invested with erotic meaning, mixing pleasure and danger in an almost constant game of *caça* (hunting) or *pegação* (cruising).

Gradually, over time, more private commercial settings began to emerge as well, offering protected alternatives to the potential dangers of homoerotic contacts in public settings. In part, this took place through the almost determined invasion of what would otherwise be perceived as nonhomosexual spaces, such as (heterosex) pornographic movie theaters in the center of most major cities. Increasingly, however, particularly during the 1960s and '70s, such spaces were carved out through the opening of establishments specifically focusing on a gay clientele, such as bars and nightclubs catering to homosexual patrons. Public baths that had long been known, at least secretively, as the focus for same-sex interactions suddenly had to compete with newer, better-equipped saunas that had opened exclusively for a gay clientele. And so on.

Like the world of homoerotic pleasures in public space, these enclosed private or commercial spaces also took shape primarily against a backdrop of sexual desire—concretely represented in the *quartos-escuros* (dark rooms) of popular nightclubs and successful saunas. Together with the transgressive *pegação* in city streets or the shadowy embraces of the parks and plazas, this growing range of commercial establishments opened yet another set of possibilities for the organization of same-sex interactions— a growing, alternative, sexual subculture, or set of overlapping subcultures, closely linked to the rapidly changing realities of urban life, in which sexual desire could open up the possibilities of pleasure at almost any moment, at least in theory, and could become, at least for some, almost a distinct style of life.

If this urban gay world initially took shape in apparently sharp contrast with the rationalized distinctions between homosexual and heterosexual identities, however, by the late 1970s and then through the '80s and '90s, the histories of these different models began to merge. The self-identified, urban, gay subculture and, somewhat more tentatively, a gay liberation movement—together with a gay-friendly AIDS activist movement—began to become significant forces in contemporary Brazilian society.[7] While this subculture continued to be organized in important ways around homoerotic practices independent of any kind of sharply bounded homosexual identity, it also came to intersect in many of the very same physical and social spaces with the conscious and articulate use of homosexual or gay identity as an equally important organizing principle. Indeed, this emerging gay subculture gradually became a point of convergence where the elite appropriation of modern medical/scientific classifications and the popular reality of a relatively open-ended, erotic field of same-sex practices could be brought together and, at least up to a certain point, integrated. Throughout the 1980s and on into the 1990s, these various currents continued to flow together and mix, increasingly merging (in some cities at least) in the growing sense of a *comunidade gay* (gay community) with its own traditions and institutions (see MacRae 1990; Parker 1989, 1991, 1994; Trevisan 1986).

With the emergence of AIDS in the early to mid-1980s, and the ongoing association between HIV/AIDS and the experience of gay and bisexual men in Brazil, the relatively gradual social and political mobilization that had been taking place within the emerging gay community over the course of more than a decade began to go hand-in-hand with intensive AIDS advocacy (see MacRae 1990; Parker 1994; Parker and Terto 1998; Terto 1996, 1997). In Brazil, as in other parts of the developing world (and, for that matter, even in the developed countries), AIDS provided an important basis, as well as a significant source of funding, for increasingly visible gay organizing and mobilization:

> AIDS had a big impact. AIDS organizations were formed, mostly by *bichas* and *gays*, at least at the beginning. And they became something of an alternative, both to the commercial establishments as well as to the gay political movement. It was almost another kind of sociability that they provided. Gay groups were also being formed during this time, but the AIDS NGOS [nongovernmental organizations] were in some ways even more active and popular— they tended to emphasize a broader vision of homosexuality in Brazil. The gay groups always had a more North American vision about being homosexual. Because of their interest in AIDS prevention, they [the AIDS NGOs] had to reach many populations that didn't identify as homosexual, but that had sex with other men. (Antônio)

Thus, from the mid-1980s through the mid-'90s, AIDS-related work and gay political advocacy would together build upon the substratum of the different cultural models described above, ironically reinforcing both the distinctive difference of same-sex relations as constituted through traditional sexual culture as well as the growing sense of homosexual or gay identity as a key foundation for gay community. The advocacy efforts had a significant impact on the progressive formation of what is now probably the largest and most visible gay subculture to be found anywhere outside of the fully industrialized West.

As I have tried to emphasize, however, and as I will continue to argue throughout this book, it would be a mistake to view this subculture as nothing more than an importation from abroad—a slightly tropical version of the gay community as it exists in Europe or the United States. It clearly has been, and continues to be, profoundly influenced by external models and forces, but this gay subculture has also continued to respond in a variety of ways to particularities of Brazil's own social and cultural context. Perhaps nowhere is this more evident than in its reproduction of traditional distinctions such as *atividade* and *passividade* in a profusion of sexual categories or types. Terms such as *viado* or *bicha* are reproduced, and other, even finer distinctions are added. Effeminate *bichas*, for instance, are contrasted with hypermasculine *bofes* (which might perhaps be translated as "studs" or, in some instances, "trade"):

> The *bofe* is the opposite of the *bicha*. He may have sex mostly with women, and only occasionally with men. Or he may have sex mainly, or even exclusively with men. It doesn't really matter. What is important is that he be really masculine, macho, full of virility. The *bicha*, of course, has to conquer the *bofe*, seduce him—with him at least pretending that it is against his will. But sometimes the *bofes* will come on to the *bichas* too. It's all part of a game of seduction. (Roberto, a forty-three-year-old informant from the working class in Rio de Janeiro)

Much the same distinction between perceived active and passive roles is even more obvious in the increasingly prominent world of male prostitution, where a sharp distinction is drawn between the *travesti* (transvestite) and the *michê* (hustler)—between an exaggerated, feminine figure who is associated primarily with a passive sexual role, and an almost equally exaggerated masculine figure thought to be generally available for the active role but unwilling to perform the passive role:

> The *travesti* and the *michê* are sort of extreme cases of the *bicha* and the *bofe*, at least in relation to prostitution. The *travesti* dresses like a woman, uses silicone breasts and hips, and plays the woman's role. The *michê* is a male prostitute—like the *travesti*, he has paid sex with other men, but he plays the masculine role. The *travesti* is a stereotype of female passivity—the *michê* has to act active. (Roberto)

An elaborate set of active/passive distinctions thus typifies this subculture and underlines its relation to traditional Brazilian culture (see Daniel and

Parker 1993; see also Kulick 1997). Yet even here, it is important to emphasize just how different this is from the traditional model of the sexual universe that continues to dominate life in rural Brazil. In the emerging gay
subculture, the implicit possibilities for playing with sexual roles are
explored and worked upon in conscious and intensive ways—the distinctions that characterize this urban subculture are never seen as absolute. It
is part and parcel of the ideology that structures this world that such
active/passive oppositions can often be inverted, that *bofes* or *michês* can
be convinced to *"dar,"* that *travestis* and *bichas* also *"comem,"* and so on:

> But it's all a kind of theater—everyone knows that a lot of the
> *travestis'* clients, and even their [the *travestis'*] lovers, really like to
> get fucked. They want to see a woman sticking it in their ass, I
> suppose . . . to be dominated and possessed by a woman. . . . The
> *michê* has to maintain his active pose on the street, but lots of
> them will also agree to be fucked if the price is right. Maybe not all
> of them, but probably the majority. It's the whole active/passive
> thing. . . . The whole thing becomes a kind of game of appear-
> ances. People play with it and manipulate it. (Jorge)

The overturning of such categorical distinctions is possible precisely
because, unlike the distinctions of traditional culture, these categories are
determined and defined from within the gay subculture itself. The *viado*
in traditional culture is in large part defined from without, stigmatized
and labeled by the other members of the wider society, and ultimately
excluded from the world of proper *homens*. Here, within this homoerotic
subculture, on the contrary, it begins to become possible to at least partially escape such externally imposed labels and to begin to define or rede-
fine oneself on the basis of one's sexual and erotic preferences and within
the community of one's fellows. And the company of one's fellows, in
turn, provides at least some form of protection from the kinds of hostility
and oppression that one might still have to face when confronting the
wider social world.

   This sense of community comes through perhaps most clearly in the
fact that all such elaborate categories can be subsumed under the more
general headings of *entendido* (literally, one who knows or one who understands) and, increasingly, *gay*. The term *"entendido"* had apparently been
present for some time within the relatively secretive, almost underground
subculture that began to take shape in the mid-twentieth century, but
began to be used much more frequently with the great expansion and the
higher visibility of this subculture in the late 1970s and early 1980s. At
least since that time, it has been used by the members of this subculture

themselves as an all-encompassing term referring to anyone who, to whatever extent, participates in—and thus, by extension, knows or understands the nature of—this specific community:

> INTERVIEWER: But how do you define an *entendido*?
>
> JORGE: The *entendido* is anyone who screws around [with other men], someone who understands the rules of the game. He can be active or passive—it doesn't matter so much, as long as he likes to have sex with men.
>
> INTERVIEWER: But does he only have sex with men?
>
> JORGE: No, no, it doesn't have to be only with men. . . . He can be bisexual. He can have sex with women. But he has to understand the homosexual world, to have desire (*tesão*) for other men. Many people who have sex with both women and men prefer to call themselves *entendidos* rather than bisexuals. Even some men who only have sex with men prefer [the term] *entendido*. For many people it feels less aggressive, less violent, than words like *homossexual* or *viado*.

Significantly, then, *entendido* applies both to those individuals who have adopted a strictly homosexual or gay identity and to anyone else who has come to take part in this particular subculture even sporadically, without necessarily limiting himself to it or defining himself solely through his relationship to it.

Increasingly, the notion of *entendido* has been juxtaposed against the growing use of *gay*, imported directly from English and applied precisely to those men whose primary erotic focus is found in their relations with other men. Interestingly, however, although the meaning of *entendido* has been constructed as all-inclusive and expansive, the use of *gay* has often been restricted and contested in a variety of different ways. In the early 1980s, when the term *gay* was originally imported into Brazilian Portuguese, it was applied almost exclusively to *travestis* or other men marked by their exaggerated feminine mannerisms, almost as if it might be understood as a kind of third gender category. Over the course of the following decade, however, particularly as the discussion of homosexuality became linked to the question of HIV/AIDS, an alternative use of *gay* as a form of self-identification began to become increasingly common among at least some men not otherwise marked by effeminate dress or mannerisms— rather unassuming *entendidos* whose self-proclaimed styles could be seen as closer to those of Anglo-European gay men than those of traditional Brazilian *bichas* or *travestis*. Again, our survey data provide some sense of these changes. In 1989, only 5 percent of the men interviewed described themselves as "gay"; in 1993, this had climbed to 10 percent—and to 17 percent in 1995.

These relatively different readings of *gay* life thus seem to coexist both in the homosexual or gay subculture itself as well as in the broader world of contemporary Brazilian culture, staking out claims on the territory of sexual life that are based on what would appear to be sharply contrasting notions of the ways in which such differences might be resolved. At the same time, the result of these contrasting readings is in many ways less closed-off than open-ended, coexisting more or less amicably in both the public and even private spaces of this urban subculture, and looking each day less like a stereotypical vision of Latin homosexuality than like the rapidly changing sexual subcultures of the Anglo-European world.

Perhaps somewhat ironically, the juxtaposition of sexual styles and life styles that draw on quite different meanings and assumptions yet bump up against one another constantly on the streets or in the nightlife of Rio or São Paulo, has begun to take shape more like the emerging queer cultures of the Anglo-European world than the world of more traditional Brazilian sexual cultures. Peopled by exotic *transformistas* and *drags* (drag queens), by *barbies* (literally, implying Barbie Dolls, and used to describe the self-conscious and exaggeratedly masculine physique manufactured only through long hours of weight lifting and aerobics), by *boys* (boys, implying both youth and a certain androgynous quality) and *bichas velhas* (aging queens), by *travestis* and *michês* as well as *entendidos* and *gays*, by *militantes do movimento gay* (gay activists) and *interventores de AIDS* (AIDS-prevention workers)—this evolving subculture has in fact spread out from Rio and São Paulo to cities around the country. A veritable boom in what has been described as the *mercado gay* (the gay market) has found firms and entrepreneurs in such centers exporting *Festas* (commercial parties) and *Shows* (musical and theatrical performances [by drag queens]) to smaller cities around the country.

In short, what seems to have emerged over the course of the past decade in large urban centers such as Rio or São Paulo—and only to a slightly lesser extent in smaller cities such as Belo Horizonte, Porto Alegre, Recife, Salvador, or Fortaleza—is a relatively complex sexual subculture (or set of overlapping and intersecting subcultures) that provides an alternative model for the organization of sexual reality that contrasts sharply with both the more traditional patterns of popular culture as well as with the rationalized sexuality of scientific discourse. At one level, of course, this emerging subculture is very much the product of a set of largely impersonal, social, political, and economic transformations taking place not only in urban Brazil but also widely in the contemporary world. At the same time, it is also very much a product of human agency—of often quite conscious action aimed at making, unmaking, and remaking the world and the possibilities that it offers, and at creating options that may not have existed previously. While this remade world may at times reproduce many of the characteristics typical of the traditional or rationalized systems of sexual meaning, it would seem to organize them and link them to the formation of identities and experiences in rather different ways. And it clearly offers those individuals whose lives it touches a very different set of possibilities and choices in the constitution of their own sexual and social lives.

Homosexuality, Culture, and Power

Taken together, these different systems of meaning begin to map out the social and cultural space, or at least the semantic boundaries, of male homosexuality in contemporary Brazilian culture. It is tempting to view them as part of a kind of evolutionary sequence, a series of phases in which one model gives way as another takes precedence. Yet while each of these systems is clearly tied to the others through a set of fundamentally historical relationships, the notion of a series of distinct phases is no less clearly inadequate a characterization of their interrelations. For all of their differences, there is little in the way of an abrupt break or rupture from one to the next. In the flow of daily life, in the lived experience of ordinary people, they tend to merge and interpenetrate in more or less confusing and often fragmentary, yet also fascinating, ways—much like the changing images of a kaleidoscope, simultaneously bringing together elements of continuity and historical transformations, old practices and new configurations, constant forms and changing patterns.[8]

Although a fundamentally historical relation exists between these socioeconomic systems and structures, they cannot be understood, in Brazil at least, as a series of neatly divided phases—modes of production (not only of goods, but also of bodies and pleasures) that fall in upon their own internal contradictions before giving way to a new historical phase. On the contrary, perhaps the key quality of Brazilian society, and certainly the quality that sometimes seems to make it most difficult for (Anglo-European) outsiders to comprehend, is precisely the fact that these systems in many ways continue to coexist even in contemporary life.

It is this juxtaposition of differences—in political economy as well as in the political economy of the body—that is in fact the defining mark of contemporary Brazilian life (and perhaps of the contemporary global system as a whole). The glittering, late capitalist, financial centers of cities such as Rio and São Paulo, connected as they are to every corner of the globe by the velocity of wire transfers and the shrinking nature of both time and space (see Harvey 1990), continue to coexist side by side with the

factories of a relatively early and still (at least in Brazil) expanding industrial capitalism, as well as with the *favela* shantytowns—the largely domestic production and the street vendors of what is typically described as the
"informal" economy. Traditional, modern, and postmodern aesthetics
and ideologies compete for space not only in the landscape of the city but
also in the images of mass media. Local cultures are necessarily situated in
global contexts, and the interaction between the two increasingly takes
shape not merely through imposition but through interlocution.

Within this simultaneously traditional/modern/postmodern world,
homosexuality in Brazil has increasingly become a key point of intersection between different systems of meaning and structures of power. It is
characterized not by its singularity, but by its multiplicity—by its interfaces and its apparent contradictions. In the chapters that follow, I will
examine at least some of the aspects that seem most striking, to make
some sense of the possibilities that exist for living in this often contradictory world—for fighting back against the very real forms of violence and
oppression that exist in daily life, for seeking some degree of relief from
pain and suffering, and, indeed, for managing to find bits and pieces of
happiness while making one's way in a difficult world.

3

Contours of the
Urban Gay World

The diverse systems of meaning that seem to organize the world of male homosexuality in Brazil have evolved through time, forming an increasingly intricate weave of intersubjective cultural frames. But they have also spread themselves out through space in a variety of diverse ways. While it is impossible to do justice to the complexity of what might be described as sexual geography in Brazil, I now want to turn from the evolving models of sexual reality that have emerged over time and to look in more detail at some of the ways in which these models have taken shape and organized subcultures and communities in a variety of settings, roughly over the course of the past decade. I want to turn at least briefly from an essentially diachronic to a more synchronic field and to look at the social organization of same-sex relations in the present as well as at their physical organization in the configuration of urban life—an exercise in mapping that is concerned, if you will, with both the social organization of sexual space and the sexual organization of social space.

With this in mind, I now concentrate on what might be described as a kind of topography of homoerotic desire across a relatively broad range of contemporary urban centers in Brazil—at the ways in which same-sex interactions take shape in public space, and at the temporary subversion of dominant and often highly oppressive (hetero)sexual norms that takes place through such interaction. From here, I look at the construction of male sex work and at the ways in which sexual subcultures organized around both male hustling and transvestite prostitution play a central role in staking out both gay (or queer) space as well as the homoerotic imagination in contemporary urban settings. I then move on to examine the recent emergence of a growing commercial network catering to a gay clientele, and the role of this commercial world in providing a focal point both for same-sex interaction and gay cultural elaboration. Finally, I review the growing presence of both gay and AIDS activism and how the politicization of sexuality and the development of AIDS-prevention activities have also helped shape emerging gay cultures and communities. Ultimately, by playing off these different contexts and settings, by offering a sense of the extent to which they are at once distinctive yet intersecting within a broader cultural frame, I seek to provide some notion of what might be described as the contours of the urban gay world in contemporary Brazilian life.

Like George Chauncey in his work on New York, I want to emphasize the extent to which this world is made up of multiple realities, of diverse social networks that may overlap but that may also be quite distinct— whether in terms of race or class, age range or gender performance, gay cultural styles or erotic practices, and so on (see Chauncey 1994:2–3). Yet precisely because the men within this world, no matter how different from one another in terms of their specific backgrounds and styles, nonetheless recognize within the range of their diversity something that they may also share in common as part of an alternative (queer, or at least slightly bent) social/sexual space distinct from the social/sexual space of the dominant, straight, heterosexual world, I want to focus on the extent to which this world structures the possibilities of (male) sexual difference in contemporary Brazilian life—as well as the interfaces and intersections that make it possible to connect male homosexual life in Brazil to a wider set of global systems and processes in the late twentieth century.

The Topography of Desire

As has become clear in recent years, the social and cultural mapping of sexual relations takes place concretely within a world of physical space, of geographical space, in which sexuality is organized and distributed (see, for example, Bell and Valentine 1995; Duyvas 1995; Parker and Carballo 1990). In all social settings, and particularly in large urban areas, there exists both a complex sexual geography as well as a high degree of local knowledge about the specificities of this terrain. Some areas of the city are inevitably the territories for female prostitution, for dating and sexual interaction on the part of young male and female couples, and so on. In few cases are the intricacies of sexual geography as elaborate as for male homosexuality, where the territorialization (as well as the deterritorialization) of sexual space is often exceptionally complex.

As I suggested in chapter 2, the development of relatively impersonal and anonymous social relations in more urbanized settings over the course of the twentieth century has led the complex space of the city to become increasingly eroticized or sexualized. City streets, plazas, parks, and other public venues become a stage for relatively impersonal homoerotic contacts—sexual interactions and adventures that surely would have been unthinkable in a more small-scale or intimate social setting. And through these homoerotic adventures, through ongoing acts of *paquerando* and *fazendo pegação* (roughly translatable as cruising), *olhares* (stares or prolonged glances), and *seduções* (seductions), the supposedly neutral space of daily life has begun to be called into question, at least momentarily, opening the possibility for the construction of a very different sexual landscape.

Indeed, what is perhaps most striking in the relationship between homosexuality and space in urban Brazil is precisely the extent to which a homoerotic undercurrent permeates urban life, though in large part without organizing sharply defined gay ghettos or neighborhoods along the lines found in many Anglo-European societies. As one informant put it in trying to characterize life in Rio de Janeiro, for example:

> Rio has that quality that everybody is familiar with. . . . Sex (*sacanagem* [implying here homo-sex]) is everywhere around you. . . . On the corner, buying groceries at the supermarket, people are always cruising (*paquerando*). . . . Anyone who feels horny (*tesão*, or sexual excitement) just has to go down [from the building where they live] to the street, to pick someone up (*arranjar alguém*). (Antônio Carlos, a thirty-seven-year-old informant from the middle class in Rio de Janeiro)

Thus, there is a homoerotic tension underlying virtually any encounter, and urban space becomes eroticized precisely because of its perceived impersonality and unpredictability. The watchful eye of social control in traditional society can thus be transformed into the gaze of desire and the possibility of seduction in urban settings:

> Lots of people move to Rio or São Paulo from small towns, or smaller cities in the interior, because of sex. . . . In a small town, you're always being watched (*vigiado*). But in the big city, nobody cares. . . . The only people who are looking (*olhando*) are the ones looking for (*procurando*) the same thing you are. You can pick people up (*pegar*) anywhere—on the street, at the beach, in the shopping center. You just have to give them that look (*dar aquela olhada*), and they know what you want. (Marquinhos, a twenty-four-year-old informant from the working class in Rio de Janeiro)

The importance of looking, as opposed to being looked at or looked after, is crucial here. By escaping into the anonymity of the city and appropriating the gaze of the other not as a form of social control but as an expression of desire, the *entendidos* in this gay world are able to transform the otherwise hostile space of the dominant, heterosexual world into a field of erotic possibilities—a field in which, at least in theory, anything can happen.[1]

The ways in which these perceived possibilities are resolved in sexual adventures, however, may vary. The exchange of glances may lead to nothing at all, serving as little more than a way to liven up an otherwise dull routine, or to kill time while waiting for an appointment, or what have you. They may lead to further contact, however, and, at least in some instances, may ultimately end in sexual interaction. This, too, can play itself out in a number of different ways. The street (beach, shopping center, or any other essentially public space), for example, may become a site for *paquerando* and *pegação*, for cruising, for making contact and picking someone up before ultimately going back to an apartment, or, in the absence of private space, a hotel or motel:

> A place to have sex can be a problem. For people who have money, they are likely to have an apartment, at least a studio, of their own or that they share with friends or roommates, so if they meet someone on the street they have a place to go back to [for sex]. . . . If they live a long way away, or don't have a place of their own, there are always motels or hotels. The motels at the edge of the city, or on the major highways, don't always let two men enter together—some do, but not all of them. Some [of the motels] even try to charge each guy for a separate room![2] But every city has an area in the center of town with "hotels for gentlemen" (*"hoteis para cavalheiros"*) that are exclusively for sex between men. They're usually old and kind of run down, but at least it's a place to fuck. (Jorge)

But perhaps even more frequently, the street itself, or other public spaces such as parks or beaches, public toilets or movie theaters, can themselves become the site for sexual interaction:

> INTERVIEWER: What about public sex? How are sexual interactions in public organized, and where do they take place?
> JORGE: Every city has a kind of network of places where people go to find partners and to have sex—it's usually concentrated in the center of town, the oldest part of the city, and the most run-

down, but even some of the outlying neighborhoods have their own places. Any *entendido* can tell you where they are. Cruising parks (*parques de pegação*), tearooms (*banheiros de pegação*), places where people go to cruise, but also to fuck . . .

INTERVIEWER: At any time of day, or only at certain times?

JORGE: No, it depends. Its very complex. Sometimes the time of day is important. In the Aterro de Flamengo [the largest park in Rio de Janeiro], for example, cruising goes on all day. But it is less intense during the day. . . . People cruise, they may even get together, or perhaps go into the bushes, or beneath the trees, out of sight of others, to jack off (*tocar punheta*), but they don't usually have much physical contact, because they are worried about being seen. At night, though, or even as soon as it begins to get dark, the sex heats up. People are much more likely to suck—and to actually fuck in the bushes. It is usually at sundown that things heat up, that there is heaviest movement, because it is when people are getting off work and can pass through the park, as if they were innocently taking a stroll or passing through on their way home. But people have to be careful at this time as well, because it is also when the police patrols are most intense. There are lots of robberies, and the police also want to control "immoral" behavior, so they are constantly patrolling from one end of the park to another. If they catch people having sex, they won't do anything really, they certainly won't take them in or arrest them. . . . They may threaten to, for an "affront against pudency" ("*atentado ao pudor*" [one of the few legal categories regulating sexuality in Brazil]), but usually it's just in order to be paid off. They earn lousy salaries, and shaking down a *bicha* for money is a way of adding to the family income. Sometimes they want to be paid off with a blow job, or to screw one of the guys who they have caught.[3]

INTERVIEWER: Are all the parks the same?

JORGE: No, not all of them—sometimes nothing happens at all. It depends on the geography. If it is just a simple square, the most that happens is cruising, looking, maybe picking people up. When the geography is more complicated, with more secluded spaces, or places where you can hide from view, it's easier. It also depends if the park is fenced in or not. When it's fenced in and closed at night no one can get in. The Aterro is really attractive because it's open, so you can go there all night long. And late at night, when the police patrols stop running, is when things get really heavy, when everybody goes not just to

cruise or jack off, but to suck and fuck, to have orgies with lots
of guys fucking together.

In cities located on the coast, beaches (which play a central role in Brazilian notions of leisure and pleasure) also take on special importance:

> RODRIGO (a thirty-year-old from the lower class in Fortaleza):
> Most of the beaches have a gay area, the gay beach (*a praia gay*),
> where the *bichas* all go. During the day, the beach is mostly for
> cruising (*paquerando*), or picking people up (*pegando*). Late in the
> day lots of people will leave together, will go back home
> together [for sex]. Later, at night, lots of the gay beaches also
> become a place for cruising, and for having sex—as well as a trap
> for anyone who doesn't take care with the thieves or the police
> who go there to take advantage of the cruising *bichas*. At night,
> because they are located near bars and restaurants, or other sim-
> ilar places that don't have anything to do with this, that aren't
> necessarily gay, it all seems innocent—you walk out to the beach
> in the dark as if you are going to pee (*mijar*), and nobody thinks
> anything of it. The people on the *calçadão* (the large sidewalk
> that runs along at least a stretch of beach in almost all coastal
> cities in Brazil) don't even realize that just a few meters away, in
> the dark, a bunch of guys are having sex.
> INTERVIEWER: But aren't the beaches used by straight couples
> (*namorados*) too?
> RODRIGO: Of course, but that's why it's important to know
> which stretches of the beach are gay, which stretches are where
> it happens (*do babado forte*, a euphemism for being part of the
> gay world).[4]

Even in broad daylight, a deserted (or largely deserted) beach can provide
a site for sexual contact, whether intended or unexpected:

> I remember once when I was at the beach at Urca [a neighborhood
> in the South Zone of Rio de Janeiro], it was late in the afternoon,
> and there had hardly been anyone on the beach all day . . . and by
> now it was completely empty, except for a fisherman working with
> his net a ways down the beach. . . . It was a really hot day, and the
> sun was just starting to go down. I was lying on my towel, on my
> belly, with my ass up (*a minha bunda para cima*). I wasn't paying
> any attention to the guy working on his net, but when I turned
> over I realized that he had moved closer, and that he had been

looking at my ass. And he started to squeeze his prick (*segurar o seu pau*) beneath his pants—you know, real macho (*bem machão*). I couldn't believe it—I hadn't even thought of the possibility of making it with him. But we wound up having sex (*transando*), right there on the beach, at the far end where it is harder for people to see you. (Robson, a twenty-four-year-old informant from the working class in Rio de Janeiro)

Whether in the nooks and crannies of city parks or the relative secrecy of moonlit or deserted beaches, the simultaneously hidden yet (potentially) exposed character of these games of seduction, and of physical contact itself, is central to the gay world that has taken shape in Brazil.[5]

Given the emphasis on impersonality, on an almost constant kind of movement in and out of the sites that serve as a focus for same-sex interactions, it is perhaps not surprising that buses, trains, subways, and similar forms of mass transportation also seem to play a special role in this construction of sexual space and homoerotic adventure:

MARCOS: The trains in from the suburban areas are famous—
they come in completely packed with workers, and go out the same way at the end of the day. During rush hour it's like a can of sardines, with everybody squeezed up together. Women complain all the time, because the macho guys are always using this as an excuse to take a piece out of them [*tirar um pedaço*, figuratively implying to brush up against them or touch them indecorously]. But gays love it. . . . Everybody [who is gay] jokes about how rush hour is the best time to take the subway or the train. There are even special wagons at the end of the train that become almost exclusively queer (*só tem viado*)—so much playing around (*tanta sacanagem*) happens that anyone who isn't gay (*entendido*) knows to stay away from them. I've literally seen people fucking. Not often, but a couple of times. Usually it's more rubbing up against one another (*roça-roça*, or, literally, rub-rub).
INTERVIEWER: But why does this go on so much on the trains and the subway?
MARCOS: I think that it's the masses of people—there are people everywhere around you, but at the same time it's like everyone is anonymous, like you were in a cruising park (*parque de pegação*) or something, where no one knows anyone else. And there's nothing else to do, anyway—the ride is always long and tedious, so playing around is a way to kill the boredom. It's the movement, too, I suppose, maybe the vibration of the vehicle. . . .

> I don't know. But it's not just the trains. The buses are famous for playing around (*sacanagem*) too, and the boats across the bay [from Rio] to Niterói—the toilets on the boats are a constant in and out [of people cruising].

Like the trains and subways, then, other forms of mass transit, and buses in particular, are a central part of the fluctuating, transgressive gay world:

> I love buses that are full, packed. . . . I always try to catch buses that are superfull, and I let myself get into my own sexual craziness (*taras*). I don't go looking for anyone—inside the bus I just let it happen. . . . I travel in the bus thinking about what I have to do the next day, and suddenly something [sexual] happens, and I forget about life and give in to pleasure (*me entrego ao prazer*). . . . I act like nothing is happening, but I participate actively in the event. . . . I feel something pleasant, coming out of me—sometimes I arrive home [with my pants] all full of cum (*esporrado*), but when this doesn't happen I go to take my bath and masturbate to the fantasy of that cock pressing up against me, against my shoulder, against my ass, against my thigh. (Alessandro, an eighteen-year-old informant from the working class in Caxias, a poor suburban area on the outskirts of Rio de Janeiro)

As in public parks or beaches, then, in the movements of the mass transit system throughout civic space, the possibilities of same-sex interaction—if not of sexual intercourse, certainly of sexual *brincadeiras* or play—is an ever-present possibility. Almost as if one were conquering enemy territory, the transgression of proper (hetero)sexual decorum becomes part and parcel of the creation of queer space, the construction of a semi-secretive (yet quite conscious) gay world within the very structures of otherwise straight society.

This emphasis on a certain kind of transgression, an invasion of alien sexual space, is clearly evident not only in the erotic undercurrents and sexual contact of open-air settings or the playful interactions of the mass transit system, but also in the appropriation of at least some indoor sites that would otherwise serve as a focus for dominant masculinity and heterosexuality. In men's toilets, pornographic movie theaters, and similar settings, homoeroticism takes shape as part of the broader range of male sexuality:

> JORGE: I'm always impressed by the different kinds of tearooms (*banheiros de pegação*). . . . They're everywhere. Sometimes it isn't

even a tearoom, just a regular bathroom, but you cruise some-one while using the urinal, suddenly a climate is created (*pinta um clima*), and it winds up happening. Then there are the bath-rooms that aren't specifically tearooms all of the time, but that people know about and sometimes check out when they want to pick someone up or have sex—like lots of McDonald's or other chain restaurants in the downtown area. You go in, and lots of times nothing will be happening, but sometimes you notice that someone has been at the urinal too long, or washing his hands for hours, so you step up to the urinal, take your cock out, and start jacking off (*tocando uma punheta*) more or less dis-creetly to see what will happen. Chances are that the guy will come up beside you to jack off too. . . . Then there are the big public toilets, like at the Central do Brasil [the central train sta-tion in Rio de Janeiro] or the Praça da República [the central square or plaza in downtown São Paulo]. The urinals are huge troughs and a dozen or more guys of all types—blacks, mulattos, whites, lower class and upper class, young, old—they'll all be there with their cocks out jacking off.

INTERVIEWER: Do people just jack off looking at one another, or do they touch one another?

JORGE: It really depends on the bathroom. At the big tearooms where there are lots of people, its like an orgy. One guy will reach over and jack off another, sometimes—but not everybody likes to be touched, and it's a whole active/passive game, the one who touches, or who sucks someone else, is always seen as infe-rior. There's a superiority in having the other person touch you! Depending on the layout of the bathroom, people can some-times find a corner for sex. I've seen people on their knees suck-ing, or getting fucked in a standing position—or they go into a stall if they want to have sex so that no one can see. But in some tearooms sex doesn't even happen, just looking. It's really crazy—there are even some tearooms where the people just jack off but don't come (*não gozam*), and others where they come in the urinal and the trough gets all filled up with cum (*porra*) by the end of the day.

INTERVIEWER: What about the police, or the authorities?

JORGE: At the small bathrooms, places like McDonald's, the secu-rity people or some other employee always goes in on a regular basis, supposedly to clean up, but really to make sure that noth-ing is going on—and they'll kick you out if they find something happening. At the bigger tearooms, the ones with room for dozens of people, like at a railroad station or a train station, the police come in every now and again, but just for show, and they go away soon. At these public restrooms, there is always an attendant—usually you have to pay to get in, and the attendant who takes the money and who cleans up is in a position to see everything that is happening. But the *bichas* pay him off—the people who go all the time give him a little something extra when they pay to go in, and he knows to shut up and look the other way. Sometimes the attendant will even take part in the game—once when I was at the international airport for a really early flight, I went in to use the bathroom, really to use it, nothing more, and the attendant, this big mulatto, was cleaning the floor. I gave him a look as I was peeing (*fazendo xixi*), and in seconds he had come over to a urinal near me and had taken his cock out and started to stroke it. He had a huge cock, but he wanted money [in exchange for sex], so I didn't do anything with him. Besides, I had to catch a plane.

Like toilets, at least some cinemas, especially cinemas that specialize in pornographic or sexually explicit (heterosexual) films, are also a focus for cruising and sexual interaction between men:[6]

>INTERVIEWER: You said that cinemas are one of the best places to go for sex? Are all cinemas used for cruising?
>
>RODRIGO: No, not every cinema. . . . Not even in every cinema that shows porno films (*filmes de sacanagem*). . . . But in almost every large city there are at least a few cinemas were people go for sex. Even in some legitimate cinemas, the toilets are a place where people cruise. . . . They can go into the toilet as if it were something natural, just going to use the facilities—they may even be at the cinema with their family, their wife or girlfriend, and they go to the toilet to cruise without anybody even knowing. But there are always some cinemas that are almost exclusively for sex. Everybody knows it—the owners of the cinema, the city authorities, and certainly the local male population, whether they're gay or not.
>
>INTERVIEWER: But what goes on there? What do people do?
>
>RODRIGO: Lots of people sit watching the film, but there is a constant circulation of people. Guys sit in the seats, jacking off or stroking their cocks beneath their clothing—especially the *bofes*. The *bichas* walk up and down the aisles looking for someone who interests them. . . . When they see someone, they stop near

them, in the seat next to them, or a few seats away. If the guy you're interested in exchanges glances, you move closer, and put your hand on their prick. The *bicha* may just jack them off, or maybe give them a blowjob (*uma chupada*). Sometimes at the back of the cinema, when there is a place for people to stand, whole masses of guys stay there, standing up—so many that you have to push your way through to pass from one side to the next. You let your hand slip down to feel there cocks, or you brush up against them. The *bofes* always act macho, playing the role of the *ativo*, brushing up against the asses of the *bichas*, who push back against their cocks. Sometimes they take their cocks out of their pants, sometimes not. But when the lights come up between one showing of the film and another, everybody goes scurrying off and acts like nothing has been happening. It's really funny.

So even the masculine, apparently heterosexual, space of public toilets and straight pornographic cinemas can be contested and reconstituted as a kind of homoerotic underside to (normal) male sexuality, which is at the same time part of a transgressive, and often almost orgiastic, gay world. And while this world may at times seem to have a kind of clandestine quality (taking place in the shadows of the night or the reflected light of the film projector), it is at best only partially hidden. In fact, it is relatively well-known to the local authorities, who may periodically (but almost never systematically) make it the object of public morals campaigns—just as they sometimes do with female prostitution. And it is certainly well-known to the male population as a whole, including those men who may prefer not to participate in it, or who consider it immoral or improper.[7]

One can read this social/sexual process any number of ways. It might be interpreted as itself a reproduction of the oppression and domination of traditional sexual life. In this system, the constant discrimination of homosexuality and sexual deviance more generally prohibits any possibility of a socially legitimate space for amusement, festivity, socialization, sharing, and so on, between men who have sex with men. This system literally expels such interactions to the dangerous world of the street, where they must be carried out clandestinely and with the constant threat of physical or verbal violence on the part of offended onlookers, the police, or vigilante groups seeking to clean up society for respectable citizens. Such a universe is also open to a second interpretation, however—the constant "queering" of straight space through innumerable acts of transgression. The creation of a world of homoerotic bodies and pleasures in precisely those social spaces in which such a possibility should be most unthinkable. Persistence and resistance in the face of the sexual oppression that defines homo-sex as unacceptable and offensive.

Whichever reading one opts for (Brazilian informants have offered both, and a nuanced reading would probably lie somewhere between the two extremes), there can be little question that sexual space, like sexual meanings more generally, is always inevitably contested—a focus for both domination and resistance that is in fact anything but neutral. Nor can there be any doubt that this homoerotic transformation of otherwise public, (hetero)sexual, or straight space is utterly essential to a more general process in which the contours of a gay world are carved out in the flow of daily life in Brazil. With its especially fluid, highly mobile, character, it may perhaps seem to be an unlikely foundation for the construction of a distinct, organized, sexual community, yet it has formed an important part of a broader sexual subculture organized above all else around a notion of sexual difference.

The Negotiation of Difference

If this homoerotic inscription of otherwise straight, public space often seems particularly fluid, however, in at least some instances it may also take more concrete and defined form through what might be described as the territorialization of specific areas and the concretization of sexual subcultures. This is perhaps most evident in prostitution or sex work, which, like male homosexuality, has been an integral part of complex sexual geography in virtually all major urban centers in Brazil. Indeed, in many cities, the geographical distribution of both female and male prostitution has often overlapped with the topography of homoerotic interactions described above—in part perhaps by choice (of both prostitutes and men who have sex with men), but also certainly by design (on the part of the local authorities). The prostitutes are relegated to what members of the Chicago school of sociology might have described as "moral (or, perhaps more accurately, immoral) zones" within the wider structure of the city.[8]

In virtually every major Brazilian city, the intricate geography of prostitution responds to a range of local conditions and circumstances, taking shape as an important part of the wider geographical map of spatial sexualities, and at the same time organizing itself around a set of social and cultural distinctions: differences in class and status, age, race and ethnicity, gender style, and so on. This is perhaps especially evident in the world of male prostitution, which has evidenced a gamut of somewhat diverse (though rarely altogether separate) constructs. The sharp distinction between *michês*, or male hustlers, and *travestis*, or transvestite prostitutes, for example, has been especially important both in marking out extremes in gender constructs within the gay world as well as in demarcating spatial territories associated with same-sex interaction.

The male hustling of the *michê* is perhaps especially curious and complicated, concretizing a range of symbolic contradictions. Indeed, the very terms *michê* (hustler) or *michetagem* (hustling) are themselves fundamentally ambiguous, referring both to the hustler himself (who is called a *michê*) in male prostitution, as well as to the payment (also called a *michê*), which is exchanged between a male client and a female prostitute in heterosexual prostitution. At a relatively conscious level, then, the world of male hustling, within the entire gay world, not only links a notion of sexual interaction to a system of economic exchange but also constitutes a complex symbolic economy in which the meanings associated with both homosexual (queer) and heterosexual (straight) experience must be constantly negotiated and renegotiated in social/sexual interchanges (Perlongher 1987; see also Parker 1993).

Within the wider context of such symbolic exchanges, the *michê* (the person) and his *michetagem* (the activity) become almost synonymous with the world of homoerotic desire unexpectedly uncovered in the otherwise apparently normal heterosexual world of public space described above. Indeed, it is almost part and parcel of the mythology of the *michê* that he is a kind of Everyman: a typical young male from the lower sectors of Brazilian society, from the popular classes and the *subúrbios*, or suburban neighborhoods, that surround major urban centers such as Rio and São Paulo. While the stereotype is of course not altogether correct, and *michês* may well come from a variety of social backgrounds depending upon a number of specific circumstances, the *michê* is nonetheless in many ways the embodiment of the surprising sexual partner that one may unexpectedly meet in cruising on the street:

> The *michê* has to be really young and masculine, virile, someone who you wouldn't really expect to screw around [with other men]. . . . If he looks or acts like a *bicha* it isn't any good—he would never be attractive to the *bichas*. It's like the popular saying, *"homem com homem dá lobishomem, mulher com mulher dá jacaré"* ("a man [having sex] with another man produces [gives birth to] a werewolf; a woman [having sex] with another woman produces [gives birth to] an alligator"). He has to be really masculine to fit together with the effeminate *bichas*. He has to be like someone who you would cruise in a park or on the street, someone who you would be attracted to and would want to have sex with. But he can't be had for free—if you are going to have him, you have to pay the price. (Reinaldo)

Typically, then, the *michês* are adolescents or young adults, between the ages of thirteen and twenty, who are characterized by youthful male virility. They often live in the poor outskirts of the city and ride the trains or buses (which, as discussed above, are a key part of the sexual circulation through city space) into the center of town, where they work, often sporadically, in different streets or plazas that are primary locations for making contact with older, more well-to-do, and often more effeminate, men (called *mariconas* by the *michês*—more or less equivalent to "faggots" in English) who will be willing to pay for their sexual services:

> JORGE: There are specific locations where you can always find *michês*. Every city has them, but they change a lot over time. In São Paulo, most of the places that I know are located near the Praça da República. In Rio it is mostly downtown or in Copacabana.
>
> INTERVIEWER: Are all of the locations more or less the same?
>
> JORGE: No, it depends a lot. At the Central do Brasil [the central train station in Rio], for example, the *michês* are really young and poor—a lot of them are street kids, or really poor boys from the *subúrbios*. The clients are usually poor too, and a place to have sex may be more of a problem because he [the client] may not have money for a hotel. The price for sex is a lot cheaper. On the gay beaches, the beach boys (*michês de praia*) tend to be a lot more expensive, and sophisticated—they may work the tourists, or the rich *bichas* who have nothing to do but hang out on the beach all day. They may be sophisticated enough to stretch out their careers longer, working into their twenties or even their early thirties. The *michês* downtown are sort of in between— older, better dressed, and more expensive than at the Central do Brasil, but not as sophisticated as the beach boys.

Depending on the specific setting, then, negotiations between the *michês* and their prospective clients, can take a variety of different forms:

> The interaction between the *michê* and the *freguês* (client) depends a lot on the kind of place that it is. If it is a plaza, like in Cinelândia [in Rio], it is a lot more constrained—the *michê* will sit on the bench with his legs spread apart, sort of showing off his merchandise, and will wait for the *bicha* to come over and strike up a conversation. They may sit talking for a really long time before finally getting to the heart of the matter and reaching an agreement. When they finally work it out, they will go off together towards

Avenida Gomes Freire [where hotels that rent rooms by the hour to male couples are located] to have sex. When the cruising takes place in a less visible location, like Via Ápia [also in downtown Rio], the *michês* will stand in the shadows beneath the trees, or leaning against the old lamp posts, with their cocks hard, jacking off (*tocando punheta*), while the clients drive around slowly in cars. A client will stop next to a guy who interests him, and they will negotiate the price, what the *michê* will do for that price, where they will go. . . . If they reach a deal, the *michê* gets in the car, and they go to have sex, in the car itself, at a motel, or sometimes even the client's home. (Excerpt from fieldnotes)

In large part, then, the general physical space of male hustling tends to overlap or at least intersect with the space of homoerotic adventure in the street—indeed, concentrating in many of the same streets, parks, or plazas that are common for noncommercial cruising and public sex. Yet although a certain mixture of venues may take place, the physical space and social interactions associated with hustling are also understood, within this milieu, as qualitatively distinct—as obeying a set of rules that also regulate the negotiation of all same-sex interactions, but that must be carried out in accord with a more rigid formula when the exchange is to be financial as well as sexual.

As in other forms of commercial sex, then, the negotiation of a *programa* (a paid sexual interaction) between the *michê* and his prospective clients is a delicate interaction, in which both the price charged and the specific sexual practices involved must be specified (and sometimes renegotiated over the course of the interaction). Indeed, it is a negotiation in which not only bodily pleasures but also subjective identities are always at stake. The question of sexual practice is perhaps particularly crucial precisely because of the meanings associated with activity and passivity, since practices such as fellating another male or being anally penetrated by a client are highly problematic behaviors that implicitly call into question masculine identity, and are therefore rejected outright by a large number of *michês*:

At least in principle, the *michê* is always supposed to be active (*ser ativo*), to fuck the *maricona* (effeminate male [client]). It's almost as if he were a kind of exaggerated representation of the *bofe*. He fucks with other men, but only occasionally, and only for money. (Jorge)

At the level of representation, then, an idealized pattern of active/passive distinctions is constructed within this world, as the expected activity of the *michê* is contrasted with the passivity of his *maricona* (effeminate) clients. And for many young males involved in hustling, this emphasis on a kind of exaggerated masculinity (concretely symbolized by sexual *atividade*) is perhaps almost a logical necessity—precisely because hustling may by a relatively limited part of their lives that must somehow be organized within the broader context of their experience. While they may work the streets a few nights a week, or even quite regularly during certain hours of the night and early morning, many *michês* continue to live with their families of origin or in the conservative and traditional neighborhoods where their families live, and to maintain ongoing social relationships and participate in social networks within such conventional settings, engaging in heterosexual interactions with partners who know nothing of their involvement in male prostitution. Sexual activity in their work as *michês* appears, for many, to serve as a kind of psychological defense, necessary in order to guarantee that their homosexual relations—performed in exchange for money or other material benefits—need not in any way call into question their heterosexual experience and masculine identity within a social context in which almost all sexual exchanges are structured in a rigorous hierarchy. Indeed, within the terms of this construction, turning a trick on Friday night may be the only way to assure the money necessary to take a girlfriend out on Saturday, and a series of relatively rigid, social, cultural, and psychological mechanisms are therefore brought into play in order to ensure that these universes of experience never interpenetrate or mix.

If a notion of sexual activity, symbolized by active penetration of the supposedly passive *maricona*, is clearly central to this construction of masculine virility, however, it is also reinforced by a close association with the constant potential, and in many instances the actual incidence, of physical violence:

> Violence is almost synonymous with the *michês*, with the whole world of *michetagem* (hustling). . . . It's sort of logical: the *michê* is an image of masculinity and machismo, and nothing is more macho in Brazil than physical violence. You're always hearing stories about violence involving *michês*. Sometimes it's because the client doesn't want to pay, and the *michê* has to beat him up to get his money. Sometimes it's because they agreed to one thing, but in the heat of the moment (*na hora H*) the client tries to do something else—like trying to fuck the *michê*, and the *michê* has to protect his masculinity. And there are lots of stories about thieves who aren't even really *michês*, but who hang out in areas where *michês*

> work and act like they're hustling in order to be picked up and
> taken back to an apartment to rob the guy [the client]. (Robson)

The symbolism of violence, always a possibility in the homoerotic world
of the street, is thus concretized and localized above all else in the figure
of the *michê* and in the physical spaces or zones in which hustling takes
place.[9] Together with the *michê*'s active penetration of his clients, this
potential for violence becomes almost a kind of symbolic norm that is
expected to structure the nature of interactions and exchanges, reproducing at a fairly obvious level the notions of male virility and the active/pas-
sive calculus of traditional sexual culture, and concretizing such notions
physically in a specific figure (the *michê*) and the sexual space that he
inhabits (his territorial streets, parks, and plazas).

This image of exaggerated, active, violent virility that is personified by
the *michê* within this system, is belied, however, by the popular wisdom
on the streets that suggests that almost all the *michês* may at some point,
in private settings, eventually engage (at least occasionally) in passive anal
sex or in fellating their clients, and that the stereotype of straight *bofes*
engaging in homo-sex only for pay is in reality far more complicated:

> The stereotype is that the *michê* is always active—a straight guy
> (*um hêtero*) who just fucks *bichas* because he is being paid. In some
> cases, this is true. But it's a lot more complex than this. Everybody
> knows that if the price is right, or the conditions are right, lots of
> *michês* will agree to be fucked—and lots really like to get fucked.
> Its almost a game for many of the *bichas* who like to have sex with
> *michês*, to see if they [the client] can wind up fucking them [the
> *michê*]. And in spite of the popular image, many of the *michês* are
> really gay—or wind up gay. For lots of young guys from poor back-
> grounds, in the *subúrbios*, or from small towns, places where the
> stigma of homosexuality, of passivity, is really strong, being a
> *michê* becomes a way of entering into the gay world. During ado-
> lescence, they start having sex for money—the money justifies the
> sex, as though it wasn't homosexual because of the payment. Over
> time, the kid begins to become more and more involved in the gay
> world, the nightlife—and winds up having mostly gay friends. By
> the time he is twenty or twenty-five years old, he isn't in much
> demand any more as a *michê*, but by this time he has already taken
> on a gay identity. And almost all of the older *michês*, the ones who
> manage to keep turning tricks (*fazendo programa*) when they are in
> their twenties or thirties, are probably primarily gay. (João)

In actual practice, then, the figure of the *michê*, and all that he represents within this particular deployment of sexual meanings, is in fact a good deal more ambiguous than he first appears. Although the *michê* seems to concretely symbolize the intervention of straight masculinity in the homoerotic world of the street, at the same time he also represents the constant possibility of feminizing, bending, or queering straight patterns through the inversion of expected norms. Perhaps more than anything else, however, the *michê*'s highly visible presence in homosexual prostitution, combined with his supposed (and often real) movement back and forth between the center city, with its homoerotic zones, and the periphery, characterized (at least symbolically) by traditional or conservative family values, coalesce to present a transitive figure who concretely links the spaces of homosexual adventure to the spaces of straight society—transforming one cultural/geographic space into the other by his own movement and transformation.

This emphasis on transformation, on slippery meanings that seem to be constantly changing into something else, is thus central to the symbolic significance of *michetagem* or male hustling within this social and cultural universe. And it also links the *michê* symbolically to what at first glance might appear to be almost his polar opposite—the *travesti*, and the world of transvestite prostitution.[10] Yet if the *travesti* is as exaggerated a version of traditional femininity as the *michê* is of masculinity, the social/sexual space of transvestite prostitution (which mediates, in a sense, as a kind of third gender option, between the extremes of male hustling and female prostitution) is in fact no less transitory and multivalent, and the play of appearances rapidly melts away as one begins to untangle an underlying reality.

Precisely because of their highly stylized and exaggerated representation of femininity, the *travestis* are among the most distinctive and visible figures in the urban gay world in Brazil—severely stigmatized by virtually every segment of Brazilian society yet at the same time strangely respected (and perhaps feared) by many for their remarkable resilience. These extreme reactions can be found at almost every turn, ranging from popular songs like Chico Buarque's "Geni"—in which the constantly repeated refrain, *"joga bosta na Geni"* ("throw shit on Geni"), succinctly summarizes the treatment that the *travesti* receives in normal daily life (see Hollanda 1978)—to intentionally ironic popular sayings such as *"para ser travesti, você tem que ser muito macho"* ("to be a *travesti*, you have to be really macho"), which acknowledges the emotional and physical strength that one must have to survive such treatment:

> The *travesti*'s life is really tough. Nobody else takes so much shit in Brazil. The *travesti* suffers discrimination all the time. It is worse

than with blacks or even with *bichas* ... [with whom] people feel like they have to be at least a little more discreet in showing discrimination. But not with the *travesti*. People look, and stare, and laugh all the time—on the bus, in stores. And the *travestis* who work the streets are threatened all the time. Death squads from the periphery [the outlying suburban areas] make them a constant target—just like they do street kids or young blacks from the *favelas*. ... It's called "cleaning up Brazilian society." (Marcelo, a twenty-six-year-old informant from the lower class in Rio de Janeiro)

In spite of the remarkable stigma and discrimination that they face, however, the persistence of the *travestis* is really quite astounding. The *travesti's* body must quite literally be produced over time through an almost constant exercise of cultural and chemical intervention ranging from more superficial make-up to long-term application of hormones and silicone:

INTERVIEWER: Are you born a *travesti*, or do you become one?

JOINHA: No, you're born with a tendency ... from the time you're born you know that you're different, that you weren't meant to be an *homem* (man). But everything is arranged to push you in this direction, so you have to fight to remake yourself. It's more like a process—it is a process, really. It starts out as a kid, when you play like a girl, or want to use girl's clothes, or lots of times when you serve as the *bichinha* (literally, little *bicha*) for the local guys, and they start to treat you as a woman. Using hormones, or silicone, to change your body, comes later, after you already have it clear in your head that you are different.

INTERVIEWER: But how do you find out about the use of hormones, or of silicone?

JOINHA: There are doctors who specialize in this, and all the *travestis* know where to find them. But usually it is an older transvestite who teaches the younger one. Like the *travecas* (perhaps best translated as little, or apprentice, transvestites) who live at my house, Mônica or Nicole. ... They came to live with me after they had been thrown out of their homes, and I taught them how to use hormones to start transforming their bodies, when they were ready to start having silicone applied, where to go to turn tricks.

INTERVIEWER: You said earlier that *travestis* use hormones and silicone, but usually don't want sex-change operations. Explain what you meant.

JOINHA: No, even if sex-change operations were legal here, most people wouldn't want then. Underneath it all, we're still males—

just different. And its important to turning tricks too. Lots of clients want us precisely because we have what women don't have. (Excerpt from an interview with Joinha, an older [perhaps thirty-seven or thirty-eight-year-old] transvestite prostitute who also maintains a kind of rooming house, located in a *favela* in the South Zone of Rio de Janeiro, for younger transvestites)

It is by remaking the body, creating the illusion of femininity without sacrificing a hidden reality of masculinity, that the *travesti* takes shape (literally) as a key reference in the gay world in Brazil—mapping out the contours of this world and defining it as distinct and opposed to the routine of straight conformity (see photo 3.1).

Photo 3.1.   Creating the Illusion of Femininity. Photo by Richard Parker.

Again, like the *michê* and the world of *michetagem*, the detail and specificity of such mapping is striking. The geography of transvestite prostitution is organized around the dual axes of activity/passivity and socioeconomic class:

> JOINHA: Where to work depends on what you want to offer—or what you are able to offer. Lots of clients, especially from the lower classes, only want to fuck you—but there are also clients who want to be fucked, especially middle-class, married men. . .
>
> INTERVIEWER: Why middle-class men?
>
> JOINHA: I don't know why, but it seems like they are more likely to want to be passive.
>
> INTERVIEWER: Why do you suppose some clients want to be passive?
>
> JOINHA: I think that it is something about being screwed by a woman—looking up at a woman's face, a woman's hair, while they are being penetrated (*penetrados*) and possessed (*possuidos*). It's why the *travestis* often call their clients *mariconas*. They say that we're *bichas*, but at least we own up to it (*somos assumidos*)—they're the real *viados*, the ones who like to get fucked in the ass, but who live a lie in daily life.
>
> INTERVIEWER: But how does this define where you work?
>
> JOINHA: No, it's that sometimes you can't fuck the guy, even if you want to. When you are taking hormones for example, there are lots of times when you just can't get it up (*o pau não soube*). So if you can't be active, then it is better to work in areas like around the Quinta da Boa Vista [a large park in the North Zone of Rio de Janeiro], where the clients are mostly working class, and where they almost always want to fuck you rather than to be fucked. If you want to fuck too, then Copacabana or Gloria are the places to go, because that's where the clients who want to be fucked drive by in their cars to pick you up.

Transvestite prostitution seems to function on the basis of a complex game of appearances and underlying realities or revelations, concretely expressed both in the physical body of the *travesti* and in the fantasies and desires of the *freguês* (client).

Like the world of *michetagem* and, indeed, of homoerotic adventure in general, this world of transvestite prostitution is marked not only by its unexpected transformations and revelations but also by its peculiar mix of both pleasure and danger. There is an undercurrent of violence, both on the part of the *travestis* as well as of the clients, the police, the drug dealers, and also the pimps who circulate around them:

> The world of the *travestis* is really heavy (*barra pesada*). . . . Even
> more than the *michês*, they live in a kind of underworld of all
> kinds of crime. They don't really have any choice. Except maybe
> as hairdressers or sometimes cleaners in really poor, marginalized
> neighborhoods downtown, no one will give them a job. They have
> almost no choice but prostitution to survive. And they tend to get
> mixed up with drugs and drug dealers—with a whole range of
> petty thieves who often serve as their pimps (*gigolôs*) just like they
> would pimp for women. To survive on the streets the *travestis* have
> to be really tough and strong. And they are too—they really have
> men's bodies, after all, in spite of appearances, and they usually
> carry knives, or razor blades that they keep in their mouths, under
> their tongues. They even scare the police, because if they get
> picked up, and if they're fucked up enough [on drugs], to get
> themselves set loose, they sometimes take the razor blades out and
> cut themselves up, bleeding all over the police station. You would
> be amazed at how quickly the police let them go when this hap-
> pens, especially now with AIDS, because everyone thinks that all
> the *travestis* are infected, and they're scared of the *travestis*' blood.
> (Jorge)[11]

For *travestis*, and the spaces of transvestite prostitution, the symbolism
of violence is an explosive potential that permeates daily life, reinforcing
the masculine (albeit queer) reality underlying the appearances of femininity. In its own way, it marks out a social/sexual space that is clearly distinct from the straight-laced world of heterosexual normality—a space
that is marked as much by danger as by pleasure, and by the constant
inversion of otherwise accepted conventions.

Much like the more fluid world of sexual adventure associated with
street cruising and unexpected encounters, the apparently more fixed
structures of street hustling and transvestite prostitution also function to
dismantle a set of normative values and expectations. Bending the dominant patterns of social and sexual organizations, they explicitly force the
issue of sexual difference as a question open to negotiation, integrating
notions of economic exchange, sexual exchange, and symbolic exchange
as part of a complicated economic and cultural system. This economic system has grown up in complex ways, in part breaking off from the street
and the world of street prostitution, to be a segment of a relatively complex and rapidly growing industry of *serviços de programa* (out-call services)
and *casas de massagem* (massage houses)—services that may mix female
sex workers, *michês*, and (though less frequently) *travestis* on the same ros-
ter, or that may offer more specialized services with a specific kind of sex

worker directed to a specific kind of client. Such services seem to function as a way of partially neutralizing the most deeply felt dangers associated with street prostitution:

> There is a lot more demand now for *casas de massagem* and telephone services. I think that it is mostly because of the danger on the streets really. There have been a lot of assaults, robberies of people out looking to pick up *michês* and *travestis*. Because the hustling areas (*áreas de pegação*) are generally really marginal, without any policing, except during shake-downs and clean-ups, it is really dangerous. Sometimes the thieves are the *michês* or the *bichas* [i.e., the transvestite prostitutes]—but sometimes they are professional thieves who go there looking for victims specifically because they know how easy it will be to roll a queer (*assaltar um viado*). And even if the *freguês* picks someone up on the streets and takes him home, it's dangerous—the papers are always full of stories of guys who have been robbed, or even killed, by *michês* who they have taken home. So the demand for telephone out-call services has gone up— it's safer, if the call boy (*garoto de programa*) works for a *casa de massagem*, or has an ad in the newspaper and a telephone contact service. It is a lot less likely that anything dangerous will happen— the police would always have a way to find them. (Robson)

The less dangerous and more relaxed format of such services, together with the generally higher prices that can be charged to the more well-to-do clients using them,[12] makes work in a *casa de massagem* or the maintenance of a telephone out-call service a form of social mobility even among the ranks of the *michês* and *travestis*:

> People who work in *casas de massagem* feel superior to people working the street. Actually, almost everybody starts out on the street, and then gets to know somebody, and manages to get into a *massagem*. Or you save up enough money to rent or buy your own phone. Sometimes three or four guys will get together, pool their money, for a *kitchenete* (studio apartment) and a phone, and start up a service together. You make better money, and it is safer, but it is hard to get off the streets. (Clério, a twenty-seven-year-old from the lower class in Rio de Janeiro, who has worked on and off as a *michê* over the course of the past decade)

Yet even here, in the face of an increasing specialization in sex services, the most important features that position both hustling and transvestite prostitution as key sites for the negotiation of sexual meanings and of sexual difference are in large part maintained, though perhaps with greater opportunity for more complex and evolving relationships:

> Even when you are working out of a *casa de massagem*, it is still pretty much the same thing. The *maricona* who hires a *travesti* still wants to get fucked—often in the bed that he normally shares with his wife. The guy who hires a *michê* still works [in his mind] on a specific kind of fantasy about muscles, masculinity, and even violence. And the same kinds of things happen—even violence. Lots of times I've gone on a *programa* (trick), and after it is all over the guy has refused to pay or has pulled some shit. Then you have to act like a tough guy (*dar uma de machão*), and threaten to beat him up. . . . Sometimes it's just part of a whole fantasy trip, but sometimes you really do have to get violent. The thing that I like better, though, is that sometimes you really like the guys, and get along . . . they call you back over time, and it almost becomes a kind of relationship—not like with a lover (*um caso*), but different than what happens on the street. You work things out, and the interaction becomes something different than what it started out to be. (Clério)

So even here, in out-call services and massage houses, at least some of the transitory and transformative character of male hustling and transvestite prostitution is preserved. Identities and fantasies are negotiated. A bridge is built between the impersonal world of the street and the intensely personal world of private homes. The social universe of highly distinct class backgrounds (and, often, racial and ethnic groups) intersect.[13] And the relatively informal sexual and symbolic economies of the street begin to coalesce into a much more organized and rationalized system of exchange that clearly reproduces itself and evolves in a number of new and different ways.

At one and the same time, the intersecting worlds of male hustling and transvestite prostitution, of telephone call services and massage parlors, seem to mark out a set of highly specific social/sexual territories along with a kind of deterritorialization of accepted cultural distinctions that would otherwise organize both gender and sexuality as hegemonic norms in daily life. By reproducing, in especially exaggerated and stereotypical form, the distinctions between masculinity and femininity, activity and passivity, and so on, the distinction between *michês* and *travestis* at one level does little more than confirm many of the most oppressive structures of what is culturally perceived as the natural order of things. At the same time, by constantly threatening to invert this order, by suggesting that a sharp distinction may exist between surface appearances and deeper realities—that transgressive pleasures may undercut accepted expectations, and that this itself may become part of what is both desired and expected—the complex world of *michetagem* also undercuts the very structures that it reproduces—calling attention to both gender and sexuality as culturally patterned performances, and suggesting, through its own exaggerated performance style, that even accepted norms may have less to do with nature than with culture. Perhaps most important, they take shape as yet another set of elements that is used in the construction of an alternative sexual universe in Brazil—a universe that may at first glance seem to have little of the institutional or organizational quality that has come to be associated with the gay communities of many Anglo-European societies, but that nonetheless plays a key role in the constitution of an emerging gay world in contemporary Brazil.

The Gay Circuit

While the sexual subcultures organized around male hustling and transvestite prostitution offer some sense of the ways in which the homoerotic flow of city life can be socially, culturally, and spatially organized, a quite different process can be found in the emergence of a variety of gay commercial establishments that center not merely eventual sexual encounters but also a more far-reaching kind of gay sociability. Like male prostitution, the gay commercial world that has come forth in recent years has clearly connected sexuality to the development of a specific economy, and gay life styles have become the convergence for more complicated economic exchanges. Although the territorialization of male prostitution has reworked the traditional symbolism of gender and sexuality in Brazilian society, the emerging gay commercial world has built upon the particularities of these systems while at the same time hooking them up to a set of organizational structures and economic enterprises that are relatively familiar in the international gay world of the late twentieth century: gay bars, discos, bathhouses, and similar establishments and business ventures that become the place not only to meet sexual partners but also to engage in a kind of (homo)sociability within a context that is in part free from the repression and discrimination found in the outside world.

The existence of such commercial establishments is not altogether new. *Pontos de encontro* (meeting places) for gay people have existed in most major cities for many years. But until quite recently, such sites have rarely been identified as really serving a gay community. On the contrary, most have been owned and operated by proprietors who are not themselves gay and have at best tolerated the presence of a homosexual clientele only because of the obvious financial interest that it offers. In such settings, whether bars, cafés, or saunas, queer and heterosexual clienteles have mixed, on more or less friendly terms, and the gay public has often been subject to strong sanctions on the part of owners or managers when their interactions have become unacceptably intimate:

> Some of the worst examples of homophobia (*homofobia*) are found right in the gay world (*o mundo gay*)—like at the Bar Maxim's, right near the Bolsa [the gay beach in Copacabana]. For years Maxim's has survived [economically] because of the *bichas*—who stop there for beer or a drink when they leave the beach, or who go at night to talk with friends and watch the *michês* hustling (*fazendo ponto*) on the corner of [the Avenida] Atlântica. But when the waiters see two men kissing, they have been instructed to ask them to stop, or even to leave. They treat the clients like shit, and because the bar is open to public view, they constantly police the tables to make sure that no one is doing anything improper. But if the *bichas* would take their business someplace else, the bar would close. (Fernando, a thirty-four-year-old from the lower-middle class in Rio de Janeiro)

Like many bars and restaurants that over time have developed a reputation as gay meeting places, many supposedly straight male saunas or bathhouses have also served as quasi-gay baths with the tacit agreement of management:

> INTERVIEWER: What about saunas?
>
> RODRIGO: Most of the saunas aren't specifically gay—they serve a straight public (*um público hêtero*). Some of them have female prostitutes who do massages, stuff like that. Almost nothing gay goes on there. But other saunas that are supposedly straight are really gay (*do babado*), and everybody knows it. The management looks the other way, because their business depends on it—95 percent of the clients are homosexual.
>
> INTERVIEWER: Is there a lot of sexual activity? And how does it happen? Is it open? Do the attendants do anything to stop it?
>
> RODRIGO: It depends. . . . Usually the sex is sort of clandestine. At the Hotel Othon, for example, almost all of the clients are always homosexual, and they are cruising the whole time in the entire sauna—in the showers and the relaxation areas by the bar—but sex only happens in the steam room, and even then the rhythm changes. . . . Most of the time people are sitting on

their own, looking, staring . . . but after a time there will be a full-fledged orgy going on. If the door opens and an attendant comes in to mop up, everybody stops, and acts like they weren't doing anything, even though everyone knows that he saw everything that was going on. When he finishes and leaves, everything starts up again.

INTERVIEWER: Are most of the saunas like this?

RODRIGO: No, only some of them, and there are differences, like at the Hotel Othon where the clients are a lot more well-to-do, because it costs more to get in. The Sauna Apolo, further out by the periphery, is a lot cheaper and the clients are more popular [i.e., from the popular classes]. In some, you have to be more discreet. In others, the management doesn't care at all, and the sex is a lot more open and constant.

The presence of cruising and even sex is often ignored by managers who look the other way as long as there is financial gain to be had; the complaints of nongay customers, however, or occasional pressure from local authorities can quickly lead to repressive measures aimed at controlling homosexual behavior within acceptable limits of propriety. In the saunas, as well as in more sedate spaces such as bars and restaurants, the tension between the behavior of a homosexual clientele and the possible objections raised by heterosexual clients has been a constant source of tension.

Given such tensions, it is not surprising that over the course of recent decades gay-owned and operated establishments have opened to meet the growing demand from a largely gay-identified clientele:

INTERVIEWER: Explain what you mean by the difference between "gay" saunas and "traditional" saunas.

JORGE: I mean the more modern saunas that are explicitly gay— rather than *hêtero* saunas where sex between men sometimes happens. They're like the saunas in the United States or Europe—not as big or luxurious as the saunas that you'd find in Amsterdam or New York, but catering to a gay public and intentionally presenting themselves as gay.

INTERVIEWER: How so?

JORGE: By the decoration, the entryway, I don't know how to describe it, but there is no way to confuse it—when you get to the front door you can tell that it is just for homosexuals. Nobody *hêtero* is going to make the mistake of entering and then being surprised by what goes on inside, which sometimes happens at straight saunas (*saunas caretas*) when people go in unexpectedly and get upset if they see something happening (*caso role alguma coisa*).

Among the earliest sites to take advantage of a growing gay market were the explicitly gay-centered saunas that opened in cities like São Paulo and Rio in the late 1970s and early '80s. While high turnover rates have persisted over the past decade, in virtually every major city in the country, at least one or two specifically gay bathhouses now coexist with other more general male saunas, where same-sex interaction may often occur, but generally in more clandestine or camouflaged ways:

> INTERVIEWER: But the other saunas haven't disappeared have they—I mean the traditional saunas that weren't explicitly gay, but where sex between men was common?
>
> JORGE: No, no . . . lots of guys prefer them. Men who don't want to be identified as gay, or who prefer another kind of partner. In Rio there are a whole range of options: saunas where the clients are mostly from the popular classes, where you find a lot of *travestis*, or where *michês* work, as well as those that are mostly gay, and gay-identified.

The gay commercial world has thus superimposed itself on the substratum of homoerotic interactions in the city, offering a specific set of options for men who are more likely to identify themselves as gay and to prefer participating in social spaces that are also self-consciously defined as gay:

> If I'm going to spend the money to go out, I want to go someplace gay—I don't want to waste my time with *machões* or *bichas enrustidas* (closeted queers). I'm gay, and I prefer to be with gays. It's logical that if I'm going to spend a lot of money somewhere— because, you know, it is very expensive to go out—I want to spend it somewhere where I can be with people who have something in common with me. (Márcio, a twenty-four-year-old informant from the lower class in Belo Horizonte)

This increasingly articulated preference for defined gay settings has provided incentive for the opening of growing numbers of bars, clubs, and discos run by gay men (and sometimes by lesbians) and intended almost exclusively for a gay clientele.[14]

It is important not to underestimate the very real emotional impact of such commercial establishments for the men (and women) who take advantage of them. While the more orgiastic and highly impersonal world

of the street obviously has its attractions for many men—particularly
those who may not identify as gay or wish to enter into more intense personal relationships—it also has obvious limitations. The threat of both
symbolic and physical violence—whether it takes the form of police extor-
tion, petty theft, or outright gay-bashing—is ever present in such public
cruising. And for many men, even if it is possible to live with this risk, the
very impersonality of such sexual adventures is often seen as negative
rather than positive, and the impossibility of more social (as opposed to
sexual) interaction is a source of frustration. The gay commercial world is
in part a response to such frustration, and has explicitly linked the search
for potential sexual partners to a broader possibility for socialization and
sociability:

> More and more, I think that what people want is not just sex, but
> a place you have more of a sociability (*sociabilidade*)—where you
> can meet your friends, converse, be together in a relaxed atmos-
> phere . . . someplace that is free from the stigma and discrimina-
> tion of the outside world. Obviously sex is still important, and
> going out to a bar or a disco is one of the main ways to meet sex-
> ual partners, but it is more than just sex. It is more a life style (*estilo
> de vida*). (Antônio)

At the same time, though, if this growing gay commercial world has
begun to open up new spaces for constructing homosexuality not just as
a sexual behavior but as a life style and a form of social expression, it is
also important to remember that this world has nonetheless been built
upon the substratum of homoerotic desires and styles, and that it continues to respond to this substratum in developing its own unique style and
character (just as it does, of course, in Amsterdam, New York, San Francisco, Sydney, or anywhere else a gay commercial world has emerged).
Sexual interaction and homoerotic sensibility continue to be central, as
witnessed in the presence of dark rooms, foam baths, and other similar
contexts that will be familiar to many readers from the gay establishments
in many Anglo-European settings:

> These days, the clubs and discos in Rio and São Paulo have every-
> thing that you have in the United States—the most popular discos
> all have dark rooms (*quartos escuros*), literally with no light, or
> mazelike structures, where people go in between dancing. The sex
> there can be like an orgy at a sauna—a whole bunch of guys, sweaty
> from dancing, rubbing up against one another in the dark, with-
> out even being able to see who is who, just bodies. . . . A couple of

years ago, foam baths became the big thing at a lot of discos. I think they must have been an import from the States, I don't know. But they would usually start only late at night, the time when the entry fee for the club goes up, so that the owners make more money. Most people would take their clothes off, or strip down only to their shorts (*ficar de cueca*), everybody bouncing up against one another, rubbing up against you in the foam—everything would happen then (*rolou de tudo*), you can imagine. And it was a problem, too—we tried to work there with an [AIDS prevention] intervention, distributing condoms, but there must be something about the chemicals that they use in the foam, because it would cause the latex to break really easily. We even talked to the owners about it at Le Boy [a popular gay disco in Copacabana]. (Daniel, a thirty-six-year-old from the upper-middle class in Rio de Janeiro)

If such settings reproduce the relatively polymorphous and often orgiastic pleasures of the homoerotic street, they do simultaneously transform it, creating a world that is largely free of the dangers that constantly surround homoerotic adventures in public space.[15] In much the same way, the traditional symbolic trappings of queer culture have also been reproduced and transformed in the creation of not only a world of sexual interactions but also a distinct cultural universe with its own forms of entertainment and performance. In the world of the clubs and discos, for example, the *bichas* and *travestis* from the streets have themselves been transformed (see photo 3.2), recreated as *drags* (from the English, drag queens) and *transformistas* (literally, transformers):

> JOÃO: The drag queen has become the new center of attention in the gay clubs. It's funny . . . the *travesti* has always been important in Brazil, in *Carnaval*, in popular culture, like in the '80s when Roberta Close[16] was on the cover of all the magazines. But in the last few years it seems like there has been a boom in popularity. Not so much the *travesti* as the *transformista*.
>
> INTERVIEWER: Describe the difference.
>
> JOÃO: The *travesti* lives like a *travesti* more or less all of the time, with silicone breasts and all . . . the *transformista* is a performer, just a normal man in everyday life, but who performs at clubs during the nights. There is a whole circuit of different clubs, which each night have a different performer—and the public knows who will be where and when . . . like Lorna Washington, every Thursday she is at 1140, on Tuesdays she performs at Incontru's.

Photo 3.2. *Transformistas* and *Drags* at a *Festa* (Party) in Rio de Janeiro.
Photo: Vagner de Almeida.

INTERVIEWER: But what about the difference between the *trans-formistas* and the *drags*?

JOÃO: That's harder to describe. . . . The *drags* have become really popular in the last few years . . . most of them are young guys who are trying to break into the business as *transformistas*, but the market isn't that big, even in Rio and São Paulo, so there is a lot of competition. New performers find it difficult, and only occasionally get jobs. One way to build up a reputation is to create a kind of persona for yourself as a drag queen, going to parties and nightclubs, performing on the street during the *bandas* (bands and gatherings organized in different streets prior to *Carnaval*), appearing on the television variety shows on Sunday afternoon, like the *Show de Sílvio Santos* or *Faustão*. . . . You begin to build up a following as a *drag* that you can sometimes manage to transform into a career as a *transformista*.[17]

Like the *bichas* and *travestis*, the stereotypical *bofes* and *michês* of the outside world have also been recreated as well, transformed into *leopardos* (literally, leopards, based on the title of an especially popular male strip show, "*A Noite dos Leopardos*" ("The Night of the Leopards"), that originated in

Rio de Janeiro)[18] and *go-go boys* (again, adapted from English, for male erotic dancers):

> DANIEL: During the last few years, one of the biggest successes has been the male strip shows, like the *Leopardos,* full of young *barbies* showing off their muscles and their hard cocks. At first the *Leopardos* was basically just a gay show—the whole audience was gay, and the guys would strut down from the stage into the audience, teasing the public with their hard-ons. I don't know if it's true, but people say that sometimes guys in the audience would suck off some of the performers—and there was always a joke in the gay milieu (*no mundo gay*) about an old *bicha* whose job was to stay backstage in the wings sucking the *Leopardos* so that they could stay hard.
>
> INTERVIEWER: But wasn't this exclusively at the *Leopardos* show?
>
> DANIEL: Yes, that's where it started, but like everything in Brazil, it became a fad. The *Leopardos* became an attraction for Carnival balls, they were featured on television shows. After a while they became so well-known that it wasn't so much a gay show anymore. If you walked by and saw the line of people waiting to go into the theater for a show, there were more tourists and heterosexual couples than anything else. Some of the tourists were gay, of course, but a lot weren't. It was just another example of sexy Brazilian-ness (*brasilidade*) made for exportation, as well as for internal consumption by straight people (*gente careta*)—kind of a modern, macho version of Carmen Miranda.

Indeed, an entertainment industry rooted in the gay subculture but extending beyond it and acquiring a certain "cult" appeal with progressive (or adventurous) straights, international tourists, and the like has developed as part of the entire entertainment industry in Brazil, and films, plays, and other works of art dealing with homosexuality or developing gay themes have been at the center of the cultural activity and attention.[19]

Given this growing range of commercial and cultural enterprises built around notions of homoeroticism, homosexuality, and, increasingly, gay identity, it is perhaps not surprising that by the mid-1990s talk in the news media as well as in gay circles and networks had begun to turn to what has been described as a "gay market":

> RAFAEL (a forty-two-year-old informant from the upper-middle class in São Paulo):   There have been lots of articles in the news-

papers recently about what they are calling the gay market (*o mercado gay*)—and I guess that it is true. . . . In the past couple of years there have sprung up a whole range of gay businesses and services, at least in São Paulo and Rio. It isn't like in New York or San Francisco, where you can go out and pick up a gay Yellow Pages with a listing of anything and everything specifically for gays and lesbians, but still it has grown way beyond the traditional circuit of saunas and nightclubs. . . .

INTERVIEWER: Is this new market focused around sex, or how does it work? And do you think it really exists, or is it just a creation of the media?

RAFAEL: No, it exists, I think, and it seems to be growing. Some of it is sexually focused, of course, like the saunas, or massage services for telephone out-calls. In the past four or five years they have even opened some phone-sex services for gays—it's all modeled on what goes on in the United States. But it goes beyond sex, really. . . . It is almost more of a cultural thing. There is MIX Brasil, a gay film festival and entertainment firm based in São Paulo, there are a couple of gay travel agencies, agencies that offer tourist packages just for gay people, a gay computer service. And there has been a kind of boom in gay publications—a lot of them are poorly produced newspapers that spring up and then disappear, nobody really knows why or who is involved. But some are expensively produced magazines for an elite audience, like *Sui Generis*, full of articles and advertisements specifically for middle-class gays.[20] There is a kind of social milieu now, I don't know exactly how to describe it, but it's different than it used to be—it is more focused on cultural things, and is more mixed, not just people looking for sex. A few years ago people started using the term *"GLS"—Gays, Lésbicas e Simpatizantes* (Gays, Lesbians, and Sympathizers), that includes people [the Sympathizers] who aren't gay or lesbian, but who like to be with them, who are comfortable with them. There is a huge business now, especially in São Paulo and Rio, in organizing GLS parties . . . like the Bitch Party, or the Valdemente Party in Rio. Every week or every couple of weeks the party is held at a different place, like the Tivoli Amusement Park. The company that organizes it rents the park, advertises the party by passing out flyers and making announcements at other bars and nightclubs on the gay circuit, and charges R$10 or R$15 [roughly equivalent to US$10–15] for admission. They make a fortune. And it isn't just rich people

who go, no—in spite of the price, people who are really very
poor save up their money all week to be able to go to the hottest
party. It's a mixture of all types of people.

INTERVIEWER: But what happens at the parties? What do people
do?

RAFAEL: Basically dancing and drinking, and a lot of people taking drugs like cocaine, poppers, Ecstasy, like at any club. But
there are performances by drag queens, and lots of people go
dressed up in drag, or *barbies* showing off their muscles. There is
a lot of cruising, on the dance floor, in the bathrooms. It's funny,
but in a way, because of the idea of Sympathizers, it sort of reproduces that traditional system where people can go, without necessarily defining themselves as gay—because they are just
Sympathizers—and can find partners and have sex, without having to define themselves really.

What is perhaps most striking about this so-called gay market is precisely
the extent to which it reproduces many of the basic features (even if on a
smaller scale) of the gay commercial world found in Anglo-European settings, while at the same time adapting these structures within the Brazilian context. Its hybrid configuration manages to respond to perceived local
needs and subjectivities that have been shaped over time by the traditional
structures of gender and sexuality as they function in Brazilian culture.

Among the most important characteristic of this growing economy—
and of the gay commercial circuit as a whole—is its capacity as a medium
for the flow not only of capital but also of signs and symbols drawn from
a much wider global system. Gay film festivals like MIX Brasil (modeled
on the New York gay and lesbian film festival) present not only largely
experimental and short format Brazilian films and videos but also gay and
lesbian films drawn largely from the Anglo-European world. Gay travel
agencies organize tours that take Brazilians to the heart of gay communities in New York and Amsterdam. And while such activities may be
restricted to a very limited, well-to-do elite (that has always possessed privileged access to the outside world), even the more popular and accessible
world of nightclubs and commercial parties becomes the point of convergence for the flow of essentially global images—videos by Michael Jackson, Madonna, or George Michael are intersliced with those of Brazilian
samba at the gay dance clubs, while videos of gay (and gay-sympathetic)
films such as *Querelle* or *Priscilla* are exhibited on the party circuit.

This commercial circuit and the rapidly growing, specialized economy
that has sprung from it have become central to the construction of a wider
gay world in Brazil. Even more clearly than the cultural forms of cruising

and prostitution (which are themselves, of course, in many ways transnational), the gay commercial circuit simultaneously links Brazilian reality to a far-broader set of international economic and symbolic exchanges, while adapting this international system to the particularities of local context and custom. It can be described as neither an indigenous construct nor as an imperialist import from abroad; instead, it is another example of the ways in which the process of globalization in the late twentieth century not only shapes reality but is simultaneously shaped by human beings who use it for their own purposes.

Politics, AIDS, and Gay Community

The political movements that have come to the fore over the course of the past decade have also been important forces in shaping the contours of gay life. A relatively small, but nonetheless intense, gay political movement had begun to take shape in the late 1970 and early '80s,[21] but its energy seemed to dissipate in the mid-1980s. A gradual revival began to take place in the late 1980s and '90s, however, as new, gay organizations began to form in urban centers around the country (see Mott 1995; Silva 1993). Following the emergence of AIDS in the early 1980s, self-identified gay groups and political organizations often hooked up with AIDS activists and AIDS service organizations, which have often defined themselves as serving a diverse general public, but in which many self-identified gay men have played important leadership roles—and through which, for the first time in Brazil, formal project activities purporting to serve *a comunidade homossexual* (the homossexual community) have been funded and implemented (see, for example, Parker et al. 1995; Parker and Terto 1998; see also Reis 1995).

By the mid-1990s, *grupos gays* (gay groups) and *ONGs/AIDS* (AIDS NGOs, the Brazilian equivalent for community-based, AIDS-service organizations) have become key referents in the social construction of the gay world—symbolic markers as well as key actors, they help define the range of possibilities that exist for the conceptualization of gay life not only as a kind of sexual behavior but also as a form of social expression. And much like the gay commercial world, both gay organizing and AIDS activism have provided especially important points of intersection between the particularities of Brazilian experience and the broader patterns of the outside world. Indeed, gay organizations in particular are seen by many as a kind of importation from abroad of what is in fact a very North American form of identity politics:

> The *grupos gays* in Brazil are almost all imitations of the United
> States—or of what Brazilians think that gay activism is in the

United States. Even though few Brazilians have traditionally identified themselves as gay or homosexual, the gay organizations all
try to use gay identity as the basis for their work. I think that this
is at least one of the reasons why they may have had a limited
impact. In 1982 or '83 there were only half a dozen *grupos gays* in
the country. The number has grown a lot, but even now [in 1994]
there are hardly more than forty or fifty. That is a lot more, but it
is still pretty small in a country of more than 150 million people.
Most of the groups aren't really collective—lots of them tend to be
the private domain of one or two leaders, sort of in the Brazilian
tradition of *coronelismo* (from the Brazilian Northeast's political
structure organized around powerful political bosses). But they still
play an important role—they call attention to the question of dignity, to the discrimination against homosexuals, and the need to
defend sexual rights. They make it easier for gays in Brazil to
understand their relationship to gays in other countries. (Jorge)

The majority of gay organizations emphasize the importance of *assu-
mindo-se* (roughly equivalent to the English-language notion of "coming
out"—of, literally, "taking on oneself [one's sexual identity]"), but there
has simultaneously been a push to open up organizations to incorporate
sexual diversity within the broader *movimento homossexual* (homossexual
movement):

The discourse of many of the gay groups often seems contradictory. On the one hand, almost all of the leaders of these groups
around the country are middle-class gay men, with an incredible
emphasis on gay identity, on coming out (*se assumindo*) as homosexual. But there is actually a lot of diversity in the people who
show up for meetings at groups like GGB [the Grupo Gay da Bahia,
one of the most long-standing gay organizations in the country,
located in Salvador] or Atobá [a largely working-class organization
located in the suburbs of Rio de Janeiro]—there are fewer guys
from the middle class than from the popular classes, poor *bichas*
and *travestis* who are completely different from the profile of many
of the gay leaders. The gay groups provide a social space for many
people who are otherwise completely marginalized—who live in
poor communities where violence and oppression is everywhere
around them, and who don't have the money that it would take
to be able to go to the clubs or bars. Weekly meetings of gay organizations give people a place to meet, to make friends, to find

lovers or [sexual] partners that they probably wouldn't have anywhere else. Obviously, it's only a small fraction of the men who
have sex with men in Brazil who participate in the gay groups, but
it is still important symbolically. And in the past few years, more
and more specific groups have been formed, like Tulipa, which is
made up entirely of *travestis*. It isn't always easy, especially because
there is always a lot of competition for influence and power, but
the gay movement has tried to make space for diversity. (Rafael)

Precisely because of the problem of using sexual identity as the primary
basis for political organizing in Brazil, many of the gay organizations have
had their greatest impact by addressing specifically the question of violence and the ways in which diverse forms of sexual violence are felt independent of identity:

> Groups like GGB, Atobá and Dignidade [Grupo Dignidade, one of
> the primary gay organizations in Curitiba] have compiled amazing
> archives of violence against gays—gays who have been murdered
> in their homes by *michês* or thieves, who have been beaten up or
> killed in the street by death squads, politicians who were violently
> murdered after news of their being homosexual leaked out. There
> are thousands and thousands of cases. The media never pays any
> attention to these cases—journalists just reproduce the myth of
> Brazil as a sexual paradise and never confront the reality of sexual
> violence. But the major gay groups have been able to put together
> remarkable documentation, and have published pamphlets with
> instructions on how to avoid being attacked, and how to protect
> yourself if you are attacked. (Rafael)

This emphasis on violence and discrimination has been channeled into
political intervention. For the first time, in 1996, in cities and states
around the country, a handful of self-identified gay candidates (almost all
leaders of different *grupos gays*) sought to dispute local municipal and state
elections. Championed by a leading feminist politician from the State of
São Paulo, and supported overwhelmingly by gay organizations from
around the country, a bill introduced in the Federal House of Deputies
would (if passed, which seems a remote possibility) offer legal recognition
to same-sex partnerships (see Guedes 1996; Lucena 1996).[22] Perhaps even
more surprising, as in the United States, the question of whether or not
gays should be allowed to serve in the military has also been debated—
drawing negative, but nonetheless entirely serious arguments, even from

high-ranking military personnel (see *NoMar* 1996; see also Segal and Casara 1996). In short, not just the gay market, but also gay politics have clearly arrived in Brazil:

> INTERVIEWER: What do you mean when you say that homosexuality has finally begun to become a political issue?
>
> DANIEL: It has always been hard to organize politically around sexual issues. It is the hypocrisy of the system in Brazil. Machismo, discrimination, and sexual stigma are everywhere, but there is also this myth of Brazil as somehow very liberated. And there are no laws, for example, condemning homosexuality—sexual oppression isn't so formal in the same way that it is in the United States, with laws against sodomy and all. . . . In Brazil there are no laws and sex goes on all over the place—everybody is busy trying to have sex instead of working against the sexual oppression that is impregnated in daily life. Its funny, but this has made it hard until very recently to organize politically around gay questions. The strongest gay groups have always been in the Northeast—because that is exactly where the tradition of machismo is strongest and most oppressive. But it is only recently that a gay movement has grown stronger in the South and Southeast.
>
> INTERVIEWER: But why do you think it is easier now to address homosexuality as a political question?
>
> DANIEL: Partly I think that it is a process, like the redemocratization of Brazilian society after the dictatorship—people are learning how to be citizens again. Partly it is because of AIDS. AIDS made homosexuality much more visible, and uncovered the incredible discrimination that homosexuals still face in Brazilian society. And the gay world (*o mundo gay*) is growing all the time. The more that people become involved in social networks, the more likely they are to also become more involved politically. Homosexuality and the rights of homosexuals have finally become part of a public debate in Brazil. Even among straight politicians—some people defend us, some people attack us, but the fact that people are publicly debating these kinds of issues is a big change in just the past few years.

By bringing questions related to homosexuality, to sexual identity, and to sexual rights into the sphere of public debate, the *grupos gays* in Brazil have begun to transform the landscape of the gay world. While the patterns of social and sexual interaction described above have in no way ceased to exist, their significance, both for the individuals involved in them as well as for the outside world, has begun to shift—to be at least partially transformed. Questions of sexual desire have simultaneously been reframed for some as questions of sexual rights. The deeply felt impact that the constant threat of violence poses in the lives of men who have sex with men in Brazil has been refigured, in part, as a demand for sexual freedom—freedom, among other things, from the impact of such threats. And the perceived sociability of the gay circuit has been reconceived as a point of departure for the construction of a *comunidade gay* that is in many ways comparable to the gay communities found in the so-called developed countries of the Anglo-European world.

If gay organizations have played an important role in contributing to an emergent notion of gay community, however, it is impossible to really think about the impact of such organizations apart from or independent of the HIV/AIDS epidemic, and the diverse cultural and organizational responses to AIDS at both the local and the global level (see, for example, Altman 1994, 1995b). One must remember that in Brazil (like many other developing countries), the presence of AIDS preceded the major growth of a gay movement—and the development of this movement was thus shaped by the epidemic in a series of highly specific ways:

> In Brazil, most gay groups have been formed after the AIDS epidemic had started. It wasn't so much like the United States in this regard, because there were very few existing groups that could respond to the epidemic. On the contrary, lots of gay groups began precisely because of AIDS—in order to respond to AIDS. The history of the gay movement is wound up with the history of the epidemic. (Antônio)

While gay groups were clearly the first organizations to offer any kind of institutionalized response to the epidemic, by the mid- to late-1980s a range of more specific AIDS service organizations had been founded, and an AIDS movement expanded almost exponentially through the mid-1990s (see Galvão 1997)—in some ways overwhelming the gay rights movement, at least in terms of its size and resources:

> The first AIDS NGO was founded in Brazil in 1985. By the end of the 1980s there were only a handful of organizations around the country—maybe twenty or so. But the epidemic has expanded so rapidly and so many AIDS NGOs have started that today some people say there are as many as 400 in the whole country. That is probably an exaggeration, but you can see how rapidly the AIDS

movement has grown. And homosexual men have played a key
role in founding and directing many of the most important organizations. A lot of them have died now, of course, but almost all
of the most important early leaders in the fight against AIDS were
homosexual. (Jorge)

Precisely because of the involvement of homosexual men within the early
ONGS/AIDS, it is hardly surprising that such organizations should have
become intersections for extensive social interaction on the part of the gay
population:

> AIDS NGOS have almost become an alternative to the nightclubs
> and saunas—it is a lot like the role of many gay groups, especially
> for men who are poorer, who don't have enough money to be able
> to go regularly to commercial places, or who just don't like the
> atmosphere in the clubs. The AIDS NGOS offer them a social alter-
> native, a place where they can go for free to meet other people.
> And the AIDS NGOS have generally had much more money than
> the gay groups, so they have had better offices or meeting spaces
> (*sedes*). They offer workshops, show videos and films with gay
> themes. When they can, they distribute condoms for free. They
> offer people a whole range of options that just a few years ago
> didn't exist. (Rafael)

In some ways, this new social space that AIDS-related organizations have
opened up has in fact fed back into the gay commercial world, as club
owners and other entrepreneurs have been called on to open their establishments up for political events and AIDS benefits. Fund-raising and safer
sex parties organized by AIDS NGOs and held at well-known sites within
the gay social circuit have become as much a part of the gay milieu in
recent years as the commercial parties organized within the space of the
gay market (see photo 3.3).

Ultimately, what is perhaps most striking is precisely the extent to
which both gay organizing and, perhaps in particular, AIDS-related work
have tended to feed back into the other structures of the gay world, in
some ways reinforcing them, in other ways transforming them, as part of
a complex system of interacting networks. Perhaps even more than the
gay movement itself, the AIDS movement has largely built upon an inclu-
sive politics of *solidariedade* (solidarity) rather than of *identidade* (identity),
and has been especially sensitive to the traditional context of Brazilian
culture, with its general emphasis on fluidity and flux in the organization
of sexual identities:

Photo 3.3.   Safer Sex Party. Photo: Emmanuelle Barbaras.

The AIDS NGOs have focused on a whole range of populations along with self-identified gay men. Different groups have developed outreach projects for bisexuals, for *michês* and *travestis*, for street kids and men who have sex with other men in prisons. In some ways it has been easier for AIDS organizations precisely because homosexual identity has been less important to them than solidarity with all groups affected by the epidemic. (Rafael)

Through such strategies, AIDS organizations have also become a point of intersection between the local and the global. The incorporation of AIDS-prevention models and the funding (on the part of agencies such as USAID, the World Health Organization, or the World Bank) of projects targeted to specific populations such as "men who have sex with men" has been one of the most visible ways in which conceptual frameworks and sexual meanings—developed in other, often quite different, social contexts—have been incorporated into Brazilian life, configuring the changing gay world in a range of highly specific ways.[23] It is fair to say that at least some forms of AIDS-related work, like gay political activism, have quite consciously been involved in building more structured and self-conscious gay communities in contexts where such communities would otherwise seem to be loosely organized and weakly articulated:

These days outreach workers (*interventores*) are as much a part of the gay scene as guys out cruising. In the interventions that we

organized [through the AIDS service organization that he has
worked with], we have sent outreach workers into cruising parks,
tearooms, saunas, discos, and clubs, handing out condoms, pam-
phlets, and information about the services at our offices (*nossa
sede*). We used to publish a lot of informational materials, but have
learned that AIDS prevention isn't just a question of information.
When people lack supportive communities, social and psychological support, responding to AIDS is almost impossible. In a country like Brazil, building a supportive gay community will do more
to stop the epidemic, at least among men who have sex with men,
than anything else. These days we are less concerned with education and information than with creating a strong gay community,
and a kind of culture of safe sex (*uma cultura de sexo seguro*). And
to be able to do this, we have to raise some dust, to create a little
controversy and debate. (Rafael)

It is important to remember that this process of appropriation is by no
means simply a passive acceptance of external imposition. On the contrary, it is a complex and highly dialectical process in which local actors
actively shape and reshape the very structures that they appropriate—
molding them to their own ends; recreating, out of both local and transnational resources and raw material, hybrid structures that respond not only
to external pressures but also to deeply felt internal needs (see photo 3.4).

The effect of both gay political work and AIDS-related organizing has
been to build up a series of linkages between a wider international gay universe and the gay world as it takes shape in Brazilian life. As much as *bofes*,
bichas, and *barbies*, or *michês* and *travestis*, *militantes do movimento gay* (gay
militants), *ativistas em AIDS* (AIDS activists), and *interventores* (AIDS-prevention outreach workers) have become part of the array of figures that
map out the social and psychological landscape of this world in the mid-
1990s. As much as *saunas*, *bares*, or *boates*, the *sedes* (bases or office spaces)
of *grupos gays* and *ONGs/AIDs* have become integral to the physical landscape of this world—opening up the possibilities not only for sexual interaction but also for social exchange and even political engagement, thus
building up gay life not just as a distinct sexual subculture (or overlapping
subcultures) but as a complex and diverse way of being within the context
of an emerging sexual community (or set of communities) in the late
twentieth century.

Building a Gay World

Ultimately, this description of these frames or contexts is necessarily
incomplete. The erotic adventures of the street, the negotiations and

Photo 3.4. AIDS Prevention Theater Workshop at ABIA in Rio de Janeiro.
Photo: Vagner de Almeida.

interactions of male and transvestite prostitution, the gay commercial circuit, and even the gay political groups and AIDS organizations that have formed in recent years, can perhaps best be understood as slices or fragments of a relatively fluid, open-ended social/sexual space. There are other, equally important fragments that might just as easily be taken as points of entry into the gay world in Brazil—the gay presence in the life of the samba schools that prepare and present *carnaval* (see Parker 1991, 1997b), the importance of homoeroticism in many forms of Afro-Brazilian religion (see, for example, Barros, Santos, and Teixeira 1985; Birman 1985; Fry 1982), and so on. My objective here, however, is to offer some sense of this world's range and dynamics and an understanding of the kinds of social and economic processes that seem to be playing themselves out through it.

From this perspective, these slices of urban gay life paint a clear picture of the complex, oppositional quality that seems to characterize this world and hold it together. Independent of the very different degrees of formality and conscious organization found in the diverse domains, each takes shape as a quite conscious alternative to the dominant straight or heterosexual world around it. Each calls into question this dominant configuration of sexual desire, offering up alternative readings of sexual pleasure, identity, and even community. While these alternatives hardly succeed in overturning the dominant heterosexual order, they do nonetheless bear witness to a remarkable resilience and determination—a capacity for resistance and a commitment to carving out a space for sexual expression even in the face of persistent sexual discrimination, violence, and oppression.

This oppositional character is critical. Because of it, the men within this world, no matter how different from one another in terms of their specific backgrounds and styles, their desires and identities, nonetheless also recognize within their diversity something in common. Above all else, it is through a shared sense of sexual difference, of being part of a social and sexual milieu that defines and articulates itself largely as an alternative to the dominant norms of a straight, heterosexual, and heterosocial world, that this notion of a gay (or queer) world is in fact built up. It is this simultaneous recognition of internal differences and, yet, commonality that is most distinctive of the *mundo gay* as it is lived in contemporary Brazilian life; identification takes shape not necessarily through the affirmation of sameness but through the sharing of otherness within a given field of power and desire.

It is also this same oppositional configuration of the gay world in Brazil that would seem to make it relatively open to interfaces and intersections that connect it to a wider set of global systems and processes in the late twentieth century—systems and processes that in other circumstances might themselves be seen as fundamentally oppressive, but that, thanks to a shared sense of sexual otherness, can sometimes be appropriated and reappropriated. While Brazilian society as a whole has always been marked by a relatively high degree of cosmopolitan *abertura* (or openness)—happy to import new fashions and innovations from abroad—this openness is redoubled in the urban gay world that has evolved in recent decades, and is especially obvious in the development of a gay commercial circuit reminiscent of the gay subcultures and communities in the Anglo-European world, as well as in the appropriation of forms of political mobilization quite consciously based on the models of western gay and AIDS activism.

We must still remember, however, that all these new structures have necessarily had to respond to the particularities of local contexts and cultures. They have been and continue to be configured and reconfigured by local actors, responding to a set of meanings and interests that are necessarily determined in highly specific ways. It is necessary to understand this interface, and the forces that shape it, as part of a more complex dialectical process if we are to make sense not only of the evolution of the gay world in Brazil but also of sexual life in general at the end of the twentieth century.

Part Two

Local Contexts /
Imagined Worlds

4

Dependent Development

As I have argued in the preceding chapters, the diverse gay subcultures that have taken shape and become increasingly visible in urban Brazil during the past decade must ultimately be interpreted as a complex and multifaceted response both to local structures and conditions as well as to the changing flows that characterize the latter part of the twentieth century. They have evolved over time as part of a more extensive intersection between local cultural traditions and social processes, on the one hand, and a set of broader, increasingly global forces, on the other. Where one side of this equation begins, or the other leaves off, is of course an open question—subject to debate, and ultimately impossible to fully resolve. What is important to emphasize, however, is the extent to which this interface has ultimately shaped the highly complex processes of industrialization, urbanization, and socioeconomic development that have all had pivotal roles, albeit in diverse ways, in structuring the gay world (or worlds) in contemporary Brazilian life. These processes, in turn, are perhaps the central factors that have conditioned the ways in which Brazilian society has interacted with, incorporated, and adapted influences from a range of other sources, and made use of them for the organization of same-sex relations and experience. The result has been the development of increasingly complex and varied gay identities and communities throughout Brazil—identities and communities that increasingly share many features in common with those of Europe or North America, but that also respond to the existing structures of local cultures, economies, and ecologies.

In this second part of the study, I want to explore more fully a number of these social, economic, and demographic processes. In this chapter, I will look briefly at the processes of industrialization and urbanization that have taken place in Brazil over the course of recent decades, that have been linked to a quite specific political history, and that together have set the stage for the emergence of gay subcultures and identities as part of urban life. In particular, I emphasize the extent to which the changes described here are not simply part of some kind of "natural" evolutionary sequence, but are in fact historically contingent social, political, and economic processes (that might easily "evolve" in quite different ways, given other circumstances) that can only be fully understood within the context of what has been described as the model of "dependent development" that has marked Brazilian life for centuries—and that has become especially pronounced over the course of the three decades from the mid-1960s through the mid-1990s (see, in particular, Cardoso and Faletto 1979; Skidmore and Smith 1997). In the chapters that follow, I will move on to look in greater detail at the emergence of gay communities in Rio de Janeiro and Fortaleza, two of the major cities in our research, as well as at the movement of both people and images that ultimately links such communities to one another—as well as to the wider world outside Brazil. As in the preceding discussion of what I described as diverse cultures of desire, the goal is not to offer a truly exhaustive description of these issues (an objective that would be far more ambitious than any single volume could hope to achieve) but, on the contrary, to highlight a number of the most powerful forces and contexts currently shaping the character of gay life in contemporary Brazilian society, and thus to draw attention to both the increasing velocity as well as the remarkable complexity of the changes that have taken place in recent decades.

Structural Dependence, Industrial Development, and Urban Growth

Although the pace of globalization and the expansion of the global capitalist economy would seem to be rapid at the end of the twentieth century, and to impact in especially important ways on the structure of Brazilian life more generally, it is vital to keep in mind that the intersection between local traditions and broader social and economic structures is in no way a new phenomenon. In Brazil, as in virtually any other part of the developing world, this interaction is surely as old as colonialism itself and has evolved across centuries through a series of distinct phases. At least three quite distinct periods can be distinguished: (1) from the initial western discovery of Brazil through the early nineteenth century, a time when Brazil was part of the Portuguese colonial empire; (2) from the early nineteenth century to the early twentieth century, when, following

Napoleon's invasion of Portugal and the transference of the Portuguese crown to Brazil, the Portuguese empire began to unravel and the commercial power of the British in large part pulled Brazil into the sphere of British influence; and (3) from the early twentieth century to the present, when the growing power of the United States progressively supplanted Western Europe as the northern center to the Brazilian periphery (see Burns 1993; see also Baer 1995; Evans 1979; Furtado 1963).

The basic structure of these dominant economic and political relationships connecting the Brazilian economy to the wider world has remained remarkably constant over time. Throughout its history, Brazilian life has been characterized by some form of what has aptly been described as "dependent development," in which local fortunes have been unavoidably linked to external interests in the European and, most recently, North American economies.[1] Throughout much of Brazilian history, the structure of dependency has been relatively simple and straightforward—linked to the absolute predominance of agricultural production and to the exportation of a relatively limited number of primary products (first sugar, then rubber and coffee) to the North Atlantic economies that dominated the world system in the late nineteenth and early twentieth centuries (see Baer 1995; Evans 1979; Furtado 1963).[2] As late as the 1930s and '40s, the state of the Brazilian economy was directly related to the international market for these products, and the domestic demand for manufactured goods was almost entirely met through the use of export earnings in the importation of products from Europe and the United States (see Baer 1995; Furtado 1963; Skidmore and Smith 1997).

This relationship began to change gradually in the 1930s and '40s, when the Great Depression, followed by World War II, seriously reduced Brazilian access to manufactured products from abroad, stimulating domestic political pressure in support of a nascent industrial growth—a strategy that would extend for most of the next fifty years and that would come to be known as "import substitution industrialization," characterized by fairly intensive state intervention in the economy in order to speed the process of industrialization and reduce the country's reliance on imported goods (see Green 1995; Skidmore and Smith 1997). By the end of World War II, the notion of social and economic *desenvolvimento* (development) had emerged as almost a universal dogma, both in Brazil and internationally. Within this framework, rapid industrialization stimulated by state investment came to be seen as the primary road to economic *prosperidade* (prosperity), and the very idea of *desenvolvimento* came to be understood, even for the general public, as largely synonymous with notions such as *progresso* (progress) and *modernização* (modernization):

Brazil has always had a strong positivist tendency, at least in theory even if rarely in practice. Like the motto on the flag from the nineteenth century: *ordem* (order) and *progresso* (progress). But progress used to be genuinely associated with order, with a more organized society, less confusion, less mayhem. Over the past fifty years though, the whole ideology of progress has changed. Today, progress means *desenvolvimento* (development), *modernidade* (modernity), *riqueza* (wealth). The whole capitalist ideology is what really drives Brazilian life. (Darcy, a twenty-four-year-old student from Rio de Janeiro)

It was primarily during the 1940s and '50s that modernist ideology began to become reality and that significant industrial growth began to expand in Brazil; a relatively aggressive program of government investment provided significant stimulus for emerging industries such as steel and automobile production. From 1947 through 1961, for example, manufacturing increased at an annual rate of 9.6 percent, but agricultural production increased at only 4.6 percent. From 1950 to 1990, the portion of the Brazilian labor force involved in agricultural production declined from 62 percent to 23 percent, but the portion involved in industrial production grew from only 13 percent to 23 percent, and the portion involved in service provision grew from 25 percent to 54 percent (see table 4.1). These changes in the distribution of labor were clearly reflected, as well, in the sectoral distribution of the gross domestic product (GDP). In 1950, for example, agricultural production accounted for 24 percent of the GDP, industry for 24 percent, and services for 52 percent. By 1980, agricultural production had fallen to only 10 percent of the GDP, services were slightly down to 49 percent, and industrial production had risen significantly to account for 41 percent (see table 4.2). By 1990, in what may signal the beginning of a transition to a postindustrial phase of development, agricultural production had fallen further still to 9 percent of the GDP, industrial production had dropped to only 34 percent, and services had climbed to 57 percent of the GDP.

Table 4.1.   Sectoral Distribution of Labor

Sector	1950	1960	1970	1980	1990
Agriculture	62%	48%	49%	30%	23%
Industry	13%	14%	17%	24%	23%
Services	25%	38%	34%	46%	54%

Source: Baer 1995.

Table 4.2.   Sectoral Distribution of Gross Domestic Product

Year	Agriculture	Industry	Services	Total
1950	24.28%	24.14%	51.58%	100%
1960	17.76%	32.24%	50.01%	100%
1970	11.55%	35.84%	52.61%	100%
1980	10.20%	40.58%	49.22%	100%
1990	9.26%	34.20%	56.54%	100%

Source: Baer 1995.

The growth of manufacturing, industry, and service provision in recent decades has been linked, in turn, to a number of major changes in social structure and demography. Perhaps most striking is the concomitant pace of urbanization—the large-scale transformation of what was once an almost completely rural society into a now predominantly urban society:

> Until only about fifty years ago, Brazil was almost completely a rural country. Not just the big *usinas* (plantation factories) that you see in the Northeast, but also smaller *fazendas* (farms) and even the small land holdings of poor country people or peasants. The city dominated Brazilian society culturally and was the center of political action, but political power came from the countryside. All of the most powerful politicians were great landholders who came from the country. And the whole mentality was really rural. But in only a few decades, this has changed completely. Today many more people live in the city than in the country, and urban life shapes the Brazilian view of the world. This change took place in just one generation, my generation, which grew up in the country but lives today in the city. When I was a kid, my family lived on a *fazenda* outside of town, but by the time I was a teenager we had moved into the city, and everyone in my family has continued to live in the city until today. It is the same story with almost everyone in my generation. In just a few years, urbanization completely changed the profile of Brazilian society—and the mind-set of the Brazilian people (*a cabeça do povo brasileiro*). (João)

During a period of less than fifty years, from 1950 through 1990, as the Brazilian economy became more industrial (and as agriculture itself became more mechanized), the percentage of the population living in rural areas decreased steadily: only 31 percent of the total population lived in urban settings and 69 percent in rural areas at the time of the 1940 census, but by the time of the most recent national census in 1991, this proportion had been altogether inverted, with 75 percent of the Brazilian population living in urban centers and only 25 percent in rural areas (see table 4.3). This shift has been accompanied, in turn, by highly differential growth in rural and urban areas. Indeed, by the 1970s, while the urban population continued to grow by a rate of 4.44 percent per year, the rural population had actually begun to decline by 0.62 percent per year—a rate of decline that has largely held steady through the 1990s (see table 4.4).

Table 4.3. Population, 1940–1991
(Urban, Rural, and Total)

Census	Urban Population	Rural Population	Total Population
1940	12,880,182 (31.24%)	28,356,133 (68.76%)	41,236,315 (100%)
1950	18,782,891 (36.16%)	33,161,506 (63.84%)	51,944,397 (100%)
1960	31,303,034 (44.67%)	38,767,423 (55.33%)	70,070,457 (100%)
1970	52,084,984 (55.92%)	41,054,053 (44.08%)	93,139,037 (100%)
1980	80,436,409 (67.59%)	38,566,297 (32.41%)	119,002,706 (100%)
1991	110,875,826 (75.47%)	36,041,633 (24.53%)	146,917,459 (100%)

Source: Minayo 1995; IBGE 1992.

Table 4.4. Population Growth, 1940–1991
(Urban, Rural, and Total)

Period	Urban Growth Rate	Rural Growth Rate	Total Growth Rate
1940–1950	3.84%	1.58%	2.34%
1950–1960	5.24%	1.57%	3.04%
1960–1970	5.22%	0.57%	2.89%
1970–1980	4.44%	−0.62%	2.48%
1980–1991	2.96%	−0.61%	1.93%

Source: Minayo 1995; IBGE 1992.

It is hard to overstate the degree to which a major "demographic transition" seems to have taken place in Brazil, as urbanization and changing social values have been associated with significantly increased contraceptive use (even in this nominally Roman Catholic nation), and as the average annual growth rate of the Brazilian population has declined significantly in recent years:

> The popular conception of a huge population explosion in the developing world is just simply wrong—at least in the case of Brazil. The growth of the population has actually declined a lot in recent decades, and family planning and contraceptive use are remarkably widespread. At least 70 or 80 percent of Brazilian women use some kind of contraceptive method, even though the range of methods is more limited than in developed countries.[3] But the big problem for Brazil isn't that the population is too large, but that its resources are distributed so unjustly. Brazil is a major exporter of food. If people die of hunger in Brazil, it isn't because the country doesn't produce enough food to eat! (Jorge)

While the total population growth rate in Brazil had climbed to as high as 3.04 percent during the 1950s, it dropped to only 1.93 percent from 1980 to 1991 (see table 4.4). The crude birth rate, in turn, declined from 44 per thousand in 1950 to 24 per thousand in 1991 (see table 4.5). Not surprisingly, these demographic changes have been associated with a range of other social transformations, as smaller family sizes have been linked to significantly more women entering the urban labor force, and to a series of important changes in the structure of gender and family relations in Brazilian society (see Barbosa 1997; Portela, Mello, and Grilo 1998; Martine 1996).

While the rate of population growth has slowed significantly, its concentration has intensified. The greater part of the Brazilian population lives not just in cities, but in bigger cities. In 1940, only three cities in the

Table 4.5.   Crude Birth Rate

Period	Birth Rate (per 1,000)
1940–1950	44.4
1950–1960	43.3
1960–1970	37.7
1970–1980	33.0
1991	24.0

Source: Minayo 1995.

country contained more than 500,000 inhabitants, and their combined population amounted to only 10.8 percent of the total Brazilian population. By 1980, there were fourteen cities with populations greater than 500,000 inhabitants, representing 32.3 percent of the total population of the country. And by 1991, as many as nine major cities registered a population of more than 1,000,000 inhabitants, with annual growth rates ranging from 1.01 percent in Rio de Janeiro to as high as 3.49 percent in Fortaleza (see table 4.6).

Over the course of the second half of the twentieth century, then, accelerating industrialization and urbanization, within the context of profound structural dependency, have been core influences on the changing nature of Brazilian life—and have characterized the nature of the relationship between Brazilian society and the outside world. While these processes, in and of themselves, cannot explain the progressive emergence of increasingly complex and varied urban subcultures organized around homoerotic desire, nor the more recent constitution of relatively self-conscious gay identities and communities, they nonetheless provide a crucially important backdrop against which these recent developments must be understood and interpreted. These economic, social, and demographic forces must also be linked, however, to a no-less-profound set of political developments that have unfolded over the course of recent decades, and that have perhaps been equally important in shaping both the limits and the possibilities for the public expression of sexuality and sexual experience as a primary basis for social organization and identification.

Table 4.6. Population and Population Growth
in Major Metropolitan Areas

Metropolitan Area	Population 1980	Population 1991	Annual Growth Rate
Belém	999,165	1,332,723	2.65%
Belo Horizonte	2,609,520	3,431,755	2.52%
Curitiba	1,440,626	1,998,807	3.02%
Fortaleza	1,580,066	2,303,645	3.49%
Porto Alegre	2,285,167	3,026,029	2.58%
Recife	2,347,146	2,871,261	1.85%
Rio de Janeiro	8,772,265	9,796,498	1.01%
Salvador	1,766,582	2,493,224	3.18%
São Paulo	12,588,725	15,416,416	1.86%

Source: Minayo 1995; IBGE 1992.

Authoritarian Politics, Structural Readjustment, and Neoliberal Reform

The acceleration in both industrial growth and urbanization following World War II was soon associated with a significant reorganization of the structures of political power in Brazilian society. Control over Brazilian politics had traditionally resided almost entirely in the hands of a very small class of landowners such as the sugar barons of the Northeast and the coffee planters of São Paulo, whose interests were in large part tied to those of their commercial trading partners in Western Europe and North America. By the 1950s and '60s, a new industrial elite, built on the foundation provided by state-sponsored import-substitution, had also emerged as a key political force, together with a small but nonetheless influential middle class (estimated as perhaps 10 to 15 percent of the national population, though as much as 30 percent of the population in many urban areas) that held dominant commercial and professional roles and maintained strong links to the military. Although the interests of these new urban sectors would at times deviate from those of the rural landowners, they nonetheless shared a significant commitment to the need for political stability in order to ensure economic growth—as well as an ongoing connection to the economic elites of the North Atlantic world (see Skidmore and Smith 1997).

Precisely because industrialization based upon import-substitution had always been structurally incomplete (since the production of manufactured goods continued to rely on the importation of capital goods, such as machine tools, from Europe and the United States), the relations of dependence that continued to tie Brazilian agriculture to the economies of Western Europe and North America were equally evident in tying the new urban industrialists and the expanding middle class into a series of alliances not only with the rural oligarchy but also with the elite sectors of the North Atlantic economies. These alliances were to prove crucial in the late 1950s and early '60s, when the industrialization strategy based primarily on import substitution began to show serious signs of weakening. Modeled on the capital-intensive industrialization that had taken place in Western Europe and North America, manufacturing in Brazil had emphasized investments in machinery, not manual labor. But an unintended consequence of this was a limited domestic market for consumer products and inadequate employment opportunities for the rapidly growing urban population (see Baer 1995; Evans 1979; Skidmore and Smith 1997).

By the early 1960s, these conditions had led to growing unrest in the organized labor movement, as well as to an ever more articulate political critique of both economic imperialism and dependency. Pressures mounted for some form of intervention aimed at ensuring economic and political stability. When the Brazilian military finally took action in 1964 (in what is ironically known as the "Revolution of '64") to seize power from the progressive Goulart government, it did so with the tacit authorization and cooperation of the U.S. government:

> Everyone in Brazil knows the role of the United States in supporting the dictatorship. It is just common sense, given the relation of power involved, that the military took action only after getting assurances of American support. And the military never would have lasted as long as it did without the ongoing aid of the Americans, both directly through the obvious formal channels, and indirectly, through the IMF and the other international financial agencies. To talk about Brazilian political autonomy would be absurd. The dictatorship always depended on the United States. (Darcy)[4]

In initiating what would ultimately prove to be a twenty-year period of authoritarian rule, from 1964 through 1984, the Brazilian military, backed both by the economic elites and the middle class, embarked upon a highly articulate project of technocratic development aimed at projecting the Brazilian economy into the modern capitalist system, and at holding firm the barricades against the threat of communism (thought to be sweeping Latin America following the Cuban revolution). It financed this bold new enterprise, of course, through massive investments, largely in the form of loans from private northern banks, for a series of quite remarkable development projects (described in Brazil as *obras faraónicas,* or "Pharaoh-like constructions"), such as the Trans-Amazon highway, the world's largest hydroelectric dam, large new nuclear-power plants, and so on:

> The *militares* (military leaders) were thoroughly committed to the idea of *crescimento econômico* (economic growth) as the road to *desenvolvimento.* Ironically, in the name of nationalism and capitalism, they initiated what is probably one of the biggest policies of state-sponsored growth that the world has ever seen, creating huge hydroelectric dams or nuclear power plants like Angra 1. In less than a decade after taking over, they had created the so-called Brazilian miracle (*o chamado "milagre brasileiro"*), with incredible economic growth. But they had done it, of course, by injecting the economy with huge amounts of money borrowed from the international bankers—also creating the most enormous national debt that the world had ever known. Brazil may have been safe from Castro and the communists, but not from the World Bank and the IMF. (Jorge)

As all Brazilians are now acutely aware, the economic policies of the military rulers resulted in both the phenomenal economic growth described at the time as "the Brazilian miracle," with an average annual growth rate of 8.6 percent in the early 1970s, and the simultaneous transformation of Brazil into the largest debtor nation in the world by the end of the 1970s.

In Brazil, as in so many other parts of the developing world, the rapid growth rates of the early 1970s were rudely interrupted in 1973, when the oil embargo of the Organization of Petroleum-Exporting Countries (OPEC) went into effect, causing a sharp rise of commodity prices in the industrialized countries and a major recession that led to significant decreases in demand for developing-country products. Brazil soon found itself faced with an excess of imports and a decline in exports, forcing the military government to respond to this loss of income by obtaining foreign credit at sharply increasing interest rates.[5] In seeking to maintain high levels of growth throughout the 1970s, the Brazilian government borrowed extensively from a range of different international lenders, and the nation's gross foreign debt exploded from only US$3.8 billion in 1968 to US$43.5 billion in 1978 and, by 1984, to US$91 billion. By the late 1970s, the cost of simply servicing the country's accumulated international debt consumed over 60 percent of the Brazil's total exports (see Baer 1995).

Unable to maintain its once impressive record of economic growth and development, the military had sown the seeds of its own undoing, and by the late 1970s international pressure had begun to bear—again, above all from North America—for an end to human rights abuses and a return to democratic rule together with effective economic stabilization programs:

> It's hard to know just how much outside influence determines what happens in Brazilian politics. It is clearly a major factor. Just like U.S. support for the military was a necessary ingredient in the coup, I suppose that all of the human rights discussion by politicians like Carter influenced the beginning of *abertura*. But it is really a question of how this influences the Brazilian elites—the landowners, the industrialists, and, to a certain extent, the middle classes. By the end of the 1970s, the economic situation had become so unstable that it became intolerable for the elites. The military was no longer managing to guarantee their interests, and the end of the dictatorship was inevitable independent of international opinion. And the banks approved, of course, because they wanted to make sure that they kept getting their loan payments regularly. (Jorge)

The history of Brazilian politics and economics over most of the 1980s (as in other parts of Latin America) would thus become the history of *redemocratização* (redemocratization), of the restructuring of the Brazilian debt, and the restructuring of the Brazilian economy more generally through increasingly intense intervention on the part of the International Monetary Fund and the World Bank:

> When the debt situation exploded, especially during the Arab oil crisis, the *FMI* (*Fundo Monetário Internacional*, or International Monetary Fund) and the *Banco Mundial* (World Bank) finally began to wake up and realize what a problem they had on their hands. If Brazil, or other large countries with big debts, were to default on their interest payments, it would undo the whole international financial system. When the military left power and the new civilian government threatened to default everyone went into shock. For most of the past decade, the biggest tension in the relation between Brazil and the *FMI* has been how to restructure the economy in order to ensure payment of the debt. (Vitor, a twenty-six-year-old student from the lower-middle class in Rio de Janeiro)

The price for rescheduling the debt was "structural adjustment"—the catch-all term used to describe the series of social and economic measures thought to be necessary in order to restructure the Brazilian economy, to open it up to foreign trade and competition, reducing protective tariffs, while simultaneously increasing exports and overall economic insertion within the global capitalist system.[6] At least seven structural adjustment loans were made by the World Bank to the Brazilian government over the course of the 1980s (Bello, Cunningham, and Rau 1994; Lurie, Hintzen, and Lowe 1995), and more general economic relations and interactions between the United States and Brazil were predicated in large part on the assumption that the social and economic modernization that would be necessary in order to transform Brazil into a truly "developed" nation would depend upon the progressive adoption of policies aimed at reducing government spending, at opening the Brazilian economy up to the outside world, and at assuring Brazil's place at the table (for instance, as a potential member of the United Nation's Security Council) as part of the global economic order at the end of the twentieth century.

This opening up of the Brazilian economy went hand-in-hand with the opening up of Brazilian politics—literally described as the *abertura* (or "opening") period, from roughly 1979 through the end of the last military government in 1984. From this initial *abertura*, and running through the indirectly elected Sarney administration (1985 to 1989), the Collor government (1990 to 1992), the Franco government (1992 to 1994), and the Cardoso government (initiated in 1995), the process of *redemocratização* united a growing focus on *democracia* (democracy) with an emphasis on *neoliberalismo* (neoliberalism) as perhaps the major forces in Brazilian life. On the one hand, the very gradual return to directly elected civilian rule (carried out over a period of nearly ten years, first at the local and state levels but not until the late 1980s at the federal level) opened up the space for democratic debate, for the importance of *cidadania* (citizenship) and *direitos* (rights). Political exiles returned from abroad, nongovernmental organizations were formed (most often with financial support from progressive religious or private-sector donors from Western Europe and the United States) to work for the *democratização da informação* (the democratization of information), new political parties were formed, and a new democratic constitution was finally ratified in 1988 guaranteeing *direitos de cidadania para todos* (rights of citizenship for all):

> The whole idea of *cidadania* became central in the 1980s. It may seem strange to you, but when you live in a society in which the rights of citizenship—like being able to vote for whatever candidate you want in a free, direct election—have been denied, the idea of *cidadania*, of being a *cidadão* (citizen), and having the rights of a *cidadão*, becomes incredibly powerful. This is what happened during the last years of the dictatorship, during *abertura*, and following the return of the exiles. *Cidadania* became the key word for organizing the redemocratization of Brazilian society. And it was at this time that the whole phenomenon of the NGOs (nongovernmental organizations) emerged. There had been NGOs even during the dictatorship, like ISER (the Institute for Religious Studies). But it was in the early 1980s, when exiles like Betinho[7] returned to Brazil, that there started to be an explosion in the creation of NGOs working for the redemocratization of Brazilian society. The whole idea of a division between the *estado* (state) and the *sociedade civil* (civil society) became central to political discourse. The role of the NGOs was to represent the social movements working for redemocratization—to serve their political goals. It was a new kind of political participation that was concretized in the 1988 Constitution. (Jorge)

Concurrently, neoliberal economic policies where implemented in order to restructure the Brazilian economy. The 1980s and early 1990s were marked by galloping inflation, reaching an annual rate of 2490 percent by 1993; successive *planos econômicos* (economic plans) aimed at controlling the rush to hyperinflation failed to do so. In 1994, however, the Minister of Finance in the Itamar Franco administration, Fernando Henrique Cardoso, introduced a new stabilization program, the *Plano Real*, which combined tight control over a new currency (the *Real*) with the aggressive limitation on government spending, the sale of state-owned businesses and industries, and the integration of Brazil into international trading alliances:

> These days, everything seems to be motivated by *neoliberalismo*—in politics, society, economy, everything. Collor was elected as a neoliberal candidate. Fernando Henrique also. The PT (the *Partido dos Trabalhadores*, or Worker's Party) positions itself against *neoliberalismo*. The PFL (the *Partido da Frente Liberal*, or Liberal Front Party) in favor. But one way or another, it dominates the public debate. At some kind of higher level, I think that this is supposed to mean the integration of Brazil into the global system—like through the *Mercosul* (literally, the Southern Market).[8] But more locally, it means the privatization of *estatais* (state-owned industries), the reduction of government spending, cutbacks in social programs such as health and education. The *Plano Real* is the most obvious example of *neoliberalismo* in practice. (Vitor)

While the introduction of the *Plano Real* managed to cut the inflation rate to only 1.5 to 2.5 percent in mid-1995, and carried Cardoso to a land-slide victory in the 1994 presidential election, the long-term consequences of this evolving model of dependent development are questionable at best. They are perhaps most succinctly summarized by the fact that the richest 10 percent of the Brazilian population still enjoys 53 percent of the national income, while the poorest half of the population divides only 10 percent. Indeed, the price of structural adjustment and neoliberal social and economic development has perhaps been even greater, since cuts in federal spending have taken their greatest toll on the education, social security, and public health systems that most directly serve the poorest sectors of society:

> At one level, neoliberal policies have obviously had some successes. Inflation has fallen incredibly after so many years, and the *Real* has been more or less steady now for months. But the price has been high. Ever since the Collor government, neoliberal reforms have been taking apart whatever was left of the social welfare system. The *militares* had started the process, of course, but the civilian governments that followed have continued the process. It

is the price that you have to pay to make accords with the *FMI* and reschedule the debt: you can have a civilian government, but only so long as they agree to implement policies that will make the world safe for capitalism. So the rich get richer and the poor get poorer. It is just what happens. Brazil has always been one of the most unjust societies on earth, but it just keeps getting worse. And all in the name of *desenvolvimento*. That was the big campaign promise that [President Fernando] Collor made: to make Brazil part of the *"mundo desenvolvido"* ("developed world"). (Vitor)

The result of these recent trends has been, if anything, not the gradual lessening of social and economic differences once promised by the champions of *desenvolvimento*, but the sharper polarization of Brazilian society between differentiated sectors. On the one hand are the elite—the upper and middle classes, whether rural landowners, urban industrialists, or urban professionals or merchants—who have seen their lives become increasingly integrated within the global economy of the late-twentieth century. On the other hand are the lower classes or *classes populares* (the agrarian peasantry, the industrial working class, and the growing numbers of unemployed migrants moving to the cities from the countryside), who may now be able to claim the rights and citizenship of political democracy, but who still have little access to anything remotely resembling either economic or social justice. While access to consumer goods, from imported automobiles to domestic electronic equipment, has surely increased, true social mobility has remained profoundly limited—and even the new liberties of political life must themselves be questioned in an age when traditional patron-client relations have increasingly been supplanted by media-based electioneering. While "modern times" have clearly arrived in Brazil, the implications of modernity remain vastly different depending on where one is situated within Brazilian society, and the possibilities for constructing meaningful lives within modern uncertainties is necessarily conditioned by the particular ways in which both *modernidade* and *desenvolvimento* have occurred.

(Dependent) Capitalism and Gay Identity

While this discussion of political and economic development in Brazil during recent decades may seem to be taking us far afield, I would ultimately like to argue that some understanding of this context is necessary in order to begin to make some sense of the recent appearance of gay communities that in some ways resemble those found in the Anglo-European world. One of the key insights that has come about in recent work on the history of gay and lesbian communities in the United States and Europe is the extent to which their particular history is linked to the development of capitalism. While this history has been recorded and examined by a number of writers, it has probably been most succinctly stated by John D'Emilio, who has argued that the shift to industrial capitalism provided the conditions for gay and lesbian identities and communities to emerge (see D'Emilio 1983). By pulling both men and women out of the household economy and into the marketplace, industrial capitalist development both undercut the traditional family as an economic unit and led to a new emphasis on individualism and individual labor power as central to notions of economic exchange. The social, demographic, and psychological implications of these changes were far-reaching: the transformation of the family from the site of economic production to the locus of emotional security and affection, the steady decline in birth rates as procreation gradually became disconnected from sexual pleasure as the central feature of sexual life, the growing emphasis on an autonomous personal life as the key to happiness, and so on. As preindustrial modes of economic production gave way to more modern forms of industrial growth and associated urbanization, these changes combined to create a social, economic, and political context in which men and women attracted to their own sex could begin to fashion a personal identity and a way of life based upon their sexual feelings (D'Emilio 1983).

As I have already outlined, many of these key ingredients also seem to be present in Brazil—although they have emerged at a slightly later point in time. Here, as in the United States and the countries of western Europe, processes of industrialization and urbanization have displaced agriculture and household production in a remarkably rapid period of time. Children and procreation have become less necessary, from an economic point of view, and a far-reaching demographic transition has taken place that is in many ways comparable to the demographic transition in the so-called developed countries. Systems of travel and transportation have made it possible to move widely and rapidly from one location to another in order to attend the demand of the labor market, and although the family has maintained profound ideological and often practical importance, individuals have nonetheless increasingly been able to pursue their objectives and live their lives independent of broader family structures. Taken together, such transformations have made possible the opening up of a social and economic space for the recent emergence of distinct gay communities in major cities around the country. Yet these transformations have taken place within the context of a model of dependent development that also presents a number of key differences when compared with the capitalist development that shaped gay and lesbian communities in the Anglo-European world.

Perhaps most important, the sharp hierarchical structures separating socioeconomic classes (and, linked to class, racial, or ethnic groups[9]) have been reinforced and reconfirmed over the course of the past thirty years as structures of social and economic inequality have widened rather than narrowed in the model of economic development that has been adopted and implemented in Brazil. The stark structures of inequality and injustice that have continued to organize Brazilian life have created impediments to a sense of commonality or unity based upon sexual desire or orientation—and the possibility for gay or lesbian communities to encompass or otherwise mediate other kinds of social and economic divisions has clearly been limited in a number of powerful ways:

> The question of social class is probably the key aspect that structures homosexual relations in Brazil—just like it structures everything else in Brazil. Where you live, what you think, what you consume, who your friends are, who your lovers are, everything is determined by class. Other things are important, of course, like educational level (*nivel escolar*) or race (*raça*), but for the most part even these are determined by class. Access to education is almost completely a function of class, and there is that saying that *"o dinheiro embranquece"* ("money whitens"). At some level, of course, homosexual desire cuts across these kinds of distinctions, creating possibilities for interaction. Sexual relations that cut across class lines are common. Class differences can even be part of the erotic game, and it is typical for middle-class *bichas* to be infatuated with *garotões pobres* (poor young men)—or for *bichas pobres* to use sexual relations with better-off partners as a way of climbing up the social ladder. But class differences are never forgotten in these relations—class is always present, and you can never escape from it, even when you don't acknowledge it openly or talk about it. It just isn't the same as in the United States, where gay identity, or even identification as gay or lesbian, seems to be more important than anything else. There may be an identification as gay, but it doesn't erase the importance of the other factors that structure Brazilian society. It simply reproduces them on another plane. (Antônio)

Indeed, just as class continues to function as perhaps the most important underlying principle for the organization of social and sexual relations, in keeping with the most basic trajectory of *desenvolvimento* and *neoliberalismo* in Brazilian society, the emergence of gay identities and communities has itself provided a new field of play for the very notion of social mobility:

At some level, even gay identity becomes part of the game of social ascendency. People ask why gay identity would be attractive—particularly to boys from the popular classes, whose traditional identities in some ways may offer them more sexual freedom than gay identity ever could. But being *gay* is associated with status. First of all, it is associated with the outside world, with foreign countries like the United States, with all of its wealth and power. Closer to home, it is associated with the elite, with the middle class, life in the Zona Sul (the well-to-do South Zone in Rio de Janeiro), a whole pattern of consumer culture. This has an incredible attraction for people who are poor, who are *fodidas* (fucked over [by life]). You shouldn't underestimate its power. To adopt the "*estilo de vida gay*" ("gay life style"), at whatever level, is a way of achieving mobility, at least symbolically. You may still have to live in a *favela*, but you save your money to go to a gay disco, and to buy the kind of clothes that all the gay boys from the middle class are using. You call yourself by a different name. You may still be subject to taunts and discrimination in your neighborhood, but this also becomes a form of resistance—perhaps not so much because you see it as part of a movement for sexual liberation, but because these styles come from a superior class, from another world that you have suddenly become part of. (João)

Gay cultures have thus come to provide an alternative to traditional or dominant sexual cultures not only because they provide a source of sexual freedom but also because they suggest alternatives in a world that has been so powerfully structured around social distinction and economic oppression. "Becoming gay" is thus part of a much broader process of "becoming" in contemporary Brazilian society, and is linked to the complex ideology of *desenvolvimento* and *progresso* in a range of different ways. That such becoming also tends to reproduce the very structure of dependency at a variety of levels is in many ways inconsequential for those who might use it as a kind of resistance against so many different forms of oppression that must be confronted throughout daily life.

The particularities of recent political history have also in many ways shaped the emergence of gay identities and communities in Brazil in recent years. For instance, the authoritarian model of political organization that dominated Brazilian life during more than twenty years of military dictatorship also seriously limited the realm of personal freedom and the very notion of personal identity (sexual or otherwise) as a model for political organization. The gradual *redemocratização* of Brazilian society over the 1980s and '90s made possible expressive political demands organized around notions of identity and community as part of a broader transformation of Brazilian life.[10] Indeed, the birth of a gay and lesbian movement in Brazil is in large part inseparable from the social and political context of *abertura*, and can only be understood in relation to the *conjuntura política* (political conjuncture) of this particular period:

> The development of the first gay groups, or at least the first ones with a political agenda, took place during the period of *abertura*. The founding of the magazine, *Lampião da Esquina (Streetlamp)*, in both São Paulo and Rio, was especially important, because it brought together a group of intellectuals and artists with a great deal of influence, and it linked the discussion of homosexuality and homosexual rights to the broader debate about Brazilian politics. The founding of Somos (literally, We Are) in São Paulo was completely linked to this context. It was a time when a whole range of new social movements had emerged—the feminist movement, and the Black movement, ecology. . . . There was a lot of optimism about the possibility of really transforming Brazilian society. . . . In Rio, Somos never had the same impact that it did in São Paulo in the late 1970s and in the beginning of the 1980s, but it was still an important new phenomenon on the gay scene. (Vitor)[11]

While Somos, in both São Paulo and Rio, was probably the most influential and visible organization, virtually all of the earliest gay political groups in Brazil were formed during this period: *Lamda* (named after the international Lambda symbol) in São Paulo, Triângulo Rosa (Pink Triangle) in Rio, the Grupo Gay da Bahia in Salvador (see MacRae 1990; Trevisan 1986; see also Green 1996). Ironically, however, as *abertura* broadened and new questions related to the details of redemocratization were raised, the complex process of political change taking place in Brazil may actually have diverted energy from more localized struggles around issues of identity:

> During the early 1980s, in 1984 and 1985, at least some of the initial energy focused on gay politics took second place to the broader political struggles, like the failed campaign for *Diretas Já* (Direct Election Now) in '84, the mobilization around the election of Tancredo,[12] the economic crisis caused by galloping inflation. There were just so many issues to deal with . . . I think that this was really difficult for the *movimento homossexual*. Important groups like Somos wound up succumbing to internal conflicts, while many

people preferred to turn their attention and energies to the broader political questions that seemed so crucial at the time. There was actually a decline in activity during the rest of the 1980s. A few early groups survived, like the Grupo Gay da Bahia, mostly on the basis of one or two key leaders, and a couple of other important groups were formed, like Atobá in Rio [see photo 4.1], which was especially important because it focused on people from the popular classes—unlike many of the gay groups which had been more middle class. But it was really only in the 1990s, after AIDS had

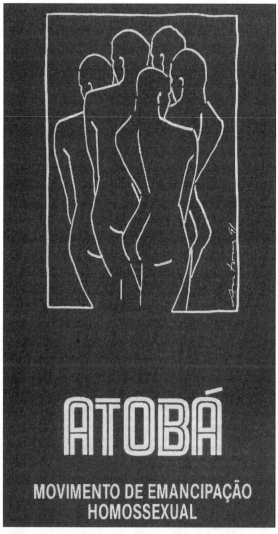

Photo 4.1.   Informational Pamphet about the Atobá Gay Liberation Group in Rio de Janeiro.

already become a major problem, and the process of redemocratization seemed more assured, that a resurgence of the gay movement seemed to take place with the formation of new activist
groups like Grupo Dignidade (Dignity Group) in Curitiba, Nuances
(literally, Nuances) in Porto Alegre, and Grupo Arco Íris (Rainbow
Group) here in Rio de Janeiro. But for the most part, this explosion
in political activism only happened sometime after an even bigger
explosion had already taken place in gay commerce, in the whole
world of bars and discos and similar commercial establishments
that made being gay into a kind of life style—almost a commodity. (Rafael)

Ultimately, it was only as redemocratization became stronger and more
secure during the 1980s and 1990s that the earliest initiatives of groups
such as Somos began to be rearticulated by other, newer organizations,
and a politics of homosexuality (self-consciously organized around a
notion of gay identity) become a growing force. At the same time, however, this resurgence in the gay movement also seemed to grow out of precisely the same neoliberal context that so consciously sought to
approximate the nature of social and economic reality in Brazil with that
of the liberal democracies in the North, such as the United States and the
majority of the other industrial powers:

It was a whole new style of activism, less oriented toward support
groups and more focused on using the media and occupying political space. You know, it's funny, but in some ways it is probably
perfectly suited to the new neoliberal order. Most of the gay
activists are progressives, of course, members of the PT or other
leftist parties, so they would surely reject the label [of "neoliberal"], but especially in the ways in which they have occupied
space in the media, they are in many ways in tune with the times.
It is almost like a marketing strategy, and the key issues, like gay
marriage or gays in the military, are being played out as much on
television and in the newspapers as in most people's lives. Everything that is fashionable in the United States, like gay marriage in
Hawaii, gets covered in Brazil, and suddenly you have gay activists
here performing public wedding ceremonies with live television
coverage, as well as a very high profile legislative project to legit-
imize gay partnerships more or less as though they were heterosexual marriages. The major players are individuals with a lot of
projeção (literally, projection, implying attention) in the media,
people who know how to manipulate the media, as well as NGOs,

most of whom claim to represent the *sociedade civil* (civil society), but who are largely funded either through external donors or through the National AIDS Program—which ultimately gets its money through a loan from the World Bank for AIDS prevention activities! It isn't that I am against any of this. On the contrary, these groups do a lot of important things. And the changes that they are working for will make Brazil a better place—for gays and for everyone. But when you start to look at it from a more distanced perspective, it is all very complex, and the relationships that are involved get very confusing. Money from the World Bank funding gay organizing in Brazil! There is something very strange about it all. (Vitor)

Self-conscious gay communities in Brazil have thus also been shaped by the broader circumstances of dependent development, authoritarian and postauthoritarian politics, neoliberal reform, and globalized capitalism in the late twentieth century, and they exhibit a number of important characteristics as a result. Perhaps most tellingly, they are almost surely even more affected by differences in social and economic class than is the case in the gay communities of the Anglo-European world—where class differences are often an important (even if sometimes overlooked) factor, but where they rarely exhibit the kind of raw, oppressive character that they often seem to demonstrate in Brazil. Although a range of other social and demographic distinctions, such as race and age, remain as forces driving social interaction within these communities, they are generally secondary to, or at best function in concert with, the more sharply dividing cleavages that organize sexuality around the lines of social class.

The role of a gay political movement, and of gay identity as a focal point for political organizing, has probably been somewhat less important to the formation of gay communities than in the Anglo-European countries. Whatever political movement there is has tended to piggyback on what already exists in gay and lesbian communities rather than to serve as the major catalyst for community organizing. On the contrary, in keeping with the neoliberal transformation of Brazilian society more generally, political struggles for emancipation and equality have thus been less central in Brazil than the recent emergence of the gay economy—the *economia cor de rosa* or "pink economy" of what even in Brazil is now clearly conceived of as a kind of gay marketplace (see Castelo Branco and Cerqueira 1995).[13]

Both authoritarian politics and the deeply rooted recession caused by international debt and spiraling inflation decisively limited the available space for gay economic development in the late 1970s and early 1980s.

The full-fledged commitment to neoliberal social and economic policies in the late 1980s and especially the 1990s, however, has led to a booming gay market, even in smaller cities outside of São Paulo and Rio. The commercial scene has taken over as the center of gay life, in part replacing the less protected and less prestigious homoerotic street life as the principal means for social interaction—and largely preceding political organizing around gay politics or HIV/AIDS as the solid center of gay consciousness. Particularly for young men from the poorer sectors of Brazilian society, participation in this commercial world has become one of the most important available sources of status—and, often, a mechanism for social mobility—and the adoption of middle-class or elite gay identities and styles has become part of a much broader struggle for ascension in a society that continues to be marked by its hierarchical socioeconomic structure and generalized class oppression.

For better or worse, it is within this context—of dependent development, authoritarianism and redemocratization, industrial capitalism and neoliberalism in the late-modern, increasingly globalized world—that the lives of gay men and women have evolved in Brazil over the course of recent decades. It is within this context that their hopes, imaginations, and struggles must be understood.

5

Tale of Two Cities

In most of Brazil's major urban centers, there has been little geographical definition of gay neighborhoods comparable to that of the Castro area in San Francisco, Greenwich Village in New York, Covent Garden in London, or the Oxford Street area in Sydney—those most typically associated with Anglo-European gay communities (see, for example, Bell and Valentine 1995; Herdt 1992; Whittle 1994). At the same time, many urban spaces, commercial establishments, and social organizations have appeared in each of the cities where we have carried out ethnographic work, and although they maintain many qualities that might be described as peculiarly Brazilian, they also share at least some characteristics with the gay enclaves and communities found in many Western European and Anglo-American urban centers. In each case, these gay communities have responded to a range of local economic and ecological circumstances, adapting more widespread forms to the exigencies of local circumstances. Yet in each case, social, cultural, and organizational structures have taken shape that provide a focus for the development of distinct life styles and identities organized around same-sex experience.[1]

In this chapter, I want to look in more detail at the gay enclaves that have emerged in the two cities where we have performed most of our work—Rio de Janeiro and Fortaleza—and to examine some of the ways in which these communities have both built upon their respective contexts as well as incorporated broader structures, symbols, and meanings found in the wider gay world at the end of the twentieth century. The choice of these two sites is of course anything but random. Rio de Janeiro has been the primary site of our research for more than fifteen years now, and together with São Paulo holds a special place as one of the major linkages between Brazil and the world system.[2] Even though Rio has experienced serious economic difficulties (and a range of related social problems) in recent years, it is still in Rio and São Paulo that the processes of industrialization and urbanization in Brazil have been most advanced, that political power and authority have traditionally been concentrated, and that the so-called modernization of Brazilian society has most clearly been realized. It is in Rio and São Paulo that the outside world first meets Brazil; that new ideas, fashions, and innovations are first introduced; and that the rest of Brazilian society invariably looks to as a model for change. It is in Rio, even more than in São Paulo, that modern communications technologies and industries have largely been centered, molding a constant flow of images and representations that through such technologies today penetrate to every corner of the country. For all of these reasons, Rio is in many ways a fairly obvious choice in seeking to examine the broader processes of change taking place in Brazilian society—and, in particular, the ways in which self-conscious gay identities and communities have begun to take shape in recent years.[3]

Fortaleza is probably not a particularly obvious choice. Fortaleza is a much smaller city, with a population of only 2,303,645 as opposed to 9,796,498 for Rio. As the capital of one of the poorest states in the country, at the heart of the traditionally underdeveloped, drought-stricken northeastern region, Fortaleza is clearly marginal at best to the broader structures of politics and economics that organize Brazilian life. At the same time, it shares a number of important features with Rio that make both comparison and contrast between the two cities intriguing. Perhaps most obviously, both are located on the Atlantic coast, with highly privileged surrounding geographies that have made them important centers for leisure for both national and international tourism—and, in the wake of tourism, business and industry. Indeed, Fortaleza, far more than Rio de Janeiro, has undergone a veritable boom of development in recent years, which has led to especially intense processes of change in a variety of different sectors (see Barros 1997). With a rate of population growth of 3.49 percent over the past decade, Fortaleza is now the fastest growing major city in the country. Not only has tourism to the Northeast generally (and Fortaleza in particular) been on the upswing in recent years (as visitors have increasingly changed their itineraries to avoid what are perceived as the urban sprawl and excessive violence of Rio), but industrial growth has also become intense as lower wages less union organizing, and a range of tax incentives have made it especially attractive for both national and international firms to relocate from the more developed Southeast to emerging financial centers such as Fortaleza. In the major hotels along the beach, Japanese businessmen and investors now mingle with German, Italian, and American tourists much as they do in Rio de Janeiro, and many of the processes of social change that have been played out over a period of decades in Rio seem to be taking place in far more intense and condensed fashion today in Fortaleza (and other similar cities in the Northeast).

In looking at Rio and Fortaleza, I do not intend to place them as representative samples that can be used to make broad generalizations, but rather as two very special cases that, through their particularities may offer some insight into more general processes that have shaped the changing character of gay life in Brazil over the course of recent decades.

Rio de Janeiro

While Rio de Janeiro has long since lost its former roles of both political primacy (supplanted by the new capital in Brasília) and economic leadership (taken over many years ago by São Paulo), it has retained its leading symbolic and practical roles in Brazilian life as a capital of culture, a primary tourist destination, and a fashion center for the rest of the country. It has been marked physically by its striking geography and symbolically by its reputation for beautiful people and romantic adventure. The geography of the city has in large part been defined by its relation to the Guanabara Bay and the breathtaking beaches and coast line to the south of the Bay.

From its original foundation at the port of Rio de Janeiro just inside the mouth of the Guanabara Bay, the city has grown both to the north in along the bay, and to the south down the coast, and is today divided into four quite clearly defined areas: the Centro (Downtown), the Zona Norte (North Zone), the Zona Sul (South Zone), and the Zona Oeste (West Zone). Oscillating between the lower sections of land (which have always been occupied by the well-to-do and have served as the centers of commerce) and the hills and mountains that rise up from the shore (traditionally the home of the poor and the site of the famous *favelas*), Rio has long been a kind of patchwork quilt of rich and poor living in relatively close proximity. Yet each of the four major zones has its own specific socioeconomic character, which in turn provides a powerful axis for social interaction more generally.[4]

The downtown area in the Centro has traditionally been the heart of commerce and finance—but also the home to any number of more marginal populations, ranging from prostitutes to drug dealers and drifters, linked to the traditional center of bohemian nightlife. As the city has grown, the Zona Sul has gradually spread down from the Centro, first to the neighborhoods known as Catete and Flamengo (along the Praia do Flamengo, or Flamengo Beach, just inside the mouth of the Guanabara Bay) and then, progressively, on to Copacabana, Ipanema, Leblon, Jardim Botânico, and Barra da Tijuca—a kind of moving frontier, initiated by the middle and upper classes as they have pushed further along the coastline in search of open spaces free from the annoying presence of the poor, and providing the key focus for Rio's well-known role as a national and international tourist center. To the north, in the Zona Norte, following the traditionally middle-class neighborhood of Tijuca, the major industrial sections of the city have grown up, mixing factories and manufacturing plants (infamous for their pollution of the Guanabara Bay) with the shantytowns and migrant populations that have flowed into Rio from all parts of the country as the job market has grown. And most recently, on the other side of the coastal mountains that so strikingly mark the geography of the city, the Zona Oeste has spread out in a kind of grand arc, stretching from the Zona Norte to the Zona Sul, providing new opportunities not only for industrial development but also for the teaming *suburbios* that today serve as home for a large part of the lower-middle class and working-class population, as well as a second catch basin for incoming migrant populations (see map 5.1).

Perhaps more than any other feature, it is this complex social/spatial structure, super-imposing both economic class and social status on geography, that has become central to the dynamic of social life in the city:

> ÂNGELO (a twenty-three-year-old informant from a working-class family living in the outskirts of Rio de Janeiro): Everything that happens in Rio is organized by the different areas of the city. The Zona Norte is much poorer. . . . There are some middle-class neighborhoods, like Tijuca, but even Tijuca is where the most boring, most traditional, middle-class people live—people with little minds. In general, to be from the Zona Norte is to be poor, to be unimportant . . . Everyone who has money or importance lives in the Zona Sul. The Zona Sul is kind of like a symbol of wealth and power, not just for *Cariocas* (people from Rio), but for everyone in Brazil.
>
> INTERVIEWER: What about the Zona Oeste and the Centro?
>
> ÂNGELO: The Zona Oeste is poorer still. It's where the *suburbios* are concentrated. . . . Because they live furthest away from the financial district and the Zona Sul, the people who live there are poorer. They have to get up at 3:00 in the morning to ride the train in [to the Centro or the Zona Sul] in time for work. It is there

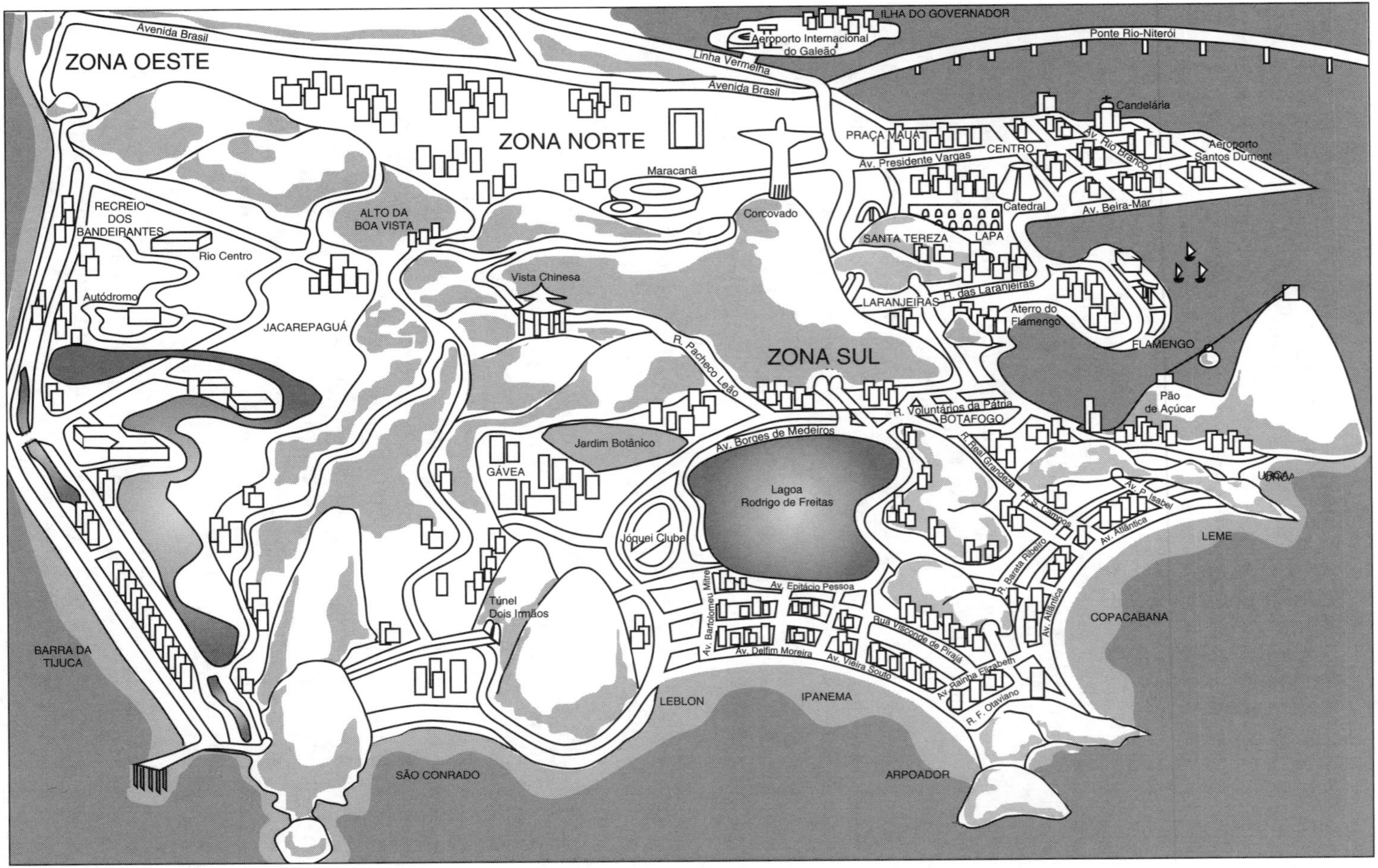

Map 5.1. Rio de Janeiro

in the Baixada Fluminense [the Rio lowlands] that the really poor people live, that organized crime is the worst, that everything is most violent. The Centro is different—it's a mixture. . . . All of the banks and financial institutions are based in the Centro, so by day it is full of people—everything from rich industrialists and bankers to office boys and secretaries. But at night everyone clears out. Some areas have prostitutes and nightclubs, like in Lapa or Praça Mauá, but the rest is just empty, like a kind of ghost town, abandoned to the beggars sleeping in the doorways of the closed banks and stores and the gangs of street kids.

Given the primacy of this spatial structure for the organization of social life and status, it is probably not surprising that the same geographical order has structured gay life. The bustling commercial and financial areas of the Centro have provided a focus for homoerotic interaction since at least the early part of the twentieth century; in his recent history of homosexuality in Brazil, James Green has documented the presence of a relatively extensive homoerotic subculture in both Rio and São Paulo, organized not only around the public spaces of parks and plazas but also through the café society that gradually grew up as these cities grew to be major centers of commerce and industry (see Green 1996).

Through the late 1970s and early 1980s, the Centro has continued to serve as perhaps the most important focus for gay life in Rio:

> The Centro has always been the most important place in the city for homosexual life. Cruising can happen anywhere, but there are many parts of the Centro that are well-known for homosexual encounters. The Campo do Santana, for example, which is a large park near the Central do Brasil [train station]—it is located by a military base and is supposed to be a good place to pick up soldiers. Or the Via Ápia, an area near the docks where the ferry boats leave for Niterói, where *michês* work at night while their clients cruise around in cars. There is also the Aterro do Flamengo [the largest park in the city], where cruising goes on all day, and where people go at night to have sex—if they can manage to avoid the police and the muggers. (João)

Indeed, the Centro can be thought of as a kind of triangle whose boundaries link the Campo de Santana and the Central do Brasil with Via Ápia and the Aterro, and running back up from the Aterro through the Lapa neighborhood, and along the Avenida Gomes Freire in the other direction (see map 5.2). Within this triangle, where street cruising is

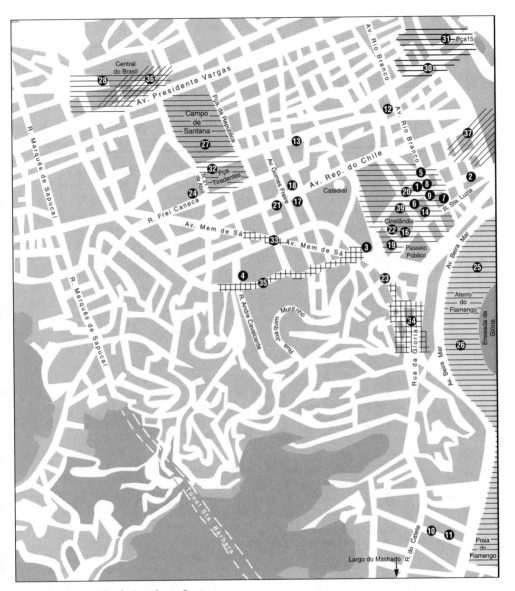

Map 5.2. Rio de Janeiro—Centro

Clubs and Discos
1. Blue Jeans
2. Boêmio
3. Casa Nova
4. Star Club

Bars and Restaurants
5. Amarelinho
6. Bar Taubaté
7. Bar Nevada
8. Verdinho
9. Vermelinho

Saunas
10. Catete
11. Flamengo

Cinemas
12. Cine Hora
13. Irís

14. Orly
15. Rex

Hotels
16. Divino
17. Gomes Freire
18. Hostal
19. Hotel 13
20. Lyp's
21. Meio Dia
22. My House
23. Souto
24. Vinte e Um de Abril

Gay Beach
25. Praia do Flamengo
 (north end, mostly
 travestis)

Cruising Areas

26. Aterro do Flamengo
27. Campo de Santana
28. Central do Brasil
29. Cinelândia
30. Estacionamento Menezes Côrtes
31. Praça 15
32. Praça Tiradentes

33. Avenida Mem de Sá (*travestis*, at night)
34. Rua do Glória (*travestis*, at night)
35. Rua do Riachuelo
 (*travestis*, at night)

36. Central do Brasil (*michê*, day and night)
37. Via Ápia (*michês*, at night)

common, the symbolic space of homoerotic desire is perhaps more intense than in any other part of the city, linking parks and plazas known for intense cruising with areas where both hustlers and transvestite prostitutes can be found, well-known tearooms, hotels for sex between men, and a wide range of gay nightclubs and bars. Perhaps appropriately, then, the heart of gay space in the center of Rio de Janeiro is Cinelândia (literally, Cinemaland), a three- or four-block area located at the center of this triangle, where one finds the highest concentration of cinemas and open-air bars anywhere in the city:

> Cinelândia is the traditional center of gay life in Rio. Many of the cinemas, even the straight ones, are well known as places to go for sex—and some of them, like the old Cine Rex or the Íris or the Orly—serve more for orgies than for anything else. Bars like the Amarelinho or the Verdinho have always been predominantly gay, even though they don't advertise themselves as gay bars. But you just have to go there and take a look to see that almost all of the clients are gay. Gay life kind of extends out from there in all directions. To the north, toward the Central do Brasil there is lots of cruising, especially with poorer men who ride the trains out to the *subúrbios*, or the poor young *michês* who work around the train station. There are lots of street kids (*meninos de rua*) too, who hang out around the Central do Brasil, looking for sex and being picked up by the older *bichas*. And the bathroom at the Central do Brasil is probably the most famous tearoom in the city. To the northwest, toward Lapa, is where most of the hotels are where gays can go for sex, especially on the Avenida Gomes Freire, and many of the low level clubs with drag shows. At night the streets around there are almost all overrun by *travestis* and their clients, from the Rua do Riachuelo to Glória [a more residential neighborhood just south of Cinelândia]. To the northeast, there is intense cruising through Via Ápia to the boats to Niterói, and famous tearooms, like the toilets on the boats or at Menezes Côrtes [one of the largest parking garages in the downtown area], and a few important nightclubs, like the Boêmio, where Laura de Visón [a well-known drag queen] performs. And to the south there is the Aterro, as well as a couple of saunas in Flamengo—one that is supposed to be popular with *travestis*, and another that caters to lower-class men. (João)

Cinelândia seems to serve as a kind of gay heart of the city, with overlapping networks of gay places and establishments stretching out in all directions:

It's kind of like a circuit. People move from one place to another—like from the bathroom at the Central do Brasil on to Menezes Côrtes or at the Amarelinho if they don't find anything that interests them, or from dinner at the Verdinho on to the Boêmio for the late night show [which usually starts only after 1:00 or 2:00 in the morning]. There is also the Casa Nova in Lapa, or the Star Club on the Rua do Riachuelo—the owners of the Star Club used to have a dive known as the *Buraco* (literally, Hole) in the middle of Cinelândia, but it was closed down and they moved over to Riachuelo, at the foot of the Santa Tereza, where there is a crazy mix of a gay club and Afro-Brazilian restaurant that caters to the Black crowd from the *favela* there. Everything in the Centro is a little like this, a kind of surrealistic mix of things that one doesn't really expect to fit together. A lot of of the circulation [i.e., circular movement from one spot to another] is just looking for sex—at night, when the financial district clears out, the large columns of the buildings and the shadows in the small streets makes it easy to have sex, even if you can't afford the price of a room in the hotels on [Avenida] Gomes Freire. But it is also the most "democratic" area of gay life in the city, the most mixed in terms of social class. Everything mixes together in the Centro—from the [extremely poor] *michês* who you find around the Central do Brasil to the middle-class gays who come into town to go to the theater and then meet afterward in the restaurants in Cinelândia or at the *pagôdes* [street performances of *samba* music] in Lapa. Or the crowd at Laura's [the Boêmio club], where the cover charge is cheap enough that almost anyone can get in, but the atmosphere is also considered kind of chic for the middle class, or for foreign tourists. Everything happens in the Centro—from anonymous sex to AIDS demonstrations. It's where everything seems to come together. (Antônio)

Characterized by its hustle and bustle and its relative mixture of social classes, the Centro has served as the traditional site for much of gay life in Rio de Janeiro. It is without a doubt the area of the city where all of the diverse dimensions of the gay subculture are most present: the homoerotic adventures of the street, the diverse worlds of male husting and transvestite prostitution, the gay commercial circuit, and even the more recent organizing of gay militants and AIDS activists. Although it is described as a kind of "democratic" mix of different types, it is simultaneously organized around an almost constant reference to class, with the spaces of homoerotic desire marked out by the symbolism of class groups, from the popular classes in the public toilets at the Central do Brasil to the more well-to-do patrons of bars and restaurants of Cinelândia. Even the interactions between classes, in the negotiations of Via Ápia or the audiences at the Boêmio nightclub, are marked by the idiom of class—precisely because of their juxtaposition of class differences.

It is socioeconomic class that seems to have had the greatest influence on the growth of gay life out from the Centro in Rio de Janeiro, both to the south and to the north. While the Centro continues to be probably the most important focus for gay interactions in the city as a whole, the Zona Sul has become a kind of elite alternative to what many now consider the somewhat seedy and dangerous character of the Centro:

> The Centro is still the place where you find the most homosexual activity—the most cruising, the most bars and discos, hotels for sex, and all that. It is the part of the city where people feel most anonymous, most free. . . . But it is also very heavy (*muito carregado*), kind of dirty and smelly, like the Avenida Gomes Freire or the area around the Arcos da Lapa, where a lot of the gay parties are held now—it is really dangerous, people are always getting mugged or rolled around there. And you never know who to be more afraid of—the thieves or the police? Especially for gays, the general level of everything makes you a constant target. I think that this is one of the major reasons that the Zona Sul has become a lot more attractive than the Centro for many gay people. It tends to be safer, and it attracts a more chic, well-to-do crowd (*um povo mais rico, mais chique*). (Rafael)

First in the Copacabana neighborhood, then soon after in Ipanema and Leblon, the Jardim Botânico, and, most recently, Botafogo, more gay meeting places and commercial establishments have sprouted up as more up-scale alternatives to the gay enclaves found in the Centro.

The most dense and varied of the newer gay areas in these neighborhoods can be found in Copacabana (see map 5.3), the first major neighborhood on the open sea to the south of the Guanabara Bay—well-known for its spectacular, banana-shaped beach—which since the early part of the twentieth century has been a middle-class residential area and one of Brazil's most important tourist centers. Although Copacabana was once one of the most fashionable addresses in the city, by the 1970s and '80s it had begun to decline (replaced by Ipanema and Leblon as the newly fashionable neighborhoods). With the highest population density anywhere in Rio de Janeiro, a heavy international tourist trade, and an especially wide array of nightlife, however, by this time Copacabana had also come

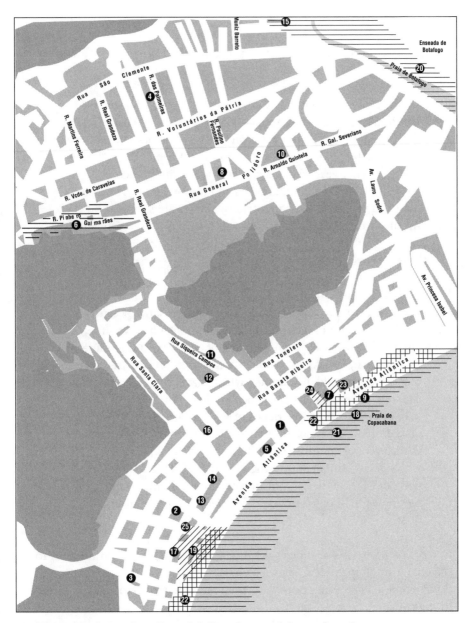

Map 5.3.   Rio de Janeiro—Zona Sul (Botafogo and Copacabana)

Clubs and Discos
1. Incontru's
2. La Cueva
3. Le Boy

Bars and Restaurants
4. Bastilha
5. Fruto do Bar
6. Jumping Jacks
7. Maxim's
8. Querelle
9. Quiosque Rainbow
10. Tamino

Saunas
11. Ibiza
12. Roger's

Cinemas
13. Art Copacabana
14. Copacabana
15. Scala
16. Star Copacabana

Hotels
17. Caprice

Gay Beach
18. Bolsa de Copacabana

Cruising Areas

19. Galeria Alaska
20. Praia de Botafogo (at night)
21. Praia de Copacabana (at night)

22. Avenida Atlântica (*travestis*, at night)

23. Rua Fernando Mendes
    (*michês*, afternoon and evening)
24. Rua Repúlica do Peru (*michês*, at night)
25. Rua Djalma Ulrich (*michês*, at night)

to offer an important, slightly more up-scale, alternative to gay life in the Centro:

> Today, the whole feeling in Copacabana isn't really all that differ-ent from in Lapa or Praça Mauá—it is kind of run-down and seedy, except that in Copacabana it is probably a lot more safe, because there is better policing due to the high number of tourists. But fif-teen or twenty years ago, Copacabana was really the center of gay life, especially for the middle class and for foreigners. The Galeria Alaska (a gallery of bars, nightclubs, and theaters located on the Avenida Atlântica) was one of the most famous spots for the inter-national jet set, and you would see Elton John or Mick Jagger, or other international stars, there. And the biggest gay beach, the *Bolsa de Valores* [literally, the Stock Market, named for the male hustlers who sell their services there] is in Copa—in front of the Copacabana Palace Hotel—so it has become a kind of center for tourism and leisure (*lazer*). It has also become a kind of little gay ghetto, with the gay beach and a number of bars and restaurants right near it, like Maxim's and La Trattoria, on [Rua] Fernando Mendes at [Avenida] Atlântica, which have a large homosexual clientele. People go to the beach during the day, then stop at Maxim's for a beer with friends or with someone who they have picked up on the beach, as they are leaving. And they come back in the evening for drinks or dinner, and to watch the hustling. The whole focus shifts. During the day, the *michês* and the *travestis* hang out on the beach, but by late afternoon and evening they move over to Maxim's or take up a spot (*fazer ponto*) around there. (João)

Indeed, nowhere is the image of Copacabana, and its role in relation to the changing shape of the gay world in Rio, more clear than in relation to the *Bolsa de Valores* (see photo 5.1), the first widely recognized gay beach in the country:

> INTERVIEWER: Has the *Bolsa* [in Copacabana] always been in the same place?
> REINALDO: There has always been some section of the beach that is gay, at least ever since I can remember, and not just in Copacabana, but all the beaches. . . . At the Praia do Flamengo, for example, it is the far end, up by the airport—but mostly for *travestis*. In Copacabana, there are various stretches that have a lot of cruising and that are well known to the *bichas*, but in gen-

Photo 5.1. The *Bolsa de Valores* in Copacabana. Photo: Richard Parker.

eral everything is very clandestine, everything happens without straight people (*gente careta*) even realizing it. The *Bolsa* is the first place that really became widely known, not only by the *bichas* but also by the *hêteros*. For at least twenty or thirty years, the *bichas* have been going there, and everyone has more or less known that this is the gay beach. If you are a mother, this is where you tell your kids to stay away from. But if you are gay, this is where you tell your friends to meet.

ALEXANDRE (a twenty-two-year-old from the lower class in Rio de Janeiro): It used to be much more elite. Because it is located right in front of the Copacabana Palace, which was for many years the most expensive hotel in Rio. Anything associated with the Copacabana Palace was very high class.

REINALDO: But during the past ten or fifteen years it has become much more mixed. More poor people come in from the *subúrbios*. There have always been *marginais* (marginals, implying either thieves or simply the poor), *michês*, and *travestis*—that is actually how it got its name, the *Bolsa de Valores*, because everyone would joke about how the prices were on that particular day. But these days, as Copacabana has become more chaotic (*mais bagunçada*), even the people at the beach have become rougher (*mais carregadas*). I think that it is partly because the *Bolsa* is the most important attraction for international tourists—the queers (*bichas*) from Europe and the United States who come to Rio, so it has also become the focus for people who want to make it with them, or who are trying to pick them up for financial reasons. This is especially intense in the summer, when the Brazilian *travestis* from Italy or France come back to avoid the European winter, and the foreign gays come for tourism or for *Carnaval*. The *Bolsa* becomes completely full with the most different types of people. And it is where everybody goes during this period to pick someone up. *Bichas* who are more out of the closet (*assumidas*) hang out right in the middle of it, for everyone to see, and the more closeted ones (*enrustidas*), or the teenage boys who are afraid to be seen by someone they know, sit around the edges, the margins, so that people won't be sure if they just sat there by accident or if they really intended to be in that kind of place.

Although Copacabana's status has declined somewhat in recent years, it still remains an important location for gay interaction. Perhaps somewhat less known for street hustling and transvestite street prostitution than the Centro, it is undisputably the center of more organized forms of male sex work in *casas de massagem* and *saunas de programa*:

Almost all of the *casas de massagem* in Rio are currently located in Copacabana. The large number of commercial buildings, together with run-down residential buildings where almost anyone with a little money can rent an apartment or a group of rooms, make it the easiest place to set up a business. The major newspapers, such as the *Jornal do Brasil* and the *Globo*, have extensive listings daily in the classified ads sections, announcing the services of women as well as of boys and even *travestis*. Most of them are actually located in Copacabana. According to Clério and Rafael, the majority are probably for out-calls, either to private residences or to hotels (*programas nas casas dos clientes, ou nos hoteis*), but at least a few have places on site for clients to go in order to have sex. There are also saunas, like Roger's, also in Copacabana, where they have a team of boys available full-time in order to give a massage, which is then expected to lead to something more (negotiated on the basis of the specific services requested and provided). Rarely, people go there by mistake thinking that it is a sauna for just picking people up—to have sex, but not for pay. But the vast majority of the clients there are actually there to hire the *garotos de programa*. (Excerpt from fieldnotes)

In addition to businesses specializing in sex work, many of the most popular gay commercial venues are also found spread throughout the Copacabana neighborhood:

> A lot of the best nightclubs have always been located in Copacabana, like the old Zoom (long since closed) at the Galeria Alaska, or The Club up by the Posto 6 (the sixth life-guard post along the beach, used, like the other posts, as a geographical marker in Rio), or La Cueva, on the Rua Miguel Lemos, which has always been frequented with an older crowd. These days the most popular discos are Incontru's on the Praça Serzedelo Corrêa and Le Boy on the Rua Raul Pompéia, which has been one of the "hottest" spots during the last couple of years. There are also a couple of saunas—the Ibiza, which used to be called the Mykonos, on (Rua) Siqueira Campos, and the Termas Roger's, just a couple of blocks from there, which is mostly just *michês* and their clients. Everything is kind of spread out, with lots of cruising on the street, especially the Avenida Atlântica and on the beach, but also at shopping centers like the Centro Comercial de Copcabana, and in cinemas, like the bathroom at the Cine Star on Rua Barata Ribeiro. (João)

Gay spaces and establishments are more or less randomly situated in the neighborhood, but in a few areas, such as in the Galeria Alaska and around the Copacabana Palace Hotel, they seem to be concentrated in what some informants describe as *polos* (poles) of activity:

> And there are a number of small nucleuses or centers—not exactly gay ghettos, but more like commercial poles (*polos comerciais*), like the old Galeria Alaska, which has gone downhill, but still has important gay revues, like Heloína's *Os Leopardos* strip show, or ABIA's *Cabaret Prevenção*. Around the Copacabana Palace Hotel there is another important pole, with lots of traffic on the gay beach during the day, as well as at the Bar Maxim's in the afternoon, when people are leaving the beach and stop there for a drink, and in the evening when it is a focus for tourists and hustlers. Right next door to Maxim's is La Trattoria, an inexpensive Italian restaurant that is really popular with lots of gays, and with the theater crowd late at night. This area has become even more popular since they opened the Quiosque Gay—in 1994, one of the *quiosques* (kiosks, or refreshment stands) on the Avenida Atlântica, right in front of the gay beach, was taken over by a couple of

lesbians, and started advertising itself as the Quiosque Gay or the Quiosque Rainbow [see photo 5.2]. They hired mostly gay boys and dykes (*sapatões*, or, literally, big shoes) to work there, and they put up a rainbow flag and a bunch of rainbow stickers like the ones that are sold at gay stores in the United States. On the weekends, and also on Wednesday nights, they have shows with drag queens, and lots of other activities, especially around *Carnaval*. It became so popular that it started to take business away from Maxim's. One of the other *quiosques* a block or so down (the Avenida Atlântica) went gay for a while too, but couldn't compete. (Vitor)

Like the Centro, Copacabana has been characterized not only by a growing numbers of gay spaces and venues, but also by the increasing diversity of gay or gay-friendly establishments and the higher visibility of gay life. In contrast to the Centro, where gay life continues to thrive on the relative anonymity provided by the hustle and bustle of the downtown business district, with most gay establishments adopting a relatively discrete or even clandestine character, gay life in Copacabana has come out into the open—and it would be hard to imagine any venue more exposed to public view and public scrutiny than the Quiosque Rainbow (more popularly referred to, by gays and straights alike, as the Quiosque Gay) in Copacabana.

Photo 5.2. Advertising for the *Quiosque* Rainbow on the Copacabana Beach in Rio de Janeiro.

Although gay life in the Zona Sul has been most intense in Copacabana, it has also followed the more general movement of the middle class in Rio over the course of the past forty to thirty years, extending gradually down along the coast as new neighborhoods have been opened up and become fashionable. By the early 1970s, at the height of the so-called Brazilian miracle—when the aggressive economic growth policies of the military regime seemed to have been successful, and before the worst impact of the international debt crisis sent the Brazilian economy into a spiraling cycle of inflation—the rapid expansion of the middle class had begun to push the focus for urban development south from Copacabana to the newer neighborhoods of Ipanema, Leblon, and Jardim Botânico (see map 5.4). By this time, Copacabana had become perhaps the most heavily mixed neighborhood in the city, at least in socioeconomic terms, with traditional middle-class family life intersecting with an influx of poorer sectors seeking social mobility, with the growing confusion caused by tourism and bohemian nightlife, with expanding markets for commercial sex work, and with the growing range of gay enclaves. Even though Copacabana had originally been an up-scale alternative to the older neighborhoods nearer the Centro, it was not long until neighborhoods such as Ipanema, Leblon, and Jardim Botânico, with their higher real estate prices and more exclusive commercial establishments, came to be seen themselves as alternatives to what was perceived as the growing decadence of Copacabana— and this was as true of gay life as it was of straight. In Ipanema, Leblon, and the Jardim Botânico (and, some years later and further down the coast, Barra da Tijuca), a middle-class Brazilian culture modeled, in many ways, on that of the United States—and especially on an image (derived in large part from television and, to a lesser extent, film) of American life in Southern California—began to emerge.[5] As ecological awareness increased, zoning laws were implemented to control the height of new building constructions and preserve trees and areas of vegetation. Youth subcultures flourished, and surfing, rock-and-roll music, and drug use all became important parts of contemporary Brazilian life. Although the development of gay styles and subcultures never received as much attention as these more mainstream trends, they nonetheless took place within much the same matrix and as part of the same general process:

> The popularity of Ipanema really exploded during the '60s and '70s. It was a special place, where Brazil met the world—the home of *Bossa Nova* music and Tom Jobim, with the most beautiful beach and the most beautiful people in the world. The new generation in music—the *Novos Baianos* (New Bahians), Gil, Caetano, Gal Costa, Maria Bethânia. Rock-and-roll music. Marijuana. The hippies. Fem-

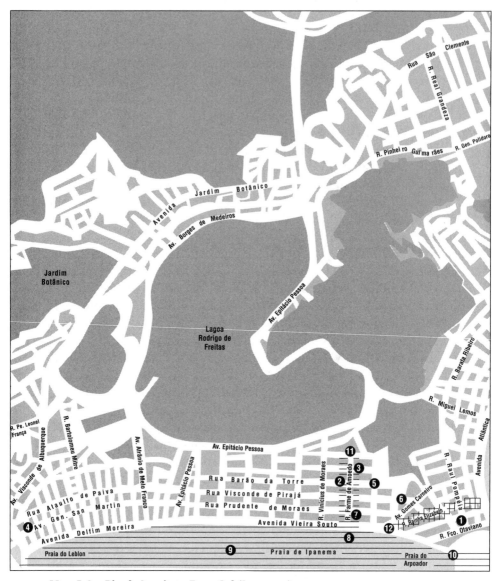

Map 5.4. Rio de Janeiro—Zona Sul (Ipanema)

Clubs and Discos
1. Le Boy

Bars and Restaurants
2. Bofetada
3. Pizzaiolla
4. Pizzaria Guanabara
   (late at night)

Saunas
5. Nova Termas
   Leblon
6. Studio 64

Hotels
7. Agris

Gay Beach
8. Bolsa de Ipenema

Cruising Areas

9. Praia de Ipenema
10. Praia and Pedra de Arpoador
11. Rua Farme de Amoedo

12. Rua Rainha Elizabeth
    (*travestis*, at night)

inism. The ecology movement. Everything "modern" seemed to arrive in Brazil through Ipanema and the Zona Sul. It was the same thing in gay culture in Brazil. All during the 1970s and '80s, all of the new gay fashions from New York and Paris arrived in Brazil by way of Ipanema and Leblon! This is an exaggeration, of course, but that is how it seemed to me at the time, when I was a teenager discovering the gay world. During the day, all of the sexiest guys could be found on the beach in front of Farme [Rua Farme de Amoedo—the street that runs into the Ipanema beach at the site of the *Bolsa de Ipanema*, the gay beach in Ipanema]. At night, they could be found mixing with the rich teenagers in Baixo Leblon [a strip of hip bars and restaurants, especially popular with young people, in Leblon]—or dancing at Papagaios (Parrots), the most popular gay dance club in the city, on the Avenida Epitácio Pessoa. In the days before it closed, everybody, even straight people (*os hêteros*) used to refer to it not as Papagaios but as Papagay! Late at night, the action was at Quarenta-e-Quatro [literally, Forty-Four, the name of the most exclusive gay baths], the hottest sauna in Ipanema. I came from a poor family, and had to save everything I could, or somehow get myself invited, to be able to go to a lot of the hottest places. But this was where it all happened (João)

Over the course of the 1980s and early 1990s, these various enclaves in Ipanema and Leblon continued to expand and to provide another important focus for gay life in Rio, offering a range of largely middle-class and upper-class options and alternatives to the areas found in the Centro and in Copacabana. These differences are perhaps most clearly symbolized in the *Bolsa de Ipanema*, the gay beach that has grown up in front of the Rua Farme de Amoedo, sometimes referred to by gay and straights alike as Farme de "AmoAIDS" because of its heavy association with homosexuality (and the strong association between homosexuality and HIV/AIDS in popular culture and representations). Although the *Bolsa de Ipanema* originally took its name from the *Bolsa de Valores* in Copacabana, it is constantly contrasted with the *Bolsa* in Copacabana as the center for a younger, richer, better-looking crowd—the body-building *barbies* and the well-to-do *bichas profissionais* (gay professionals) who frequent the *Bolsa de Ipanema* by day and make the party circuit and the commercial scene "boil" (*ferver*) by night:

> In comparison to the Centro, or even Copacabana, you find a whole different crowd in Ipanema or Leblon—people who are younger, better looking (*gente mais jovem, mais bonita*). Like at the

beach: the *Bolsa* in Ipanema has people with more money, in better shape. At the *Bolsa* in Copacabana, you find a lot more hustlers (*michês*), old queens (*bichas velhas*) and poor queens from the suburbs (*bichas suburbanas*). The whole atmosphere (*ambiente*) is different in Ipanema—more modern (*mais moderno*), better looking (*mais bonito*). It's the same thing with the clubs, and even the saunas. (Rafael)

While sharp class differences have continued to characterize these different areas, over time the areas have developed into a kind of interacting circuit. Without altogether abandoning the importance of class distinctions, as gay commercial establishments and events have multiplied and become more varied, the possibilities for circulation and mixture on the part of participants also seems to have increased, perhaps most vividly in the neighborhood of Botafogo (see map 5.3), which in the late 1980s and early '90s emerged as the focus for a new, more concentrated gay scene:

> In the past couple of years, Botafogo has become one of the hottest neighborhoods. Botafogo has always been a fairly mixed neighborhood, with people from all different classes, and with lots of public transit, the subway and buses, providing good access. Some of the oldest surviving gay bars, like Tamino on Rua Arnaldo Quintela, are located there. But a whole range of new places have opened in recent years, like Jumping Jack's, which is probably the most popular bar in the city right now. It is turning into a kind of gay ghetto, and has even been getting attention as such in the newspapers. The *Globo* newspaper just ran an article about it as the new "*gueto gay*" (gay ghetto) in Rio. (Excerpt from fieldnotes)

Commercial events, such as the popular *Festas* or Parties organized by commercial entrepreneurs, have created a social circuit that has sown together distinct spaces as well as social classes:

> ANTÔNIO: The *festas* that have become so popular are a good example of how gay life in Rio has changed.
> INTERVIEWER: How so?
> ANTÔNIO: Well, it isn't really all that different from the gay party circuit in the United States: big dance parties, paid admission, lots of drugs, like Ecstasy, sex, of course, and all of the beautiful people competing to see who is most beautiful.
> INTERVIEWER: But the parties are still really exclusive, aren't they? Because of the cost, most people probably can't afford them.

ANTÔNIO: Yes and no. They're expensive. *Festas* like Valdemente or the Festa Bitch can cost as much as R$25, or R$20 if you have an invitation [with a discount], which is a lot of money. But it depends on your priorities. Even people who are quite poor can save up money for this if they decide not to spend it on other things. Or they can find other ways to get in—performing, working there, even volunteering to do AIDS prevention work! Obviously, for people who are really down and out (*fodidas*), the cost makes it impossible, but I am always impressed by how many people I know who prefer to spend money on the gay social scene rather than on other things. For a lot of them, I think, it is the most important thing in life.

Although this gay commercial circuit hardly undercuts the spatial distribution and class differences that have tended to shape much of gay life in Rio, it has still rearranged the ways in which such distinctions have traditionally functioned. Rather than simply being excluded, as might have been the case in the past, the poorer sectors (or at least some parts of them) seem to have been increasingly incorporated into the growing gay economy—the *economia cor de rosa*—that organizes the possibilities for both sexual and social interaction. While this gay economy is clearly neither synonymous nor coterminous with homosexual life more generally, it has penetrated further and further into the most basic structures of the gay subculture in recent years, and has provided the terms of reference for many of the most important developments in the more visible gay communities found in cities such as Rio de Janeiro—certainly for the middle and upper classes, but, increasingly, for the poorer or popular classes as well.

We can get a sense of how prevalent these changes are by turning to the poorer areas of the Zona Norte and the Zona Oeste, where some trends similar to those in the Centro and the Zona Sul have presented themselves. The social and cultural characters of these regions are typically a good deal more constrained and conservative, characterized by the "traditional" values of the rural areas or small towns in the interior. Yet both the Zona Norte and the Zona Oeste (see map 5.5) have also developed their own gay spaces and subcultures. Many of these spaces have been carved out of traditional life through the construction of homoerotic territories:

The Zona Norte is supposed to be this whole other world—another planet or something. . . . But it really isn't all that different. There are just as many places for cruising (*paquerando*) and picking people up (*pegando*) as you find in the Zona Sul. The Quinta da Boa Vista (a large park in the Zona Norte where the Museu Nacional is

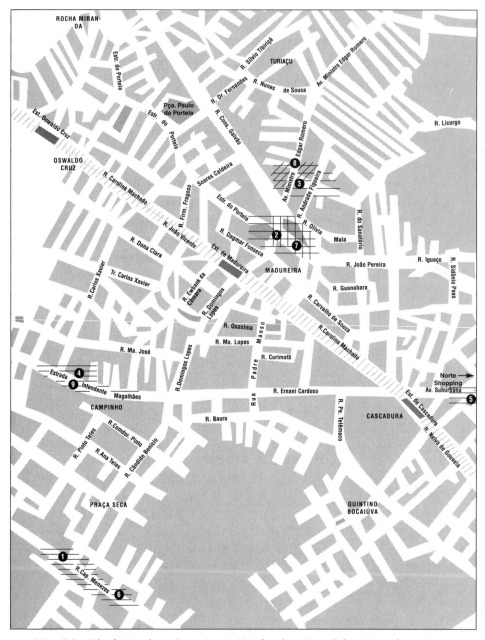

Map 5.5. Rio de Janeiro—Zona Oeste (Madureira, Campinho, Cascadura, Praça Seca, and Quintino).

Clubs and Discos
1. Boite 1140

Bars and Restaurants
2. Botecos/Botequins

Cinemas
3. Astor

Hotels
4. Jumbo

Cruising Areas

5. Avenida Suburbana (*gays*)
6. Rua Capitão Menezes (*gays*)
7. Rua da Lama (*gays* and *travestis*)

8. Avenida Ministro Edgar Romero (*michês* and gays)

9. Estrada Independente (*gays*)

located) is a good example. During the day, there is every bit as
much cruising and sex as in the Aterro or the Campo do Santana.
And it is especially popular for some men, because it is used a lot
for training by the army—it is supposed to be especially easy to
pick up a soldier boy (*um soldadinho*). Because it is fenced in, and
closes at night, it isn't like the Aterro—but all around it on the
sidewalks there is a constant movement of cars and *travestis*. At
night, a lot of the homosexual cruising moves over to the area
around Maracanã (the major sports stadium), where there are lots
of areas to practice sports and exercise bars (for public use)—and
around UERJ [the State University of Rio de Janeiro], where there
are a lot of hot spots (*buracos quentes*, or, literally, hot holes) where
people can have sex. It is like that everywhere in the Zona Norte
and the *subúrbio*. The streets are a lot darker than in the Zona Sul—
there are less streetlights, and less movement too, which in some
ways makes it easier to find places for sex. (João Carlos)

Although many of the same kinds of spaces or territories for homoerotic
sexual encounters can be found in the Zona Norte and, perhaps to a lesser
extent, the Zona Oeste, the ways in which they are structured and controlled is distinct from such modes in the Centro or the Zona Sul:

The division of things is a little different in the Zona Norte and the
Zona Oeste. There is a sharper separation of [residential] neighborhoods and commercial or industrial areas. The neighborhoods
and communities in the poorer parts of the city tend to be a lot
more conservative than in the Zona Sul. People have to be much
more discrete. Everybody may know that you are a *bicha*, and they
don't really treat you any differently as long as you are discrete
about it. But if you act swishy (*dá pinta*), or dress too outlandishly,
you are likely to get beat up. In some communities, especially
those that are more traditional working class (*classe trabalhadora*),
there is no way that a *travesti* could live, let alone work! Most
homosexual interaction has to be reserved to areas that are more
commercial and impersonal—where it won't mix with proper family life. It is probably a little easier in the *favela*, where everything
is so marginal that the *bichas* and the *travestis* just mix together
with the *traficantes* (drug dealers) and other *marginais* (marginal
types, implying thieves and other sorts of social outcasts). But generally there is probably much less tolerance for individual differences than you find in the Zona Sul—even though the community
can accept people who are different if they are integrated into com-

munity life, like *bichas* who are *Pais de Santo* (Afro-Brazilian religious priests), and so long as they behave themselves properly. In the community, everyone can know that the *Pai de Santo* is a *bicha*, but he has to be a little reserved—he can't walk around like a *bicha louca* (crazy queen). And he can't go fucking around with the boys from the community. He can have "intimate" friendships, so long as they are discrete, but nothing too bold (*escancarado*). For that, he would have to go outside of the community. (Joel)[6]

The more tightly knit, local, community structures, representing traditional and conservative cultural values, are thus seen to be characteristic of the more residential areas in the Zona Norte and the Zona Oeste. Even so, the rather uniquely Brazilian ability to divide or separate even quite proximal spaces into distinct (private and public) moral universes has made possible the existence of gay spaces and commercial venues even in the poorer areas of the city:

For the most part, in the Zona Norte you don't find so many places that are specifically identified as gay—you know, bars or discos or what have you. Everything is a little more clandestine. There are lots of saunas, for example, but they don't advertise themselves as gay saunas—just as saunas for men. People go there as if it were nothing special. In the steam room everybody fucks around, and nobody would go who doesn't want to fuck around—at least not more than once, because they would immediately find out what kind of place it is and would be scandalized. So it is all much more camouflaged than in the Zona Sul, where saunas or bars are much more likely to announce themselves as gay. But even in the Zona Norte in recent years, this has begun to change. Clubs have begun to open in places like Bangú and Nova Iguaçú [poor suburban neighborhoods in the Zona Oeste]—places like Casa Grande or Batom Vermelho [literally, Red Lipstick] which everybody knows as a gay bar. And a whole bunch of fairly visible and well-known places have become the focus for gay cruising and socializing. The Shopping do Meier [Meier Shopping Center] has as much open homosexual cruising as the Rio Sul [Rio Sul Shopping Center in Botafogo], maybe more. But it is still very different from gay life in the Zona Sul, or even the Centro. Even though the atmosphere is changing, becoming more modern, much more traditional patterns still exist here. At the Casa Grande, for example, the old style of *bichas* and *bofes* still exists very strongly. The *bofes* do a whole *macho* number, with jeans and T-shirts showing off their muscles, wearing tennis shoes and the shirts of different football (soccer) teams. They say that the *bofes* have more success [in picking up sexual partners] if they are wearing football shirts, because it makes them look more *macho*. The *bichas*, on the contrary, are either *travestis* or quasi-*travestis*—very effeminate gay boys who sometimes cross-dress. Like Beto. He goes [to enter the club] dressed as a *boy* (a term adapted from English, and implying a young, somewhat androgynous, yet still basically masculine, appearance), with jeans and a T-shirt, because the young *bofes* get in for free. But in his backpack he takes another set of clothes. He runs to the bathroom as soon as he gets in, and changes into a miniskirt with a bra and a wig, and spends the rest of the night as a *traveca* (a little [or perhaps young] *travesti*, or a *travesti*-in-training) picking up *bofes*. At the entrance to the bar is what they call the *Corredor da Morte* [literally, the Corridor of Death—essentially equivalent to the notion of "running the gauntlet" in English], with the *bofes* leaning up against the wall on one side and the *bichas* passing back and forth on the other, fondling them (*pegando no pau deles*) and trying to pick them up. Everyone is very poor, completely fucked over (*fodido*), especially in comparison to the wealthier crowds that you find in the Zona Sul, at bars like Jumping Jacks or *festas* like Bitch. And the whole *bicha/bofe* thing is typical here where people are poor, typical of the Zona Norte and the Zona Oeste, and very different than what you would find in the Zona Sul. (João)

Gay-identified venues have thus become more common, even in the Zona Norte or the Zona Oeste, throughout the lower-class *subúrbios* that surround the city, but they remain highly distinct from the more up-scale gay circuit found in the Centro or the Zona Sul. Indeed, the gay establishments and enclaves that have developed here might well be described as in many ways very different from those of the Zona Sul or even the Centro—characterized by at least one of our informants as an "archaic homosexuality" (*homossexualidade arcaíca*) in contrast to the more "modern" and "middle-class" homosexuality of the better-off sectors of town:

When you go to the Zona Norte, it feels a little like going to another world, or back in time maybe to a kind of archaic homosexuality. There are clubs and bars, and the cruising can be just as intense there as anywhere else in the city, especially in well-known public places like the Shopping de Madureira or some of the cinemas where men go to cruise (*fazer pegação*) with other men. But there is also something much more clandestine about it all. There is one house for boys that I know of, for example, out in the *sub-úrbio*, full of young kids from the neighborhood who turn tricks (*fazer programas*) there with older *bichas*—the *bichas* come mainly from the *subúrbio* too, and with good reason, because there is absolutely no advertising. It is nothing like a modern *casa de mas-sagem* with advertisements in the newspaper or magazines. Every-thing is word of mouth. There are no signs or anything, so you could never find it if you didn't know where you were going. Inside, it has been divided up into a bunch of little cubicles where the boys go with the clients to have sex. The *freguês* can pick the boy he likes, and they go into the cubicle to screw. Everyone in the neighborhood knows about it, and knows what it is, but nobody complains, probably because a lot of the families supplement their income by having their kids turn tricks there. Since the boys always fuck the *bichas*, nobody really worries much about it, and it brings money home that otherwise they wouldn't have. Since it is located not far from our center, we have done some AIDS pre-vention work there—taking condoms to the old *bicha* who runs the place and asking him to distribute them to the boys. (Paulo, a forty-three-year-old member of a gay-rights organization that has been involved in a range of HIV/AIDS prevention activities)

The homoerotic world that has taken shape in the poorer, more suburban areas of the Zona Norte and the Zona Oeste seems to preserve at least some of the more traditional patterns characteristic of a quite different cultural system. At some level, it may seem to be as different from the gay enclaves of the Centro and the Zona Sul as the world of *travestis* and *michês* is from that of *ativistas* or *militantes*. And yet, as the words of the gay activist engaged in AIDS prevention work might suggest, these worlds are some-times not nearly so distant as they might at first appear. On the contrary, both are very much in the midst of highly complex processes of change, and the interfaces and exchanges that constantly take place between them are in fact intense.

Movement between these different spaces is a constant part of daily life. Couples who meet in a club or bar in places as distant as Copacabana or Nova Iguaçú are likely to end up at a hotel *"para cavalheiros"* (for men) on Avenida Gomes Freire if they need a private place to have sex. Poorer young men from the Zona Norte may well work the streets in the Centro or out of the *casas de massagem* that are concentrated in the Zona Sul, where their clients are as likely to be middle-class gay men from Copaca-bana or Ipanema as closeted married men (*homens casados*) or aging queens (*bichas velhas*) from the *subúrbios*. Many of the most popular commercial settings, like the Boêmio nightclub in Cinelândia, the Casa Nova or the Star Club in Lapa, and Incontru's or Le Boy in Copacabana, are characterized by the mix of different social types and backgrounds that are found among their clientele:

> You can never escape the differences of social class, but that doesn't mean that the classes live in completely separate worlds, one for the elite and another for the popular classes. This exists, of course, at the extremes, but the gay life (*a vida gay*) is one of the principal places in which mixture and interaction takes place. Not so much in the *subúrbio*, because people from the Zona Sul are not so likely to go all that way. But certainly in the Centro or the Zona Sul, where people from the Zona Norte always come to party (*para se divertir*). The public that frequents clubs like Boêmio or even Le Boy is completely mixed. There are young people and old, rich and poor, white people and black people. Indeed, the mixture is part of the atmosphere at places like Laura's (Laura de Visón's nightclub, the Boêmio). You have everything there: *marginais* (marginal people, i.e., poor people or people involved in some way in crime), *bichas ricas da Zona Sul* (rich queers from the Zona Sul) looking for excitement. . . . Sometimes you even get foreign *bichas*, who come to make fools of themselves by trying to imitate the *transformistas* (drag queens) who perform. This kind of mixture adds to the fun. It also creates a kind of transgressive atmosphere where people can leave behind the problems of life, at least for a while. (João)

Such intermixing is vital to the the gay economy, which depends upon it for its continued success:

> In part, it is a purely economic question. If a gay club is going to succeed, it has to cater to the largest possible public. Many of the bars and discos go under quickly. They open one day and go under the next because they have been unable to attract a diverse enough public. But not the really successful ones, like Incontru's in Copacabana, which has always managed to attract both foreign tourists and Brazilians looking to climb (*subir*, implying climbing up the social ladder), or La Cueva, which has been around for years specializing in old *bichas* and young boys who like to hustle (*fazer michê*) with the old *tias* [literally, aunts], or like Laura de Visón (the Boêmio club), that has always mixed poor with rich. Those are the places that just keep going. (Clério)

In a sense, the importance of such intermixture is in some ways concretized as part of the annual cycle of life in Rio by becoming a feature of
the summer holiday season and the remarkable cultural industry that has
grown up around the *Carnaval* festivities immediately prior to Lent:

> Social life in Rio has always revolved around summertime and *Car-
> naval*. The *Carnaval* is the gay fantasy of life in Rio! Both in popu-
> lar culture in Brazil as well as for *bichas estrangeiras* (foreign
> queers). Gays have always been central in the *Carnaval*. Ever since
> the '40s or '50s, many of the most successful *Carnaval* balls in Rio
> were organized by *travestis* and *transformistas*. They used to call
> them the *bailes dos Enxutos* (the fairies' balls) or *bailes das bonecas*
> (dolls' balls), and they would be widely reported in the popular
> press, the *hêtero* press. Since the 1980s, though, they have gotten
> much more complex. Some, like the Gala Gay, are organized by
> the major promoters of nightlife in Rio, like Chico Recarey, and
> have become very elite because the cost of the ticket is very high.
> They are "big business" [in English] run by *hêtero* promoters. They
> are held in the most elite clubs in Ipanema and Leblon. But oth-
> ers, like the traditional ball at the Elite, continue to have a com-
> pletely mixed crowd, and a much more authentic feeling. It is
> really incredible. People of all colors, sizes, and shapes packed in
> like sardines, dancing *samba* all night long. With so many hot
> sweaty bodies and so many queers together (*tantas bichas juntas*)
> you can imagine the sex that goes on (*a sacanagem que rola*). And
> gays have a central place in the festival as a whole in Rio, even in
> the traditional *escolas de samba* (samba schools). Some of the *esco-
> las*, like Estácio de Sá [a samba school located in the Centro, by the
> Praça Onze, at the foot of the Morro de Santo Cristo (a *favela* in the
> downtown area)], are special favorites with the gay public. Groups
> of gay friends get together every weekend during the summer
> months and go to the rehearsals at Estácio. Things really cook [*fer-
> ver*, literally "to boil," which is a common slang expression among
> men who have sex with men, suggesting a hot, exciting social set-
> ting as well as intense sexual activity] there, on the dance floor and
> in the bathrooms. Not just Estácio, but many of the *escolas de
> samba*. These days, all of the *escolas* have *alas gays* (gay contin-
> gents) that play a key role in the parade of the *escola*. And they mix
> together all kinds of people, *bichas ricas* with poor people from the
> *favelas* and the *subúrbios*. It is part of the whole logic of *Carnaval*.
> (Jorge)[7]

Just as it is part of the reinvention and reformulation of traditional culture (such as *Carnaval*) in Rio, this interaction and intermixture is also part of the reframing of social, economic, and political life that has taken place over the course of the past decade. Perhaps nowhere is this as evident as in the rapid growth and transformation of both the gay rights and the AIDS advocacy movements, which have been especially important in Rio de Janeiro since the mid-1980s:

> In the late 1970s and early '80s, much of the gay organizing was really focused in São Paulo. Somos is a good example: there was a group in Rio, but the heart and soul of Somos was always much more in São Paulo. There were a number of other groups in Rio, which in some ways were competitors [with Somos], but they were mostly very small and narrow—the private kingdom of one person or another, usually some middle-class gay, rather than organizations with any kind of community base (*base comunitária*). But things changed radically after the end of the dictatorship. Probably the most important change was the creation of Atobá in Magalhães Bastos, in the *subúrbio* of Rio. It was founded by a group of friends, poor men from the *subúrbio*— men who had suffered a lot, because of where they came from, from the *subúrbio*, from poor and very marginalized families, living in very traditional neighborhoods where violence against effeminate *bichas* happens all the time. Violence and class oppression was really what gave Atobá a sense of identity. The group even took its name from this, in a way, because the group of friends had gone on a picnic and had found a wounded *atobá* (albatross). They took the bird back to the house that would become their *sede* (office or center), and cared for it until it was well. And they got to talking about the kinds of violence that they had all suffered in their lives. It was out of this discussion that the idea of forming a gay group emerged, a group to work against violence, and with a self-conscious Marxist ideology, at least in the early days when Rodolfo [Skarda] was president, as a group from the working class, and even with a kind of emphasis on ecology—even today, their *sede* is almost a zoo, there are so many animals there. It was very hard for them to get organized, because they had very few resources. They also confronted real hardships, since a number of their early presidents, like Rodolfo [Skarda] and Paulo [Roberto Nogueira], became sick with AIDS and had very difficult deaths. That is probably one of the main reasons that they became involved very quickly in AIDS prevention work.

But you have to understand what an unheard of thing this was—
a leftist gay group from the working class, when all of the gay
groups before had basically been middle class. It gave them a great
deal of influence with poor *bichas* from the Zona Oeste and the
subúrbios, because they could really claim to understand the conditions that these people had to confront. And they were able to
take advantage of some of the things that were happening politically at the time. Most of the guys in the group had limited edu-
cations, but Paulo had studied law and worked in the office of a
politician from the PDT [the *Partido Democrático Trabalhista*, or
Democratic Workers Party], the leftist party that [Leonel] Brizola
had founded when he came back from exile at the start of the '80s.
The PDT had invested in a big way in the Zona Oeste, making it the
center of its power base, and people from the PDT helped Paulo
and Atobá to get set up as a nongovernmental organization, to
write their legal statute and get incorporated, to meet all of those
bureaucratic regulations in order to become an NGO. This was
probably in 1985 or 1986. It could have never happened just a few
years earlier, but by the mid-1980s it made perfect sense politically.
And Atobá has played a key role since then in creating a notion of
gay rights and gay community in Rio. Precisely because they have
always been based in Magalhães Bastos, but have also worked
throughout the city—doing AIDS prevention work and outreach
on the beaches of the Zona Sul, during *Carnaval* at the parade of
the *escolas de samba*, or in Cinelândia during major political
demonstrations. (Jorge)

Like Atobá, many gay and AIDS organizations were formed rapidly during
the late 1980s as part of a veritable population explosion of nongovernmental organizations following the dictatorship:

The AIDS Program in the State of Rio de Janeiro was very slow to
get started and very inefficient. . . . One of the consequences of
this situation, though, was that many nongovernmental organizations were either founded or in some way reorganized to take on
AIDS. In the late 1980s, many of the most important organizations
were founded. ABIA [the *Associação Brasileira Interdisciplinar de
AIDS*, or Brazilian Interdisciplinary AIDS Association] was first
founded in 1986, and I think that GAPA-RJ [*Grupo de Apoio à Prevenção à AIDS-Rio de Janeiro*, or Support Group for AIDS Prevention-
Rio de Janeiro] must have been founded more or less at the same
time. ARCA [*Apoio Religioso Contra AIDS*, or the Religious Support

Group Against AIDS] was started as a project of ISER [*Instituto Superior de Estudos de Religião*, or Institute for Religious Studies]. The *Grupo Pela Vidda* (Group for Life), which was the first organization anywhere in Brazil of people living with AIDS, was founded by [Herbert] Daniel when he became ill in 1989. None of them was specifically gay, and some, like GAPA and Pela Vidda, explicitly wanted to avoid being labeled gay, but they all had activities that more or less explicitly addressed homosexuals, and they were especially important in raising issues about homosexuality in the media, on television. And some groups, like Atobá, were specifically gay and became involved in AIDS work. Atobá probably survived financially because of AIDS work. They got a grant from the Ford Foundation in 1988 in order to set up an AIDS hotline. ABIA and GAPA had gotten funds from Ford a year earlier, and Pela Vidda was set up with a grant from Ford to ABIA in 1989, but Atobá was the first gay group to be funded. Later they got additional funding from the AIDSCOM Project of USAID [the United States Agency for International Development] for educational materials and outreach work, as well as from the National AIDS Program. Today, almost all of the groups in Rio get support from the National AIDS Program. (Rafael)

In the late 1980s and early 1990s, many of these organizations began to be key players both in providing an organizational focus for homosexual and bisexual men in Rio as well as in raising the question of sexual rights as part of a broader focus on human rights. Much of this work was possible at least in part due to support provided by international development cooperation agencies, such as the Ford Foundation and the U.S. Agency for International Development, mentioned above, as well as other North American and European agencies that had made a strong commitment to the process of redemocratization and to the reconstruction of civil society.

Drawing on such sources of support, both AIDS prevention work and gay rights activism has provided a key point of intersection not only for diverse nongovernmental organizations but also for organizations and the growing network of commercial and leisure establishments that have provided the focus for gay social life throughout the city:

Projeto *Homossexualidades* [the Homosexualities Project], the AIDS prevention project at ABIA, was the first really large-scale project. It started out as a partnership between ABIA and the Grupo Pela Vidda in Rio de Janeiro and in São Paulo, and with participation

Photo 5.3.   AIDS Prevention Materials Developed by the Brazilian Interdisciplinary AIDS Association (ABIA).

of a number of gay groups in both cities, to do outreach work and to set up services for men who have sex with men. Funding came from the AIDSCAP Project of USAID in Brasília, as well as from the National AIDS Program and a number of private donors. The idea was to do a kind of community-based activism, with educational materials that were less about information than about eroticizing safe sex and addressing homophobia (*homofobia*) and sexual oppression. There were post cards with erotic images, and posters with well known slogans like *Silêncio* = *Morte* (Silence = Death) and *Ação* = *Vida* (Action = Life). The idea was not simply to imitate what is done abroad, but to consciously proclaim participation in a broader global movement. And most of the outreach work and project activities were based in the most popular bars and discos that are a focus for the gay community in Rio—not only in the Zona Sul, but also in the Zona Oeste and the Zona Norte. There was a kind of partnership between the NGOs and the commercial establishments, which let the outreach workers in for free, and which sometimes sponsored parties or other events related to the project. More recently the *Projeto Praça Onze* also has some of these same qualities, working in the community through institutions like these, although this project is less political—in some ways, it is more medicalized because it is linked to HIV vaccine research. It has less of an obvious political agenda. (Rafael)

By the early to mid-1990s, consistent with the kind of logic driving such projects as well as with the rapidly evolving nature of Brazilian political life, there were more organizations responding to both AIDS prevention and gay organizing:

In the 1990s, there has been a whole new wave of organizations and organizing styles. In the 1980s, everything was much more influenced by *abertura*, and by the process of redemocratization. The bigger issues related to *democracia* and *cidadania* were central, and the model for organizing was in large part the model established by the redemocratization movement—by NGOs like IBASE [the *Instituto Brasileiro de Ánalise Social e Econômico*, or Brazilian Institute for Social and Economic Analysis] or FASE [the *Federação de Orgãos para Assistência Social e Educacional*, or Federation of Agencies for Social and Educational Support]. Most of the AIDS

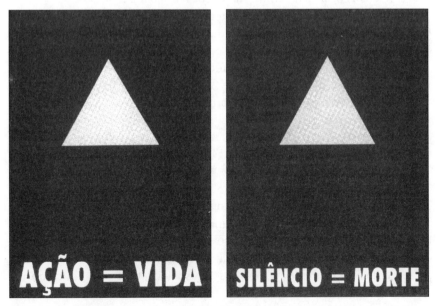

Photo 5.4. AIDS Activism (in Brazil and the World).

organizations, and even some of the gay groups, were heavily
influenced by these models, and were very concerned not just
about questions of identity but about broader political issues
affecting all Brazilians—and as an extension of this, affecting people with AIDS or gay or lesbians in Brazil. By the early 1990s,
though, the process of redemocratization had been more or less
consolidated, even if economic inequalities had never been successfully confronted. Indeed, things had only gotten worse as
neoliberalism had become more dominant. But many people
began to turn attention more other things, to more localized struggles (*lutas mais localizadas*). Questions of identity began to become
much more important. A whole range of new organizations
emerged with a completely different character. NGOs like NOSS
[*Núcleo de Saúde Social*, or Nucleus for Social Health] are an example of this. They are a kind of mix between an AIDS NGO and a gay
organization—first they ran the *Programa Pegação*, an outreach
education program directed to *michês*, then they started a gay
newspaper called *Nós por Exemplo* (Us for Example), which lasted
for a few years before it went out of business, and which tried to
introduce a new kind of aesthetic style, with a mixture of first-
world eroticism and exotic tropicalism (*tropicalismo exótico*). Then
they opened a gay bar, called the Safe Bar, which was funded as an
AIDS prevention project as well as a commercial enterprise. Or
there is PIM, which I think stands for *Programa Integrado de Marginalidade* (Integrated Program on Marginality), which started out
as a unit of ISER, one of the traditional NGOs that struggled for
redemocratization. A few years ago they created a new entity . . .
in order to do AIDS prevention and mobilization for *travestis* and
female prostitutes. And even gay groups, like the *Grupo Arco Íris*
(Rainbow Group), which have formed in recent years, have been
very different—much more focused on gay identity, and what are
perceived to be "modern" gay issues like the struggle for gay marriage or the importance of electing openly gay political candidates.
(Vitor)

Together, these organizations seem to have been built on the foundation
already provided by the more traditional homoerotic world of the street
in Rio de Janeiro, and the rapidly growing pink economy of commercial
enterprises, as a nonprofit sector that offers employment opportunities,
public education, and new options for socialization and community
mobilization.
   By the mid-1990s, then, an increasingly complex and diverse homo-

sexual community (or set of overlapping communities) has emerged in Rio de Janeiro that, while still distinctly and identifiably Brazilian in many ways, nonetheless shares a number of features in common with gay communities and queer subcultures in other parts of the world. It has quite clearly and consciously incorporated many of the symbolic representations (such as pink triangles and rainbow symbols) and organizational structures (such as similar types of commercial venues and community-based organizations) that have been central to the organization of gay communities in the Anglo-European world. But it has done so in ways that respond to the social, economic, and political conditions of a particular historical period—marked, as it has been, by issues related to the redemocratization of Brazilian society, structural adjustment, and the opening of the Brazilian economy to the outside world, and the ongoing (even if largely frustrated) attempts to build a more just social order. While the gay subcultures and communities that have emerged in Rio over the course of recent decades resemble those of the so-called developed world, they are also marked by profound and largely continued inequalities—in particular, those related to socioeconomic class and, by extension, race or ethnicity that changing times seem to have done little to alter.

Fortaleza

While cities such as Rio de Janeiro and São Paulo, by virtue of their size and complexity, have clearly been the most important centers of gay life in Brazil for many years, over the course of the past two decades increasingly visible gay cultures have also emerged in a range of smaller Brazilian cities such as Belo Horizonte, Porto Alegre, Curitiba, Recife, and Fortaleza. Precisely because of its smaller size and its location in the poorer northeastern region of the country, Fortaleza offers an excellent opportunity to examine the evolution of changes that have already been identified in Rio. Nearly two decades ago, Peter Fry's seminal work on the historical construction of homosexuality in Brazil drew an important contrast between the social organization of same-sex experience in the far less-developed North and Northeast of Brazil and the more urban and industrial Southeast, where Rio and São Paulo are located (see Fry 1982). Yet today, after at least ten to fifteen years of rapid change, the starkness of this contrast has been mitigated in many ways, offering some sense of how broader patterns of social transformation have increasingly linked what once might have appeared to be altogether distant and distinct realities.

While Ceará is still one of the poorest states in the country, over the past decade it has become one of the most important centers of economic development in the Northeast. Indeed, as the *Jornal do Brasil* recently suggested, "at an accelerated pace of economic development, with balanced public finances, poverty in decline, and without any news of involvement in [political] scandals, Ceará has become a kind of model for the country" (Barros 1997). Governed since 1987 by the center-left PSDB (*Partido Social Democrático Brasileiro*, or Brazilian Social Democratic Party), which in recent years has championed the restructuring of the Brazilian economy as well as the control of inflation through neoliberal strategies, Ceará has become a model for other Brazilian states in keeping a tight lid on public spending and ensuring that state expenditures never exceed revenues. From 1987 to 1995, Ceará's economic growth has been remarkable: at a time when the gross national product of Brazilian economy as a whole grew only 12.2 percent, with an annual growth rate of only 1.5 percent, the state of Ceará registered growth of 40.9 percent, with an average of 4.8 percent per year. This impressive growth rate has been linked to both rapid industrialization as well as urbanization over this same period. As industrial growth has exploded across the state, the total consumption of electric energy has gone up by 90 percent and the consumption of cement used for construction by 58.3 percent. From 1990 to 1996, 320 new businesses either started or relocated in Ceará, representing US$3.7 billion in new investments. Equally important, Ceará has emerged as one of the most important tourist centers in Brazil, and by 1996 was the fastest growing tourist destination anywhere in the country, with an increase of 15.3 percent in international visitors and 27.2 percent in passengers on international flights departing from the state, as well as an 11.2 percent increase in tourist revenue (Barros 1997).

Although poverty has remained a persistent problem in Ceará in spite of such rapid growth, it too has been on the decline; the poor accounted for 52 percent of the population in 1990, but for only 33 percent in 1996 according to a study commissioned by the World Bank (cited in Barros 1997). More generally, the adjustments in social and developmental indicators have been striking. From 1985 to 1995, for example, illiteracy in Ceará fell from 46.7 percent to 36 percent. The percentage of the population with an income lower than the minimum legal wage (approximately US$100 per month) fell from 33.5 to 27.2 percent. Availability of running water increased from 31.2 percent of all residences to 47.6 percent, and the availability of electricity grew from 53.1 percent of all residences to 73.3 percent (Barros 1997).

Over this period, Fortaleza, the capital of Ceará, has been the fastest growing major urban center in the country. Located on the northern coast, at the edge of the Sertão, a desperately poor interior region characterized by cycles of drought and economic despair, Fortaleza has been the site for some of the largest development projects in recent Brazilian history—such as the rapid construction of an extensive irrigation system aimed at guaranteeing the city's supply of water even during periods of extended drought. Throughout the 1980s and 1990s, it has been marked by the highest population growth rate of any of the major cities in the country, and its large population and relatively low wages have made it an attractive site for businesses and industries seeking to relocate from the more expensive centers (with their more unruly labor unions) in the South and Southeast, as well as for multinational firms and international investors, particularly from Japan and the United States. Equally important, given its proximity to especially beautiful beaches along the Atlantic Coast and its reputation for year-round sunshine and warm weather, Fortaleza has dominated the tourist industry in Ceará and has emerged as one of the primary centers outside of Rio de Janeiro for both national and international tourism. Indeed, in almost every sense, Fortaleza has come to be seen as a kind of geographic and economic oasis in the otherwise poor northeastern region.

Like Rio de Janeiro, Fortaleza has grown up along the coast and has been marked by intense construction of high-rise apartment buildings for the middle and upper classes, mixed together with dozens of new hotels and flat services, stretching from the Praia Formosa and the Praia de Iracema to the north, around the port area of Mucuripe, on down the Praia do Futuro to the southwest (see map 5.6). It has also grown inland, from the traditional downtown commercial area around the Nossa Senhora de Assunção fort and the Passeio Público park, in to more middle-class residential neighborhoods such as Aldeota and Papicu. Further inland still, at the outskirts of the city, one finds the cluster of poor *subúrbios* that serve as a kind of catch basin for migrants from the rural Sertão (just as the *subúrbios* in Rio serve as a catch basin for migrants from the North and Northeast).

In comparison to the much larger cities such as Rio de Janeiro, São Paulo, or Belo Horizonte, gay life in Fortaleza has always been far more circumscribed and restricted, marked by what is described as the more traditional and conservative character of Brazilian society in the Northeast:

> RODRIGO (a thirty-three-year-old from a working class background in Fortaleza): The main difference between the cities in the south [of Brazil] and Fortaleza, or other northeastern cities like Recife, is the traditional character of family life. Family is much more important in the Northeast . . . and much more oppressive for gays. Children are expected to live with their parents until they get married, no matter how old they are. There isn't even the possibility of anything else. Family is so strong that even the

Map 5.6. Fortaleza.

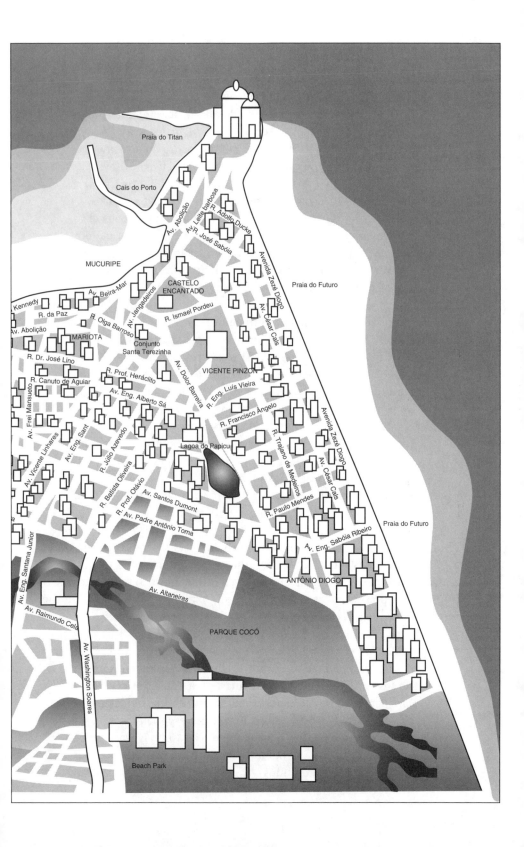

architecture of the buildings reproduces the family system. There are hardly any buildings with smaller, less expensive apartments that single people could afford, because hardly anyone would buy them. All of the apartments are made for married couples or families with children—a one-bedroom apartment is the smallest that you can find, and most have two or three bedrooms. People are expected to live at home until they marry, and only move to their own apartment once they have married.

CARLINHOS (a twenty-six-year-old informant from the lower class in Fortaleza): Even family houses follow a traditional pattern that makes any notion of privacy impossible. In the traditional architecture, all of the rooms have doors that open up so that they all connect, and everyone can see everything that happens. The space inside the house is completely controlled by the mother—the watchful eye of the mother.

INTERVIEWER: But if life is so controlled, what do homosexual sons do? How do they meet people? How do they organize their lives?

RODRIGO: Most people have to live a double life—they don't come out at home, they stay in the closet, but they live another life away from home, in the street. The family may really know, especially as they get older and fail to marry and have children. But nobody says anything. Everyone maintains a kind of fiction. And at some level, I think, everyone may even kind of accept it. A homosexual son even has an important social role, because he stays at home and takes care of his parents when they get old. He often provides their main source of financial support.

Thus, the limited local housing market that allows for the construction of a gay life style has meant that the homoerotic interactions of the street and, increasingly, homoerotically charged interactions in commercial settings—some presumably straight and others explicitly gay—have been the focus for gay life in Fortaleza:

WILLIAM (a twenty-four-year-old informant from the lower class in Fortaleza): People meet mostly in public places, cruising on the street, at tearooms and cinemas, or at dances or discos. . . . *Forrô* dances [a traditional, sexually charged form of dance typical throughout Northeastern Brazil] are especially popular— probably even more than gay bars or discos. Nobody wants to be seen going to a gay disco, but they can go to the *forro* without anybody thinking anything—there is constant cruising, even the guys with their girlfriends. It's kind of like a game, which is what lots of people prefer.

INTERVIEWER: But what happens when you hook up with someone? What do you do? Where do you go for sex?

WILLIAM: Sometimes it doesn't come to anything. But if you manage to hook up, you may arrange to meet later, or make a date for another day. There are a few cheap hotels where you can rent a room for sex—or you can go to the beach, especially out by the Praia do Futuro where it is darker, or at the Quebra-Mar [the largest breakwater sheltering the port area, which is a major area for homosexual cruising and homoerotic encounters].

As in Rio, the sexual geography of homoerotic interactions has been concentrated in the bustling commercial areas in downtown Fortaleza and cast as semi-secretive or clandestine precisely because it is intermixed within the legitimate flow of city life (see map 5.7):

RODRIGO: A lot of the cruising areas are concentrated in the Centro, around the Praça do Ferreira, and the Praça dos Leões—also around the Praça do Passeio Público, the Praça da Santa Casa, and the Praça José de Alencar. Each location is a little different, depending on the time of day. At rush hour, or during the days, things are more mixed, with lots of people coming and going. The Praça dos Leões has a lot of *putas* (whores) working during the days and early evenings, for example, and some *michês*, but at night it is mostly *travestis*. By the Fortaleza de Nossa Senhora da Assunção, there is a mixture of *viados* and *travestis* at night. At the Praça José de Alencar there are lots of *caboclos* [people from the interior of the *Sertão*]. But during the day, everything sort of mixes together.

INTERVIEWER: What about tearooms?

RODRIGO: They change a lot over time. The toilet at the Lojas Brasileiras [a downtown department store] has been famous for years. And at movie theaters, like the old Cinema Jangada, which has been closed down now, and the Cinema Rex, where there is always a lot of cruising.

INTERVIEWER: Are there places to have sex?

RODRIGO: There are a couple of hotels in the Centro, like the Casa de Cômodos Novo Brasil, between the Praça dos Leões and the Praça do Ferreira. And there is also the Motel Charme, out by the Shopping Iguatemi [the Iguatemi Shopping Center].

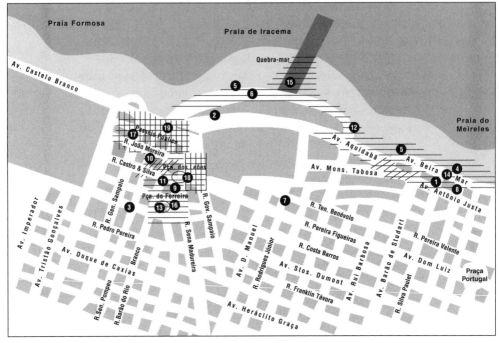

Map 5.7. Fortaleza (Centro)

Clubs and Discos
1. Medhuza
2. Rainbow
3. Style

Bars and Restaurants
4. Barraca do Joca
5. Pirata
6. Tributu's

Saunas
7. Apollo
8. Mormaço

Cinemas
9. Rex
10. Star

Hotels
11. Casa de Cômodos
Novo Brasil

Cruising Areas

12. Calçadão, Avenida Beira-Mar (*gays*)
13. Lojas Brasileiras, men's room (*gays*)
14. McGay (McDonald's) (*gays*)
15. Quebra-Mar (breakwater) (*gays*)
16. Praça do Ferreira (*gays* and *michês*)

17. Praça José de Alencar (*travestis*)
18. Praça dos Leões (*travestis*)
19. Praça do Passeio Público (*travestis*)

Just as in Rio, however, the gay subculture has also tended to expand along with the city, linked in particular to areas of general leisure and nightlife:

These days, most cruising and socializing takes place at the beaches, or along the *Calçadão* [the sidewalk running along the beach]. There is cruising all day on the *Calçadão*, from Iracema [known as a bohemian or alternative neighborhood] down to the Praia Meireles. The best known place is the Quebra-Mar [a long, stone breakwater protecting the port], where people cruise and have sex all day. It is kind of a prohibited zone, where young people go to smoke dope and the *bichas* go to cruise. There are lots of places to hide down in the rocks, where you can have sex but still see who is coming out along the rocks. Even though the police patrol it, it is still fairly safe, because you can see them coming from a long distance away. The whole *Calçadão* from there to *McGay* [local gay slang for the McDonald's restaurant on the Avenida Beira-Mar], where the gay boys hang out in the afternoon and evening, is really intense [for cruising]. At night there is a small stretch where *michês* work the street just a block in from the Avenida Beira-Mar. And on the beach in front of the Clube Náutico, the Barraca do Joca [Joca's Hut—a kind of cabana bar directly on the beach] has been a gay meeting point for years. (Vinícius, a thirty-nine-year-old informant from the lower-middle class in Fortaleza)

Stretching from Iracema to Meireles, this strip along the beach has also become the nightlife congregating place in Fortaleza (see map 5.7). Tourists from the beach-front hotels mix together with female sex workers and hawkers, and a mix of restaurants, bars, and nightclubs have opened up. It has become the locus for *Carnaval* in Fortaleza, which is held primarily along the Avenida Beira-Mar, as well as for other popular festivals and events organized by the municipal government:

Because of the importance of tourism for Fortaleza, you can imagine how much emphasis there is on *Carnaval*. The *Carnaval* here is very different from in Rio, without the big spectacle of the *Desfile das Escolas de Samba* (Parade of the Samba Schools). It is much more of a street *Carnaval*. Most of the music is by *trios elétricos* [loud electric music bands that play atop trucks or trailers in the streets]. And there is cruising everywhere, of course, especially along the beach where people can always find a secluded spot to have sex. The whole spirit of *Carnaval* is reproduced as well in other popular festivals, like the Fortal, when the tourist bureau sponsors a kind of mini-*Carnaval* during the winter, but with the same style of music and the same kind of spirit. (Vinícius)

The gay commercial scene, which is still a good deal more limited than in Rio de Janeiro, is largely situated in Iracema and Meireles. Many of the small bars and restaurants in Iracema have become popular with young people, and with young gay men in particular. The Pirata (Pirate) dance club has become a focus for *forró* dances with a mixed (but nonetheless heavily gay) crowd, and the most exclusively gay and lesbian nightclub, pointedly named the Boate Rainbow (Rainbow Club, with the term Rainbow used in English rather than its Portuguese equivalent), opened in late 1995 and decorated with images of masculine gay men that might easily be found in New York or San Francisco. A second, slightly less well-to-do commercial enclave has also emerged in Meireles, where the traditional Barraca do Joca (now marked by a rainbow flag) has been joined by the explicitly gay sauna, the Termas Fortaleza, as well as the mixed Sauna Mormaço in the Hotel Othon, and the Boate Medhuza, a nightclub featuring drag shows and male dancers (see map 5.7):

> The people who frequent Iracema tend to be more middle class. Iracema has always been popular with an alternative crowd—students, artists. . . . During the summer it is always full of tourists, some from abroad, but especially young people from other places in Brazil who come to spend their holidays in Fortaleza. Gay people feel comfortable here because of the general bohemian atmosphere. Like everywhere in Fortaleza, there is a lot of mixture of gays and straights (*hêteros*). People who are in the closet (*enrustidos*) can go there without being so afraid of being identified, and gays who are out (*gays assumidos*) are the major clientele at the [Boate] Rainbow. The level is a little lower down (*mais barra pesada*) by the Praia de Meireles—there is more of a mixture with tourists looking for prostitutes, adolescents looking for tourists. But it is still a lot better than in the Centro, where at night the only people there are much poorer and everything is more dangerous. (William)

Now well integrated within the tourist economy in Fortaleza, both of these commercial areas have become essential to the emerging sense of gay community. They provide a setting not only for seeking sexual partners but also for the interaction of overlapping friendship networks, in which not only sex but also more varied and general forms of sociability have become increasingly important. At the same time, while they provide a kind of circuit comparable to those found in like Rio or São Paulo, the relative protection that they offer to their clienteles is not always clear, and the threat of police repression is always present:

> At 23:00 we went to the Boate Medhuza (formerly known as Capitão Gancho [Captain Hook]), which is located on the Rua Oswaldo Cruz 46. The club was full, with many *travestis* and many effeminate men from the popular classes. It doesn't seem to have many clients from the elite, perhaps because of its location squeezed between two nightclubs for straight men with a crowded

entryway full of female prostitutes and other "marginal" types who might scare off a more up-scale crowd. Some of the men we have interviewed have described the Medhuza by saying that it tends to attract *"gente de baixa renda e perigosa"* (low-income, dangerous people). The low income level was evident, though nobody in the place looked particularly dangerous. The show only started very late, at about 1:30 in the morning, with a series of *transformistas* dubbing songs and a master of ceremonies named Ailex. Along the walls, and up on some platforms, there were three go-go boys who danced. They were dressed in "tiger skin" bathing suits, more or less imitating the styles of Heloína's *Leopardos* at the Teatro Alaska in Rio. At about 2:30 in the morning there was a police blitz, with three female and four male officers. They had some documents, and apparently the order to close the place if there were any minors present. It appeared that this wasn't a particularly unusual event, and the "regulars" just went on drinking their drinks calmly while the confusion sorted itself out. The most hostile to the police were the drag queens, who continued to dance without stopping, making increasingly more outrageous gestures. The police observed them and made comments among themselves (we couldn't hear what they said, but it was pretty clearly derogatory about everyone there). After checking Identification Cards, they finally were satisfied and left without any further problem. Most of the clients who were there stayed until dawn, when the buses would start running again for the return trip home. (Excerpt from fieldnotes)

These gay establishments offer only a limited degree of safety for individuals who may not want to be publicly identified as gay, or who prefer to mix together in spaces that are self-consciously both gay and straight at the same time. Still, in spite of potential public scrutiny and police repression, these commercial venues do offer at least some possibilities for constructing an increasingly open gay life style in Fortaleza:

At 12:30 we made a visit to the Barraca do Joca (Joca's Hut). There are about fifteen tables (located around the bar on the beach at the water's edge), and they were all more or less full with men sitting in the sun and drinking beer. It is a hard place to find without someone local to point it out to you or to differentiate it from the other bars along this stretch of beach, since they all look more or less alike. It has a thatched roof, with white plastic tables and chairs, and an outdoor shower for bathing after coming out of the salt water. The only difference in comparison to the other bars is a small plantation of banana trees just to the left of the hut itself. As one comes down the path from the *calçadão* and through the clearing in the banana trees, however, there is a discreet rainbow flag that has been hung from a rope strung between two bamboo posts—something of an "X marks the spot" for prospective customers (and perhaps a warning for the unassuming). During the day, when the crowd tends to be a bit more mixed, the basic behavioral pattern is somewhat more reserved—definitely and obviously gay, but not overly outrageous or transgressive. No kissing or other open expressions of affection or sexuality. At night, or at the end of the afternoon, interaction tends to be more intimate, with people kissing, holding hands, and caressing. The Barraca do Joca is known locally as a place for lovers, and there are many pairs in the evening simply "*namorando de beijos e abraços*" (more or less like "making out with hugs and kisses," an expression that implies an almost innocent adolescent dating). (Excerpt from fieldnotes)

Much the same open quality is also present in the Boate Rainbow, which of all the commercial venues in Fortaleza is by far the most self-consciously gay:

The largest and most successful gay club in Fortaleza is currently the Rainbow. The name really says it all. It is located up near the Praia de Iracema, with its slightly more bohemian/intellectual/upscale mixture and relatively tolerant atmosphere. It is a little difficult to find, and the first time that we went we wound up losing our way and wandering into a number of straight clubs and music halls and having to ask for directions (which were offered in good spirits, respectfully, and without the kinds of looks that sometimes are given when one asks how to find a gay address). Once you find the place, though, there can be no mistaking it. The whole aesthetic is "First World Gay." As you come through the door, the walls are covered with paintings of naked or semi-naked men in various sensual poses, effectively lighted with some kind of track lighting. There are two different areas, upstairs and downstairs, with a carefully lighted and designed stage area in the center for dancing. The bar itself is toward the front, with the restrooms toward the back. The color scheme is carefully designed, with soothing tones of gray and green that combine with the careful lighting. Everything about the place, including the crowd itself, contrasts with more popular or traditional homosexual clubs (like the Medhuza). It is largely a middle-class crowd, and lesbians mix together with homosexual men (which is still fairly uncommon in most popular bars or clubs). There is a lot of cruising, and some sex in the men's room, but little of the *travesti*-show atmosphere that dominates at Medhuza. The whole feeling is much like Le Boy or the other more middle-class gay clubs in Rio—and the place is apparently equally successful, with packed crowds on weekends and weeknights alike. It appears to be by far the most popular of the gay clubs in Fortaleza. (Excerpt from fieldnotes)

While the success of the Boate Rainbow may mark an important alteration in the style of gay life in Fortaleza, it is one of only a very few places that currently offers this particular style to its clientele. In general, little in the way of the more explicitly gay bars and discos found in the larger cities of the Southeast has yet developed:

In comparison to cities like São Paulo and Rio, there is very little choice of places to go in Fortaleza. There are only a few *boates* and *saunas* that are really gay, like the Rainbow, for example, and even these are always precarious. They are always opening and closing. The Rainbow opened only a year ago, and it seems to be doing well, but it is always hard to tell. And now it has competition, because a new gay club has just opened only a block or so away. There isn't the variety and the options of different places to go that you have in Rio. But there are many places that aren't specifically gay, but that have a kind of tolerant atmosphere, and where many gays and lesbians go because they feel good there, like the restaurants in Iracema, or the bars out at the Praia do Futuro. (Rodrigo)

As in Rio or São Paulo the scale of gay life in Fortaleza seems to be closely linked to questions of class and status. Although the commercial scene in Iracema and Meireles is significantly more well-to-do than the atmosphere in the downtown region, an even more upscale gay population has also developed apace with the Praia do Futuro (see map 5.8). Much like the successive advance of fashionable neighborhoods such as Copacabana, Ipanema, and Leblon in Rio de Janeiro, in recent years the Praia do Futuro has become an important leisure spot for the middle and upper-middle classes in Fortaleza, and has been marked by a growing presence of more well-to-do lesbians and gay men:

A lot of the hottest spots now are along the Praia do Futuro. There are bars at either end of the beach that have a growing gay

> crowd—mostly young people, especially if they have money. It is
> more chic than the older part of town. The Gato Pardo Bar at one
> end of the beach is especially popular with *lésbicas*. There is also
> Chico Carangueijo at the other end. The crowd is more mixed
> there, and it is popular with tourists, so it is a good place for peo-
> ple who want to pick up tourists. During the days, the beaches in
> front of these bars aren't completely gay, but a lot of the people
> are. At night, the crowd drinking and dancing is also mixed, but
> with lots of gays. And there is always heavy cruising (*pegação forte*)
> on the beach in front, where it is dark and people go down by the
> water to make out (*namorar*) and have sex (*trepar*). (Joaquim, a
> thirty-one-year-old informant from the working class in Fortaleza)

Again, as in the case of Iracema and Meireles, the Praia do Futuro is
characterized by a relatively mixed crowd, free from the potential stigma
of the more exclusively gay beaches and establishments found in larger
cities such as Rio. As a drawing card for a relatively young, well-to-do public with significant numbers of gays and lesbians, it has become important
within the broader ecology (as well as the class structure) of gay life in Fortaleza—similar, in some ways and on a smaller scale, to the role of the
Zona Sul as a key marker of the gay geography in relation to socioeconomic status and social mobility in Rio de Janeiro.

Many of these changes seem to have been reinforced in Fortaleza (as in
Rio) by organizing and community mobilization for gay rights as well as
HIV/AIDS-related issues. These activities have taken place on a much smaller
scale than in Rio and at a slightly later point in time, yet they have begun
to add to a sense of community among homosexual men in particular:

> There are really only a few important organizations. The major
> gay group is Asa Branca [literally, White Wing, which was the title
> of an especially moving popular song about solitude, loss, and
> hope, originally written by Luiz Gonzaga, a famous northeastern
> musician]. Like in many of the cities in the Northeast, it has been
> important to have an organization that works especially on ques-
> tions of violence against homosexuals. To be homosexual in the
> Northeast is more difficult than in the Southeast. In São Paulo it
> is much easier to be homosexual than here in Fortaleza. In places
> where there are more contradictions, where there is more vio-
> lence ... this is where there are more negative attitudes of soci-
> ety, and more thought and ideas, more action is necessary.
> (Denilson, a twenty-one-year-old informant from the lower class
> in Fortaleza)

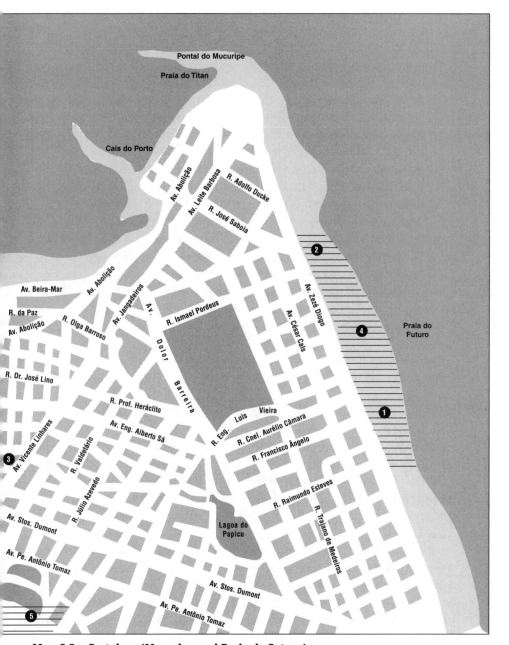

Map 5.8.   Fortaleza (Mucuripe and Praia do Futuro).

Clubs and Discos
1. Chico Carangueijo
2. Gato Pardo

Sauna
3. Iracema

Cruising Areas

4. Praia do Futuro (gays)
5. Shopping Iguatemi (gays)

Perhaps even more than gay activism, AIDS prevention work incorporating questions around men who have sex with men has been key:

> AIDS prevention work in Fortaleza is fairly recent. Groups like GAPA-Ceará [the Grupo de Apoio à Prevenção à AIDS-Ceará, or Ceará Support Group for AIDS Prevention) started up only in the early 1990s, and many of the more recent groups have started just in the past few years. But in many ways they have been more visible than gay groups. In part, it is simply because of resources. AIDS is seen as an important social question, and there is funding available for AIDS-related work that isn't available for gay organizing— you know, from international donors as well as from the government. Organizations like GAPA have been able to print materials and develop projects for prevention and research on gays that are often much more visible than the work of small gay organizations. (Artur, a forty-three-year-old informant from the middle class in Fortaleza)

Organizations like Asa Branca and GAPA have helped to contribute not only to a growing sense of gay identity but also to an awareness of the gay community as being an oppressed minority population in a society (in this case, the Brazilian Northeast) that is especially marked by stigma, discrimination, and violence against perceived sexual deviants. This work has tended to reinforce the alternatives offered by commercial establishments, overcoming some of the traditional limitations of life in the Northeast (ranging from economic scarcity to conservative family values and constrained living situations), and creating the possibility of a distinct gay life style in spite of the very real impediments to such a life that continue to exist.

Just as in Rio de Janeiro and other major Brazilian cities, the development of complex homoerotic subcultures and gay communities has taken place in Fortaleza at an accelerating pace in recent years. Framed by the specific ecology of Fortaleza's geography, these changes have responded to the exceptionally rapid development of the city (and the state of Ceará more generally), expanding progressively from its original base in the downtown area to newer poles along the booming waterfront, bringing together the more generalized homoerotic possibilities of public space with commercial meeting places largely oriented to a gay (and sometimes lesbian) public. While this gay subculture necessarily opens itself up to a certain fluidity, to a mixture of types and classes, it is also clearly marked by generalized notions of social class as well as race and ethnicity. The traditional downtown areas have remained consigned to the lower classes, the dark-skinned *caboclos* from the interior as well as largely poor *michês* and *travestis* involved in sex work. A wider mixture can be found along the beach from Iracema to Meireles, at the Quebra-Mar, along the Calçadão, or even at the Barraca do Joca or the Boate Medhuza, where poor young men may mix together with the more well-to-do, with tourists and tour guides, hawkers, female sex workers, and an assortment of other types, in what is perhaps now the center of interaction. The Praia do Futuro, on the contrary, has begun to offer an up-scale alternative—popular with a crowd that defines itself as young and hip, with well-to-do tourists and middle-class straights as well as gays and lesbians. Together, these various regions of activity provide a backdrop for the changing shape of gay life in Fortaleza, drawing attention to the extent to which the development of gay subcultures and communities is also linked to the broader processes of development taking place in society—in the case of Fortaleza, a veritable boomtown on the rise more generally.

Becoming Communities

The extent to which the subcultures that have emerged in cities such as Rio and Fortaleza can in fact be described as gay communities, in the full sense that the expression has taken on in settings such as the United States, is of course open to question. Indeed, precisely what the notion of gay community (or communities) may mean even in the fully Anglo-European world is itself exceptionally vague. Even careful researchers tend to use the notion of community in highly imprecise ways, and what in fact distinguishes a "community" as opposed to a "subculture" or even an "enclave" is for the most part unresolved (see Gelder and Thornton 1997).

To the extent that gay communities in settings such as San Francisco or Sydney rely heavily on a shared sense of gay identity as their key defining characteristic (see, for example, Murray 1996), then the gay worlds found in Rio or Fortaleza would only partially qualify for the use of such a term. As we have seen, although gay identity has become more prominent in recent years, and more individuals as well as organizations and commercial establishments have begun to self-consciously adopt some notion of gay identification, this is nonetheless hardly uniform or universal, and the adherence to a notion of gay identity as the glue that holds together a sense of community is surely very different in Brazil than in the best known gay communities of the Anglo-European world. Similarly, even though the gay worlds in cities such as Rio and Fortaleza do exhibit at least some of the spatial features found in more "developed" settings, they tend to lack the kind of geographic specificity of determined residential neighborhoods that have been so important in the definition of a sense of gay community in many parts of the Anglo-European world. Gay groups and

AIDS-service organizations, as well as some publications and community-based enterprises, have begun to form and potentially to play a critical role in local political life, but their institutional development is very limited when compared to the far more extensive organizing that has taken place in other parts of the world.

And yet, in spite of their limitations, these various developments have nonetheless combined in important ways to create, if not a full-fledged community in every possible sense of the word, at least a state of mind, a symbolic map, of what would certainly appear to be a community (or perhaps multiple communities) in formation—in Fortaleza no less than in Rio, São Paulo, or the other larger cities of the southeastern and southern regions of the country. It is perhaps most useful to think in terms of communities (like identities) in the process of becoming. In this sense, without predetermining the ways in which such formations will evolve, we can at least begin to think about emerging communities as central to the constitution of gay life in contemporary Brazil.

What is really crucial here, however, is to avoid the temptation of conceptualizing this process as if it were part of some kind of unilinear evolutionary progression. On the contrary, as I have tried to emphasize, although the gay communities found in Brazil resemble many of those found in the Anglo-European world, they nonetheless also respond to highly specific economies and ecologies in their own right. They clearly are part of a broader, interacting system—which is itself part of the world capitalist system that has become so dominant globally during the waning years of the twentieth century. But they simultaneously respond to the specificities of local contexts and circumstances, whether at the level of Brazilian society as a whole or at the level of regional and even municipal realities. The emerging gay communities found in cities such as Rio and Fortaleza would thus be unthinkable (at least in their present form) were it not for the gay communities and cultures that have previously formed in cities such as New York and San Francisco. But they are equally unthinkable outside of the highly specific context of dependent social and economic development, of authoritarian politics and the redemocratization of Brazilian society, or of the neoliberal restructuring of Brazilian life in recent years aimed quite explicitly at bringing it into accord with the structures and practices of the contemporary global system.

Although such weighty issues have rarely been conceptualized as being crucial to the development of anything as seemingly inconsequential as homosexuality (or even sexuality more generally), the fact of the matter is that it is within their context that both bodies and their pleasures take shape in contemporary Brazilian life. Perhaps most important, it is this interface between local contexts and processes, on the one hand, and global forces, on the other, that places the emergence of gay communities in settings such as contemporary Brazil in a social and political history rather than in a natural process of evolution. And it is the largely unpredictable quality of history, as opposed to the apparently natural unfolding of evolution, that makes it possible for us to wonder about the ways in which these communities will continue to develop in the future within such a rapidly changing world.

6

Changing Places

As should be clear from the preceding discussion, if increasingly complex gay subcultures and communities have taken shape in cities such as Rio de Janeiro and Fortaleza (as well as other large urban centers such as Belo Horizonte, Porto Alegre, Recife, Salvador, and, above all, São Paulo) in recent decades, they have not emerged in a vacuum—nor can gay life in any specific location be understood in isolation. On the contrary, each of these sites is clearly part of a broader, interactive system which links different communities in distinct locations through the ongoing flow of capital, people, and ideas. In this chapter, I want to look more closely at how this flow plays itself out, focusing on the question of movement and on the ways in which complex patterns of movement shape the changes taking place in the organization of gay life in Brazil. First, I will situate this question in terms of patterns of migration and population movement that have characterized Brazilian society in recent years and that have clearly played a key role in the transformation of what was once a predominantly rural, agrarian society into the overwhelmingly urban, industrialized (and increasingly postindustrial) society—a society with room for urban gay subcultures and enclaves. Then I look at the extent to which this pattern of dislocations has played into and supported a particular pattern of *sexual* movement—a migratory flow in which questions of sexual desire and notions of sexual freedom, particularly in relation to men who have sex with men, often play an important role. Finally, I examine the interfaces between gay cultures and communities in Brazil and those of the international, gay world—I focus on the roles of travel, tourism, and even immigration (of diverse types) in interconnecting local and global cultural contexts, and assess their importance in enabling the imagination of sexual worlds.

Dislocation

As we have seen, no change in the last century of Brazilian society has been as dominant, or as consistent, as the processes of industrialization and urbanization. As the Brazilian economy has become more industrial (and agriculture itself more mechanized), the percentage of the Brazilian population working in the urban-centered sector of the economy (including industry, but also related areas such as commerce, finance, communications, and government) has increased proportionally. In the late nineteenth and early twentieth centuries, some of this population growth stemmed from immigration from abroad, as immigrants from many countries—including Italy, Portugal, Spain, Germany, and Japan—arrived in significant numbers.[1] For most of the past fifty years, however, the major source of supply for the industrial work force has come from internal migration, although immigration from abroad (especially, other Latin American countries such as Argentina and Paraguay) has continued to play a minor role (see Bacha and Klein 1986; Martine et al. 1990; Minayo 1995).

Until quite recently, the dominant rural-urban migration pattern has been periodic, resulting from seasonal changes, agricultural cycles, and, particularly in the Northeast, extended periods of drought. As industrialization has been consolidated and the urban job market has offered steadier opportunities for employment and social mobility, however, this flow has become more constant. It has also taken on a decidedly generational character, as the younger members of rural families have made their way to the cities in order to earn a better living and to send financial support back home to relatives.

Such movement seems to take place in steps or stages. The first stage is almost always intraregional, or even internal to a given state, with migrants moving from the interior to the capital city of a state or the major urban center in one of the five major geographic regions of the country—for example, from the interior of Ceará to Fortaleza or Recife, or from the interior of São Paulo to the city of São Paulo.

Movement from one region to another often represents a second step. Despite booming construction and industrial growth in secondary centers such as Fortaleza, the image of wealth and prosperity in primary centers such as the megacities São Paulo and Rio de Janeiro continues to hold out hope of a better future. Migratory patterns have thus been established from the poorer northern and northeastern regions to the richer agricultural and industrial states of the South, Southeast, and central-west—in particular, to the major cities of the Southeast, such as São Paulo, Rio de Janeiro, and Belo Horizonte, as well as the newer "frontier cities," such as Brasília, of the central-western region (see map 6.1).

Map 6.1.   Interregional Migration Routes

Not surprisingly, this influx of population has tended to concentrate in the most economically and socially marginal areas of the large urban centers. The poor, outlying suburbs have grown far more rapidly than the center in almost all Brazilian cities: from 1980 through 1991, for example, the center of Fortaleza grew at a rate of 2.73 percent, but the periphery grew at a rate of 6.35 percent; the center of São Paulo grew at a rate of 1 percent, and the periphery 3.08 percent; the center of Rio grew at a rate of 0.43 percent, the periphery at a rate of 1.34 percent (see Minayo 1995). Within the centers of such cities, migrants have tended to settle principally in the heavily overcrowded and underdeveloped *favelas*, as well as in the rundown and partially abandoned tenements known as *cortiços* of many inner-city areas. Attracted in some instances by kinship ties, by lower housing costs in such areas, and by the informal job market that is often their only option, migrants are thus largely concentrated on the margins or periphery of urban life and urban services.

In spite of this, even in the face of often appalling conditions, the movement continues. What is perhaps most striking is the extent to which, even when face-to-face with remarkable hardships, the image or imagination of a better life, a better world, continues to draw people into the urban, industrial centers:

> Even during the worst periods of recession, the growth of industry and of the job market in the cities has offered an option to people from the interior. Especially in São Paulo, where the civil construction business is really large, or in smaller cities like Brasília or Maceió . . . The *nordestinos* (people from the Northeast) who come to Rio and São Paulo face all kinds of difficulties, but most of them manage to find some way of earning a living, as *camelôs* (street venders) or construction workers. And the ones who are lucky manage to get good jobs—or sometimes their children do—working in factories or stores. Brazil is a really unjust society, and the success stories shown on the television are a complete fantasy, but it is still possible to find better jobs and have a better life in the big city than in the interior of the North or Northeast. (Rafael)

These purely economic concerns (and possibilities) are integrated into other crucial factors that direct patterns of migration. The very idea of *movimento*, or movement, in and of itself, seems to hold a special significance, offering a hope not only of *prosperidade* (prosperity) but also of *modernidade* (modernity):

Brazilian society has always been based on movement. In the colonial times, it was the movement of discovery, of peopling the colony. Or the movement of the frontier in the interior—the Amazon highway and the gold rushes that take place even today with the *garimpeiros* (miners in frontier regions). Movement has always been considered important. Nobody wants to live where life is always stationary (*parada*)—like in small towns in the interior, where everything is backward (*atrasado*). People want to be where the action is (a*onde tem ação*)—where there is movement (a*onde tem movimento*). It's one of the main reasons why people keep coming into the cities. Life is hard . . . sometimes you can get a job, sometimes you can't. But life in the city is always more exciting than in the interior, even when you have to go through hard times. (Cleber, a twenty-eight-year-old from the lower class, who migrated from the interior of Minas Gerais to Rio de Janeiro at the age of seventeen)

The push and pull of very real economic hardship in the rural interior and of no less real opportunity in the markets of the industrialized cities are undeniable, even given the difficulties that are often associated with migration. But it is thus also impressive the extent to which notions of economic betterment, social mobility, and modern comforts have been constructed symbolically as synonymous with urban life—and with the dislocations that are often necessary in order to achieve it:

Everybody wants to live a modern life (*uma vida moderna*). And today it doesn't matter where you come from—even if you are from a small town in the interior, you have seen television, watched the *novelas* (nighttime soap operas) of Rede Globo [the dominant Brazilian television network], and you know what modernity is. You have an image of success, of development, of life in the Zona Sul of Rio or São Paulo. It may be mostly a fantasy, a creation of television, a fiction, but even very simple people still have very complicated ideas about what it would be like to live like that, and why they want to. And they know that to be able to have the kind of life that they imagine, they will have to move, to escape where they are and find something better—to run risks. Especially for young people—you have to gamble (*você tem que jogar*). (João)

Life in the city takes shape in the imagination as being synonymous with modernity, with economic and social development, in opposition to the backwardness of rural life in the interior. Even urban life is in many ways imagined on a continuum of modernity, with the possibilities offered by smaller cities such as Fortaleza or Salvador being seen as an important step above the stagnation of small towns or rural villages but nonetheless a cut below the truly metropolitan/cosmopolitan images conjured up by Rio and São Paulo.

What is perhaps most important about such images, however, is that economic options are not the only factors involved in constructing an attractive image of urban Brazilian life. It is widely recognized, based on the empirical experience of hundreds of thousands of migrants over many decades, that images of success and social mobility are often an illusion. Even for individuals living in situations of relative hardship, the diversity and velocity of urban life are understood, in and of themselves, to be positives:

> It isn't just work that makes life in the city attractive—on the contrary, lots of people who migrate into the city are unemployed or underemployed (*desempregadas ou sub-empregadas*). But even for people in really bad situations, living in *favelas*, or in the *subúrbios*, life in Rio or São Paulo, or even in smaller cities, is still a million times better than in rural areas or small towns. There are so many more options of things to do. Even if you don't have any money. There is more going on, more things are happening, there are more interesting people. You never know what will happen. The city can be dangerous, but it is also exciting. There are all sorts of possibilities. And the chances of finding a better job always exist. (Carlos)

Some perceive the dangers of urban life, together with its relatively high degree of anonymity and social atomization, as profoundly negative. For others, it becomes part of a positive notion of openness and unpredictability—an image of the opportunities inherent in urban life that goes far beyond strictly economic concerns:

> JÚNIOR (a twenty-one-year-old informant from the lower class in Fortaleza, who originally migrated to the city from the interior of Ceará at the age of nineteen): Living here is much better than where I grew up.
> INTERVIEWER: Why? What is it that makes it better?
> JÚNIOR: It's because there is always something to do. The little town where I was born, and where most of my family still lives, is so small that nothing ever happens. It is completely dead. It's

different here. There are always things to do. Even when you don't have any money, you can go to the beach. Or you can spend the day at the popular festivals that the municipal government organizes on the waterfront to attract tourism. There are movies and shopping centers, like the Iguatemi, where you can go to spend time looking at all the people and the stores. Where I grew up, there was only one cinema, and the films that were presented were always completely out of date. Not here. Everything here is modern, and I feel a kind of freedom here that I never felt [in the town] where I was born.

INTERVIEWER: Have you ever thought of moving from Fortaleza to some other city? To Rio or São Paulo?

JÚNIOR: Not really. I like it here. I don't even have much interest in traveling out of Fortaleza. Sometimes I think that it would be interesting to visit there, though, to see what its like. Just from watching [the] Globo [television network], I have an idea. . . . But I would like to see if it is really like that. I have a friend who went to work in São Paulo. He sends postcards and letters sometimes. I might visit him some day.

Within such images, then, space and time seem to meet in building up a vision of urban life. The space of the city, as opposed to rural areas or small towns in the interior, becomes synonymous with modernity and modernization. The search for novelty and progress is physically embodied in the dislocation from rural to urban, from smaller regional capitals to the more cosmopolitan megacities. And such understandings are built up out of a bricolage of diverse fragments: one's own experiences and memories, the letters of a friend, the images of film and television, and so on.

One must emphasize here (as so many informants have themselves) the importance of electronic media in constructing the imagination of urban reality—in particular, television's impact on Brazilian life today (see, for example, Staubhaar 1996). There are probably few societies, including those of the Anglo-European world, that are so thoroughly penetrated by television as is Brazil, which is one of the top ten countries in the world in terms of television sets (Clark 1996). With more than 200 television sets per 1,000 inhabitants, and with three Intelsat and 64 domestic satellite stations (Buckman 1996), the rapidly expanding television industry has helped produce a sense of unity and integration even into the most remote reaches of the country. Much of this is due to the strength of Rede Globo, which is the fourth largest commercial television network in the world (behind only the three major U.S. networks), and leads even the American networks in claiming the single largest viewing audience, of between 60 to 80 million viewers nightly (Buckman 1996; Staubhaar 1996).

Much of the expansion of the Brazilian media, and of the television industry in particular, took place during the 1970s and the early 1980s, when it served as a major mouthpiece for the Brazilian military, providing an effective mechanism for government propaganda as well as for an ideology of social mobility and consumer satisfaction (Staubhaar 1996). From the mid-1980s to mid-1990s, television has continued to be a major vehicle for constructing notions of *modernidade* and *prosperidade*, with both their possibilities as well as their associated ills, as well as a new sense of *liberdade* and *direitos* on the part of civil society within a newly "free" political regime. The life styles of the rich and famous, so often characterized in the nighttime *telenovelas*, mix together with political debate, with images of crime and violence as reported on the nightly news or the many television "magazines" modeled on North American "real life" police reporting. Sports programs about the campaigns of the most important football (soccer) teams from Rio and São Paulo intersect with entertainment reports and cultural agendas. Transmitted even to the most distant regions of the country, this cacophony of images becomes part and parcel of the imagination of modern urban life as a potential alternative to the oppressive realities of the interior, of small towns and villages, or even of smaller cities. And people continue to move.

Ultimately, then, the range of factors involved in the remarkable dislocation of population in Brazil over the course of the past fifty years extends far beyond the most obvious questions of economic interest and need. Indeed, as Arjun Appadurai has argued, it is necessary to move beyond overly simplistic push-and-pull models in migration theory in order to begin to understand the range of forces that may ultimately shape such movement (see Appadurai 1996). Although the search for an economically better life is almost always present as motivation in migration and movement, other issues may also be present: the search for excitement, for freedom, or even modernity can all be there as well. And even though such issues have often been examined more closely in relation to topics such as ethnicity, much of our recent work in Brazil suggests that they may be equally relevant to sexuality as well—that sexual movement, and the recreation of sexual realities as part of other dislocations, may also be an important factor currently shaping the reconfiguration of gay life in Brazil (as elsewhere) as the twentieth century comes to a close.

Sexual Migration

Within the broader patterns of dislocation, this ongoing movement of population from rural to urban areas, from smaller cities to larger ones, and so on, it is difficult to define the precise role that sexuality plays—the extent to which sexual migration, movement motivated by sexual interests or concerns, may exist as a discrete social phenomenon. As Murray has suggested in examining the migration of gay men to the "gay mecca" of San Francisco in the United States, even in such a specific setting, sexuality seems to be only one among a number of other (often much more important) concerns, and the diversity of experiences recounted by informants shows that migration can never be treated as a single, normative process (see Murray 1996). At the same time, it is also undeniable that sexuality, and perhaps homosexuality in particular, is a factor within the migratory equation to a far greater extent than has often been realized—whether among gay-identified men in San Francisco or among men who have sex with men (of many very diverse types) in settings such as contemporary Brazil (see Parker 1997a).

At some level, this should come as no great surprise. To the extent that urban life is constructed within the social imaginary as a site of relative freedom and opportunity, as an alternative to the oppressive quality of life in the interior or in small towns, it is perhaps to be expected that such images should translate into sexual freedom. Just as the media, and television in particular, paint a picture of cities as centers of economic opportunity, they also illuminate their sexual diversity and freedom. Sexuality has become an almost constant topic on news programs, documentaries, and talk shows, as well as in the story lines of the nightly *novelas* and similar fictional genres; images of prostitution, discussions of the changing sexual morals of adolescents, or interviews about the homosexual subculture have become relatively standard fare on national television. Particularly in the wake of AIDS, public discussion and debate focusing on homosexuality, and documenting the emergence of urban gay subcultures and communities in some detail, has become frequent, often reproducing the contradictory character of urban imagery and portraying the city as the key site for both sexual (and especially homosexual) freedom and danger (particularly in sensationalist stories about the spread of HIV infection).[2]

Although not independent of other factors, such as employment options or financial interests, this notion of the alternative homosexual freedom of urban life has become part of the calculus underlying movement and migration for some of the population of men who have sex with men in Brazil. In life story after life story of the men who we have interviewed, the repression associated with family reactions to sexual difference is also linked to the setting of small towns or smaller cities, and the recourse to movement becomes an escape (often achieved at great difficulty) from a range of intertwined oppressions. The case of Mário, a thirty-nine-year-old informant from the lower class who grew up in Teresópolis, a smaller city to the north of Rio de Janeiro, is in many ways typical:

> Like lot of people, I came to Rio to escape life in the place where I grew up. In smaller cities, like in Teresópolis, everything is so repressed. Everybody knows everybody. Everybody keeps an eye on everybody else's life. It's like you can never escape—the gossip, the intrusion in your life. Sexual life is completely oppressive. Everything is oppressive! When I moved to Rio, it was mostly to escape. I had fought with my family, and had more or less been thrown out of the house. We had been fighting for years really, because I had started working in theater and wanted a career as an artist, which everybody criticized. They wanted me to get a steady job—to go to work in a supermarket, packing shopping bags, or something like that—and to spend the rest of my life that way. It finally got so bad that we fought all the time and my mother told me never to come back. So I came to Rio to try to escape. At first I didn't think I would even survive—I slept on benches in parks for about a week, I guess. It was horrible at first. . . . Obviously, I was hoping to find work, and there were a lot more options here—because of the theater world and the television industry in Rio. But more than anything else, it was to escape the repression of where I grew up. (Mário)

In the vast majority of the interviews, the men themselves saw the larger urban centers with developed gay subcultures as being in direct opposition to the repression of the interior, as offering a liberty that spills over even outside of the boundaries of the gay world itself. For Júnior, for example, the decision to move from a very small town in the interior of Ceará to the urban Fortaleza was in large part motivated by the search for work and for better living conditions, but was also directly linked to the relative openness and tolerance that is found with relation to homosexuality:

> INTERVIEWER: When did you come to Fortaleza?
> JÚNIOR: It's almost two years now that I have been here. . . .
> INTERVIEWER: What is homosexuality like in the interior of the interior of Ceará?
> JÚNIOR: It's really repressed.
> INTERVIEWER: But it exists?
> JÚNIOR: It exists! For sure, there are some . . . you can count the number on your fingers, who do it openly, but there are a lot who are hidden (*encubados*).

INTERVIEWER: What is the relationship like between those who are hidden and those who are open?

JÚNIOR: The ones who are openly declared [as homosexuals] stay on one side and the hidden ones on the other. . . . There is a great distance between them. It's very difficult.

INTERVIEWER: So you feel afraid to speak about your homosexuality in the interior?

JÚNIOR: For sure. I was afraid. But now I feel more liberated. I learned a lot coming here to Fortaleza. When I arrived here from the interior to live with my sister I decided to talk to her—and she understood me and gave me a lot of support. And I talked to another friend who had come from the interior too, who had been almost a foster brother of mine.

INTERVIEWER: So your sister in Fortaleza knows about your homosexuality?

JÚNIOR: Yes, she knows, and she is superopen about it. She is married here, and has four children. Her husband is superopen, too—he doesn't discriminate. He has even seen pictures of my boyfriends (*namorados*) with declarations of love written on them.

Even when the economic prospects offered up by the image of the city fail to materialize in practice, the discovery of sexual freedom can at least partially compensate for the ensuing frustration. In Júnior's case, even when unable to find a steady job, the "openness" of his life in the city, together with the existence of gay networks and subcultures, made his life bearable.

Yet this notion of freedom and tolerance is relative. Interestingly, for at least some of our informants who were born and raised in Fortaleza, the same freedom experienced by Júnior in Fortaleza is sought out precisely by leaving Fortaleza for the Southeast. This is clear in the case of Roberto, a twenty-six-year-old informant from the lower class, who was originally born and raised in Fortaleza, but who had moved to Niterói, in greater Rio de Janeiro, seeking both financial as well as sexual escape:

INTERVIEWER: What made you decide to leave Fortaleza for Rio?

ROBERTO: Partly it was to find work. My father was pressuring me to find a job, to not be a vagabond. . . . And I had a cousin here in Niterói who had offered to help me if I came to Rio.

INTERVIEWER: How old were you?

ROBERTO: I was seventeen years old when I left Fortaleza.

INTERVIEWER: Had you already started to have sex with other men?

ROBERTO: That was one of the reasons why I left. My father had
discovered me screwing with one of the guys from the construction site near where we lived. Life had become a kind of
hell. Fortaleza isn't like Rio. Everything is very conservative,
repressive. I wanted to get away, to be somewhere else.

INTERVIEWER: Was it difficult to establish yourself in Rio?

ROBERTO: It is always difficult, you know, but my cousin helped
me a lot. Through him I was able to find a job working in the
kitchen of a restaurant, and I had a place to live. . . .

INTERVIEWER: Is he an *entendido* too?

ROBERTO: Yeah . . . that was one of the main reasons that I
decided to come.

For men who have grown up in the interior, in rural areas or small towns,
the new openness, anonymity and tolerance of larger state or regional
capitals such as Fortaleza can come as a tremendous relief. For men who
have grown up in such cities, however, the weight of family vigilance,
neighborhood social pressure, and so on can be too much, and escape to
larger cities such as Rio or São Paulo becomes an alternative. In both cases,
however, dislocation becomes a central part of seeking a better life, and
the notion of what in fact constitutes "better" takes account not only of
economic opportunity but also of social milieu and, fundamentally, sexual freedom.

Migratory movement between small towns or the interior and larger
cities with established gay subcultures can even become a way of dealing
with unresolved sexual ambivalence—just as happens in the movement
back and forth between different moral zones within the city (between
gay cruising areas or gay commercial areas in the center city and the
straight family environments of outlying neighborhoods). The case of
Vinícius, a thirty-nine-year-old informant from the lower-middle class
who was interviewed in Fortaleza, illustrates how much migration and
remigration can be used to separate distinct sexual lives. Vinícius was originally born in the Northeast but was raised in a small town located in
Goiás, one of the states in the Central-West region of the country, where
his family had migrated when he was a small child. Married with two children, he had been involved in occasional same-sex relations since he was
a young adult. Over time, it had become increasingly difficult to manage
clandestine homosexual relations without being discovered, and his wife
had even come to ask him about his apparent interest in men, including
the excessive intimacy in his relationship with at least one man from work
(who had become his occasional lover). Although he had firmly denied
any kind of homosexual involvement or interest, Vinícius and his wife

eventually divorced, and when the need arose to look after family interests in Fortaleza, he jumped at the chance, leaving his children behind
temporarily. In Fortaleza, freed from the constraints of his life in Goiás,
however, his social life became centered in the network of homoerotic
encounters and the emerging gay subculture:

> VINÍCIUS: Here in Fortaleza, everything about my life is different
> than in Goiás.
> INTERVIEWER: In what ways? You mean your sexual life?
> VINÍCIUS: In part. . . . In Goiás, I would have to be much more
> careful [about having sex with other men]. I would have to find
> excuses to travel into Goiânia or Brasília to have sex. Here, there
> is nobody keeping an eye on me, so I have much more freedom.
> I go to the sauna, to the Cine São Luís, there in the Praça do Fer-
> reira, in the center of Fortaleza, to the sauna or the discos. . . .
> My life is completely different here.
> INTERVIEWER: And when you return to Goiás?
> VINÍCIUS: No, there it is another world. It is like my life in Fort-
> aleza never existed.

Alternating between his small town home and Fortaleza, then, Vinícius
has effectively built up two distinct lives—one that is essentially heterosexual and the other homosexual. While in Goiás, occasional trips into
the cities of Goiânia or Brasília sometimes lead to same-sex interactions,
but for the most part his life revolves around his role as a father. In
Fortaleza, freed of other obligations, he is able to have regular sexual interactions with other men. Migration and remigration on a seasonal basis
has become a way of managing or administering the vicissitudes of desire
and the reality of social control in the same way that many behaviorally
bisexual men separate their sexual selves within the physical space of a
single city.

Yet if sexual migration becomes an important way of escaping from the
oppression of one's past (and sometimes of one's present), it is also a road
to the freedom of an imagined future. To escape sexual oppression in their
community of origin, to have more frequent or easier access to sexual contacts, to seek a community of sexual peers, and so on—all play important
roles in motivating men who have sex with men to move from one setting to another. Yet it is important to emphasize that it is not merely sexual oppression that pushes people to migrate, but also the image of a
better future—sexual as well as economic. As more visible homosexual
subcultures and communities have become part of urban Brazilian life, the
motivations for sexual migration and the experience of many migrants

have also become more complex. Sexual oppression, home-town stigma, and repression all continue to be major spurs to migration, but they have also come to function in concert with an increasingly complicated but largely positive image of the freedom and liberation that can be found in evolving gay communities:

> These days, it isn't just to escape that people come to Rio and São Paulo. It is to find themselves (*para se achar*)—to find what they are looking for. The idea of a gay life (*uma vida gay*) has become important. People have an idea of the gay ghetto (*gueto gay*) in these cities. For some people it seems very closed. But for other people it offers a sense of liberty—of companionship (*companheirismo*). (Rafael)

This vision of freedom now seems less focused on the possibilities for sexual interactions inherent in anonymity and social isolation and more reliant on a growing sense of shared community—an alternative social space in which it is possible to *achar a sua tribo* or, literally, find your tribe (see Parker 1997a). Such nuanced understandings of the overlapping, multidimensional networks that constitute evolving gay community structures in Brazil, and the growing image of community not simply as a physical reality but also as social and political idea have clearly become increasingly important.

The growth of gay subcultures and communities in virtually all major Brazilian cities has thus begun to make possible ever more complicated patterns of movement and adaptation. For many men, movement back and forth between different urban centers has become a way not simply of separating distinct realms of experience (whether gay and straight, home town and new reality, or what have you) but also of taking advantage of community structures in order to maximize life possibilities and experience—professional, social, and cultural as well as sexual. Within this context, the question of male sex work takes on an especially important role. For many young men who migrate but are unable to find work, or who may be subemployed in low-paying jobs, hustling becomes one way of adapting to life in the city and entering into a new set of homosocial networks:

> A lot of the guys who work as *michês* have come from the interior, or from other regions [of the country]. In Rio and São Paulo for example, people always say that many of the *michês* are *gaúchos* [literally, people from Rio Grande do Sul, the southernmost state in Brazil]—I don't know if it's true, but it is what everybody says.

Actually, there are probably as many *michês* in Rio who come from the Northeast. What is important is that turning tricks (*fazendo michê*) is a way of surviving, and it pays better than many jobs. It is also a way of getting to know people. It is an important part of migration that people don't normally talk about. (Milton, a thirty-six-year-old informant from the middle class in Rio de Janeiro)

Sex work among the *travestis* is also linked to migration patterns:

Even more than the *michês*, I think, the *travestis* seem to move around a lot from one city to another. There isn't really any kind of space for the *travestis* in small towns. There may be effeminate *bichas*, but not *travestis*. *Travestis* only exist in the city—and the bigger the city the better. It is kind of like the fantasy of elegance— the notion that in bigger cities like São Paulo, or better yet, in the exterior [i.e., abroad], the world of the *travesti* is much bigger and better. So the effeminate *bichas* from the interior go to the city and become *travestis*—they enter into the underworld (*submundo*) of the *travestis* and transform themselves into *travestis*. And the *travestis* from smaller cities try to get to big cities like Rio. It is a whole kind of circuit of movement with a kind of hierarchy of places that are considered better than others. (João)

Thus, the subcultures formed around transvestite prostitution become the key points of entry and adaptation for movement from one setting to another, forming a "circuit" that interweaves cities in a network, as well as links specific, localized networks that exist in each of these cities. Sex work, whether among *michês* or *travestis*, becomes part a sexual migration pattern in which the urban sexual marketplaces are among the primary attractions.

Even outside of the context of prostitution, however, sexual reasons may be central to the decision to move from one place to another, and the breadth of homosocial contacts can be essential to the organization and adaptation to life in a new location. The case of Artur, a forty-three-year-old informant from the middle class in Fortaleza, is perhaps exemplary of such back and forth, which took him originally from Fortaleza to São Paulo in the late 1970s, but then back again to Fortaleza in the late 1980s:

ARTUR: I lived for nearly ten years in São Paulo at the end of the '70s and beginning of the '80s.
INTERVIEWER: What made you decide to move from Fortaleza to São Paulo?

ARTUR: I wanted to escape the *machismo* of the Northeast. At the
time, São Paulo seemed like a kind of gay paradise (*paraíso gay*).
In São Paulo, I even participated in the original Somos.

INTERVIEWER: But why did you move back to Fortaleza, especially if gay life in São Paulo had so much to offer?

ARTUR: In fact, it really had to do with the kind of [sexual] partners who I like—I really prefer partners from the interior, men
who aren't gay. That isn't to say that there aren't lots of men like
that in the interior of São Paulo, or even in the city. . . . I met a
lot, and they were very good! But it is much easier to find the
kind of people who I like for sex here in Ceará. And by the time
I came back, Fortaleza already had begun to have many of the
things that I had originally gone to São Paulo to find.

If it was the search for sexual freedom that originally led Artur to leave the
more conservative Northeast for the modern and progressive Southeast, it
was thus also a question of sexual desire (in this case his erotic preference
for nongay-identified and nonurban sexual partners) that ultimately led
him to return to Fortaleza in the late 1980s, by which time both the effect
of AIDS and the new homosexual/gay subculture gave him networks in
which he could structure his professional and social life (though in large
part not his sexual life):

ARTUR: After I came back [to Fortaleza] from São Paulo, I worked
for a while in a number of different hotels, in tourism. . . .

INTERVIEWER: When did you start working with AIDS?

ARTUR: Around 1990, when the first AIDS NGO was founded
here. At first it was mostly part-time volunteering, but more and
more of my time has been involved since then.

INTERVIEWER: But the kind of partners you say you prefer are no
more easy to find in AIDS NGOs in Fortaleza than in São Paulo.

ARTUR: No, but there is always time for that on the weekends!

For other people, the motivations for movement may ultimately be
much more financial than sexual, but sexual networks nonetheless
become major sources of support, facilitating movement and accommodation in both directions. The case of André, a twenty-four-year-old informant from the lower class in São Paulo, is in many ways typical of the
experience of many young gay men who move from one urban center to
another. André had arrived in São Paulo from Belo Horizonte less than a
year before being interviewed. Although he knew almost no one in São
Paulo at the time of his arrival, the gay commercial circuit and gay social

networks were largely responsible for his adaptation in his new home, providing him with the key contacts that he would use in finding a place to live, a job, and a circle of friends:

> When I arrived [in São Paulo], I didn't have a job, and I didn't even have any idea of how to find one. I didn't know anybody in the city really, and I had never even visited São Paulo before I moved here. But I met people really quickly. I started going out to discos and clubs, and that's how I met almost everybody I know. I met Rogério [André's roommate] at Night Boy's [a popular gay disco]. And he was the person who introduced me to Carlos, the boss of the firm where I started to work. (André)

For André, then, even access to work in São Paulo was ultimately possible because of the existence of gay commercial venues. The gay circuit thus becomes a major point of entry for urban newcomers operating in much the same way that previously migrated relatives or friends do—as a support network for new migrants. The wider connections between networks facilitates movement from one center to another, or back and forth between different cities.

Some sense of these intercity connections is clear, for example, in the case of Júlio, a twenty-one-year-old from the lower class, who originally was an informant in Rio de Janeiro before moving to São Paulo. Júlio and his mother had migrated to Rio from the northeastern state of Pernambuco when he was only nine years old. After his mother's death when he was fifteen, he lived by himself in Rocinha, the largest *favela* in Rio de Janeiro. Some years later, he was an outreach worker in an AIDS prevention project for men who have sex with men that was developed by ABIA, the Grupo Pela Vidda-Rio de Janeiro and the Grupo Pela Vidda-São Paulo, which opened up contacts in the gay world that would ultimately make it possible for him to move from one city to the other:

> JÚLIO: Working on the project was really the way that I got to know more gay people and places.
>
> INTERVIEWER: What was your role in the project?
>
> JÚLIO: I was an intervention worker (*interventor*). I would go to the clubs, saunas, sometimes the gay beach, distributing educational materials and condoms. Before the project, I had never spent much time in these kinds of places, because they are so expensive. Through the project, I got to know a whole new group of people.
>
> INTERVIEWER: Why did you decide to move to São Paulo?

JÚLIO: When the project ended, I wanted to make a change. I
didn't have work, and I couldn't find anything in Rio. Because
of the project [which had been working in both Rio and São
Paulo], I had thought a lot about going to São Paulo. So I just left
everything and went.

Ultimately, in São Paulo, Júlio was finally able to find work as a ticket salesman in a pornographic movie theater that was known for sexual interaction between men in the audience. Much like the gay commercial circuit
(in the case of André), gay political work and AIDS activism thus provided
another set of networks beyond the boundaries of specific sites, connecting one city to another and providing ready-made avenues for movement
back and forth as well as for more permanent migration.

Obviously, the different examples briefly described here are in no way
representative of the motives or considerations that determine what leads
some individuals to migrate from one place to another, but they do suggest that, for many gay or bisexual men, questions related to sexuality are
integral both to the decision to move as well as to the experiences they
encounter after having moved. As urban gay subcultures and communities become more prevalent, they make it possible for many men to
imagine a new and different life, and they clearly propel some men to
relocate. The structures that sustain these communities in turn reinforce
those men who do move—offering them access to friendship networks,
employment opportunities, housing options, and the like. Dislocation
from one site to another might well have taken place (in keeping with the
general pattern of population movement in Brazil over the course of the
past fifty years) outside of or apart from the existence of such communities, but the fact that they do exist has surely changed the dynamic in
recent years.

Crossing Borders

Over the years, Brazil has maintained a relatively open relation to the outside world. Its cosmopolitan orientation enabled Brazilian society to
incorporate waves of Japanese, German, Spanish, and Italian immigrants
in the first part of the twentieth century, as well as significant cultural
influences derived from Europe, North America, and Southeast Asia and
the Caribbean in more recent years.[3]

Such movement has been bidirectional, involving not only the arrival
(at least temporarily) of outsiders in Brazil, but also the departure (again,
at least temporarily) of Brazilians to the exterior. Both through short-term
travel and tourism as well as more extended periods of migration and, in
some instances, immigration, the interface between Brazil and the outside

world has evolved as a process of interpenetration between intersecting social, cultural, and economic structures. These processes of interpenetration and openness concretely executed through the back-and-forth passage of people across international borders and the resultant integration of their cultures in Brazilian life, is as evident in relation to homosexuality and gay life as it is in relation to any other area.

At first glance, when one speaks of the globalization of sexual meanings and styles, it is almost commonplace to think of international tourism as perhaps the key mechanism through which external sex/gender systems impose themselves on local systems—a kind of cultural imperialism in which international gay culture (and gay tourists) are supposed to play a prominent role.[4] Although there is no doubt that patterns of gay tourism and travel have been present in Brazil, they are highly specific and differentiated. One should be careful not to overemphasize their significance, in particular when seen from Brazil rather than from abroad. Foreign gay tourism and travel impact in divergent ways on different urban centers, and their overall influence intersects with other patterns of movement that must also be examined with some care:

> The importance of gay tourism is completely different in Rio, for example, than in São Paulo. In São Paulo, people may travel for business, but very few people come from abroad for tourism—even if there is a large gay population, there isn't any beach or anything much to attract international tourists. In Rio, on the contrary, the whole tourist industry revolves around *Carnaval*, around the beach in Copacabana, and all that, and it has always been a major attraction for gay tourists from Europe or the United States. More recently, some people have also started to discover the cities of the Northeast, like Salvador, Recife, or Fortaleza. But Rio is still the major capital of tourism. Gay tourists who go to the Northeast are almost more likely to be Brazilians rather than from abroad—or if they are foreigners, they are most likely to spend time in Rio first before going on to these other places. (João)

The influx of gay tourists (like all tourists) is surely greatest during the *Carnaval* period, but it has now begun to be extended throughout the year, with high seasons from January to March, during the northern winter, and in July and August, when many Anglo-European tourists take their summer holidays:

INTERVIEWER: What is the high season for tourism?
RAFAEL: During the [Brazilian] summer, in January and February,

when everything revolves around *Carnaval*. *Carnaval* has always given a central place to homosexuality, transvestism, and transgression, so it is almost natural that it would be a major attraction for gays from abroad. Gay people travel to Brazil all year long, of course, but *Carnaval* is surely the high point.

INTERVIEWER: Where do most of the gay tourists come from?

RAFAEL: There are a lot from the United States, of course, especially from places with large gay populations, like New York, San Francisco, or Miami. But I think that even more probably come from Europe. Some from England and Holland, and especially from Germany, France, and Italy. But many come from other parts of South America, like Argentina, Chile, and Paraguay.

INTERVIEWER: Do they stay mostly in Rio, or do they travel to other parts of Brazil?

RAFAEL: No, Rio is the center, for sure. . . . But lots of people also buy package deals. They may arrive in Rio, but then go to Salvador or some other city for a week or so before returning to Rio for the days of *Carnaval*. People from different countries seem to prefer different places. Salvador and Recife are very popular with the French and Italians, for example.

The interactions between these foreign tourists and local Brazilians are neither as simple nor as straightforward as one might expect, being complicated by language barriers, cultural differences, and, of course, in many instances, immense differences in terms of social class, economic resources, and so on:

MÁRIO: There was a time when I used to go to the beach a lot, especially the *Bolsa* in Copacabana, and I met a lot of foreigners—tourists who were here in Brazil for vacation, and for the boys on the beach!

INTERVIEWER: What is the relationship like between gay tourists and local people?

MÁRIO: It depends a lot on who the tourists are—and who the Brazilians are! The tourists, especially if they are here for just a very short time or don't know much about Brazil, they usually prefer to go to the beach in Copacabana rather than Ipanema, mostly because the Brazilians on the beach in Ipanema are usually more middle class, more self-sufficient. . . . They are less likely to be impressed by the money of a foreigner, and foreigners who go to Ipanema are more likely to have a deeper involvement with people here. In Copacabana, where the poorer *bichas* go, the tourists *fazem festa* (to have a party, have a field day). For the price of a few beers they can buy company for the afternoon—or a tourist guide for the whole week. Sometimes they just pick people up for sex, taking them back to their hotel for a couple of hours of fucking. But sometimes they really will wind up spending a lot more time, letting the Brazilian guy show them around, or sometimes even traveling together. When I was a kid hanging out on the beach, a couple of times I met foreigners who wound up paying for me to go to Salvador or other parts of the Northeast with them.

INTERVIEWER: But do they pay for services rendered?

MÁRIO: No, it isn't really prostitution, at least not like with *michês*. Well, sometimes it is, of course—especially in Rio there are a lot of *michês* who specialize in foreign clients. But in general it is more complex. The *gringos* (foreigners) realize that they have more money, so even if they don't hire you as if you were a prostitute, they will probably pay for food, or for your ticket to go to a show together, or your air fare and hotel if you travel together. And of course you have sex, but it isn't a direct exchange, raw and naked (*nua e crua*), like you think of in prostitution. It is more like an understanding, on the part of both sides, that one has more money and can afford to pay while the other can offer other things—local knowledge as well as sexual pleasure. It's funny. It sounds kind of strong. But it isn't just exploitation. Both sides get something. When I was younger, it was through this kind of contact that I learned a lot about human beings and about the world. Often, these relationships become very strong. I still have many friends who I met this way, who I later visited in Europe, in England and in Belgium and Italy.

Although the structure of inequality may seem to be in many ways implicit in such interactions, it is also impressive the way in which both cultural differences and socioeconomic hierarchies can be broken down through the medium of sexuality. As different as European or North American gay styles may seem to be when compared to the traditional, highly gender-based structures of Brazilian homosexuality, Anglo-European gay tourists or travelers are typically reinterpreted within the Brazilian system of homosexual meanings. A gay American tourist on the beach in Copacabana, for example, becomes a *bicha americana* (an American *bicha*) in the references made by local Brazilians. A gay couple from Belgium will be described as *bichas belgas* (Belgian *bichas*). Or, more generically, simply a *bicha gringa*—a foreign *bicha*. The same language games with which Brazilians typically play upon notions of masculine and feminine gender are inevitably applied to foreign gay men, who, no matter how masculine in style, will inevitably be referred to laughingly as *ela* (she) or *aquela* (that one [woman]). And the presumed superiority of socioeconomic status will typically be relativized in an active/passive calculus of gender hierarchy— *aquela mona holandesa deve dar igual à uma cachorra no cio* (that Dutch girl probably gives [lets herself get fucked] like a bitch in heat), or similar references that clearly level out what would otherwise be an apparent hierarchy. In short, through a range of different strategies, cultural differences and relations of economic dominance can in some cases be at least partially overcome or inverted, as a "shared" sexuality becomes an idiom of exchange.

Indeed, sexual interaction between tourists or foreigners and natives or locals becomes a concrete, embodied metaphor for crossing otherwise intricate cultural boundaries:

> You may not even speak a common language, but sex itself becomes almost a form of communication. It's strange, but sex becomes a way of bridging differences, or crossing frontiers (*atravessando fronteiras*). I think that for many people there is a kind of fascination in relations with people from other places, other cultures. Through sex, cultural differences, and language differences, are partially wiped out—they get translated in the language of the body. (João)

Thus, sexual interactions with tourists or travelers become a medium through which many local gay men can overcome cultural difference and otherness, which would perhaps be impossible—or at least fundamentally more difficult—with any other strategy. To what extent such short-term interactions between relative strangers in fact make possible a greater degree of mutual understanding is of course questionable. Yet in at least some instances what is presumably a relatively short-term cultural contact may also grow into a more long-term interaction. The vast majority of the tourists who travel to Brazil probably do so only once in a lifetime, but in at least some cases, a much more complex relationship seems to develop with Brazil and Brazilians that brings people back on and off over a period of many years:

> Some people who I met decades ago have been coming back year after year, or every couple of years. I know an Italian guy, Giovanni, a hair stylist who has a salon in London, who has come to

Rio every two or three years. He loves black boys with big cocks—
the bigger the better! He comes to Rio, and usually he goes up to
Salvador because of all the black men there.[5] Once he came with
his lover (*namorado*), an English guy. But usually he prefers to
come by himself and go wild for a few weeks before going back to
his proper London life. Or a couple of Belgians, two boyfriends
who have been together for twenty years or more. They come
every year. The last few years they have been coming twice a year,
in July and at New Year's. I think that they still love each other
after all these years, but probably don't have sex. Each of them
goes out with other people during the month that they stay here—
sometimes they will both find boyfriends and will go out either
together or separately. During one period they seemed to share the
same boyfriend, José, a Brazilian guy who even went back to Belgium with them for awhile. It's funny though, he told me that
they would never have sex together, the three of them, but always
separately with one or the other. They come every year, and by
now they have a fairly large group of friends—not to mention old
boyfriends. (Mário)

If the contacts between gay travelers from abroad and Brazilian men are
usually fleeting in at least some instances, longer-lasting relationships
form that may ultimately lead Brazilian men to travel abroad, to visit,
spend time with, and, on some occasions, even live with men they have
met while traveling in Brazil. A relatively complex cultural flow is initiated, with sexuality as its most concrete medium of interaction and
expression. While it is problematical to evaluate the impact of outside
tourism and travel in influencing changing patterns of gay life in Brazil,
it is nonetheless important to look at the ways in which such movement
potentially plays into more complex processes of change at both global
and local levels.

Just as the interaction with short-term tourists or travelers constitutes
an important point of intersection between international gay styles and
local Brazilian homosexualities, the presence over more extended periods
of foreigners who have migrated, or in some cases immigrated, to Brazil
to live and work also constitutes an increasingly important influence on
the changing shape of the gay world (see map 6.2). Long-term visitors are,
of course, considerably fewer in number than are short-term tourists, precisely because of the more complex nature of their interaction with Brazilian society and culture, the potential impact of their presence may well be
even greater. Although we typically focus (from a fundamentally northern
perspective) on the importance of population movement from developing

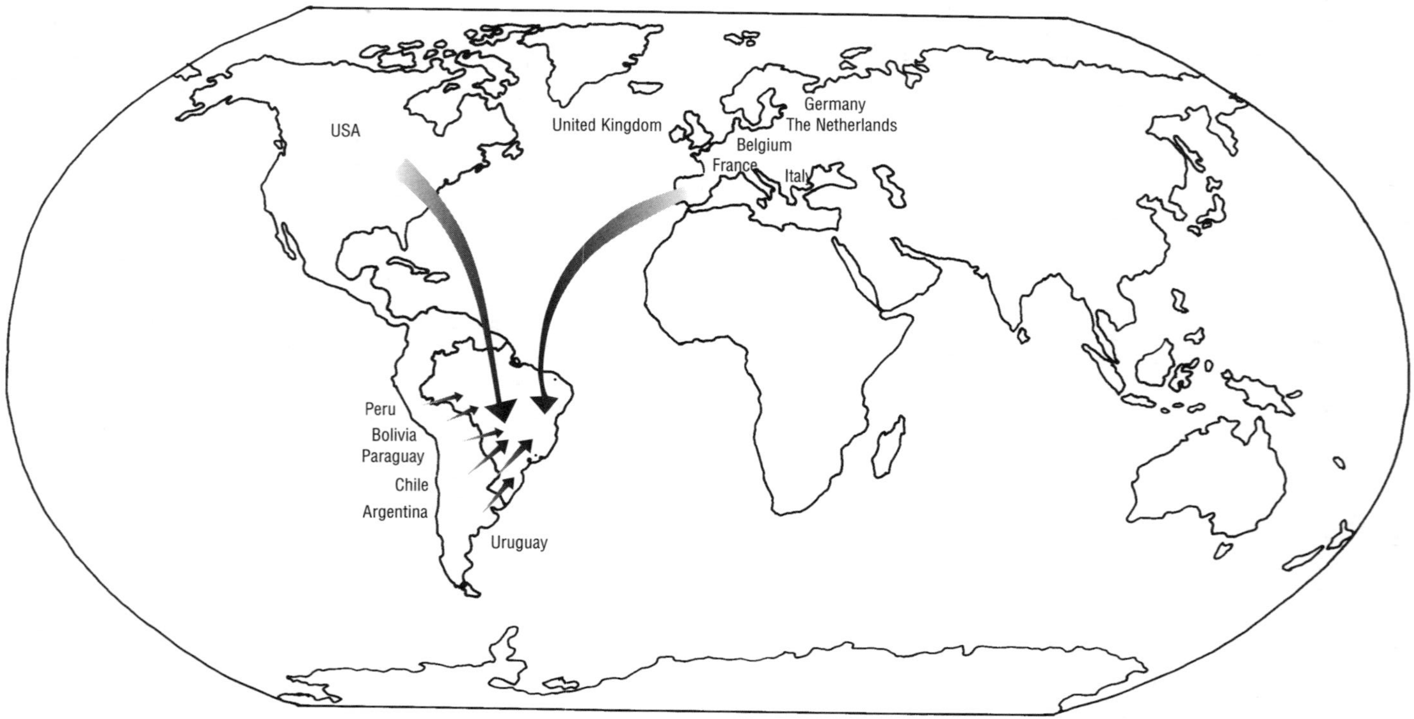

Map 6.2. Major Routes of Gay Tourism and (Im)migration to Brazil

USA

United Kingdom

Germany
The Netherlands
Belgium
France
Italy

Peru
Bolivia
Paraguay
Chile
Argentina

Uruguay

countries to the industrialized West, we should not underestimate the eventual movement from North to South as well as the largely overlooked movement that often takes place from South to South.

These two currents are evident in the movement of gay men to Brazil over the course of recent decades. In the 1970s and early '80s, for example, during the worst years of authoritarian rule throughout most of Latin America, Brazil became an important refuge for homosexual men fleeing the even more repressive regimes found in countries such as Argentina, Chile, and Peru:[6]

> Even during the dictatorship [in Brazil], the political repression here never had the moral overtones that it had in many other Latin American countries. There was some repression, certainly, but there was never as explicit an attack against homosexuals as there was in other countries, like there was in Argentina for example. So many homosexual men from other Latin American countries sought exile in Brazil—especially from Argentina and Chile, but also from other countries like Paraguay or Peru. There are also large populations of gay men from Uruguay and Bolívia. Not so many from Colombia or Venezuela, I think, but some, and also from almost every other South American country. (Walter, a thirty-six-year-old informant from the middle class in Rio de Janeiro)

Following the gradual redemocratization of most Latin American societies, similar patterns have continued—particularly in the 1990s, when they have been facilitated by governmental policies of greater social and economic integration (especially through the *Mercosul* or Southern Cone trading alliance) and "horizontal" collaboration between many Latin American nations.

The presence of gay men from western Europe and North America has also been influential in the gay world in Brazil:

> For decades now, Brazil has always had a certain attraction for gay men from places like Europe and the United States. I think that in the past they often came because of academic connections, to do research or teach. There is a long list of famous French intellectuals who have come as visiting professors mostly because they are intrigued by the gay life in Brazil, for example people like [Michel] Foucault and [Felix] Guattari, [Michael] Pollak. . . . But there are also many people who wind up staying for long periods of time and playing an important role in Brazilian culture—like Peter Fry, who was part of the original *Lampião* [the first gay publication in Brazil],

or yourself [the author], with your work on AIDS. And in just the past few years there has been almost a boom in gay American graduate students who have been here in Rio, or in São Paulo or Porto Alegre, to do research. More and more, though, it isn't so much gay intellectuals who have had an impact, but also people who come for commercial reasons. Many gay [commercial] places in recent years have been owned by foreigners who have immigrated to Brazil. There was an American who owned a bar called Rick's during the 1980s, or Gilles, from France [actually from a French colonial family in Algeria], who owns Le Boy. Foreigners have always had an important influence here, and it has become much stronger in recent years as the interaction between gays in Brazil and gays in other countries has become more intense. (Rafael)

Whether for political, intellectual, or commercial reasons, the influx of gay foreigners to Brazil has been a feature of gay life over the course of the past fifteen to twenty years. Although the numbers of men who have in fact migrated or immigrated to Brazil are significantly fewer than the numbers of tourists who arrive for *Carnaval* each year, their more long-term interaction with Brazilian culture (as well as with their countries of origin) has a significant impact on the gay world in Brazil. They have become key conduits for the flow of international capital and changing cultural meanings between the international gay world and the gay subcultures and communities in Brazil.

If gay tourism, travel, and migration or immigration from abroad plays an extremely important role in translating international gay cultural meanings and styles for Brazilian consumption (and reinterpreting them in terms of local meanings), serving as one of the major ways in which many homosexual men in Brazil come into immediate contact with the outside (gay) world for the first time, however, its importance also should not be overestimated. Indeed, at least in recent years, the travel of gay or bisexual men from Brazil to the exterior, and particularly to the major gay capitals of Western Europe and the United States, may well be far more frequent and extensive than gay travel from abroad to Brazil:

Travel abroad used to be much more restricted than it is today. . . . It simply cost too much. Only people who were very well-to-do, at least middle or upper-middle class, had enough money to travel to the exterior. Homosexual men may have had a little bit more money to spend on travel, because of not having so many family obligations, but still, even for homosexuals, domestic tourism in

Brazil was probably more common—people from São Paulo and Rio, especially, would be more likely to spend their holidays in the Northeast rather than in Europe or the United States. In recent years, though, this has changed a lot. Especially since the *Plano Real* [the economic stabilization plan initiated in 1994], everything in Brazil has become incredibly expensive. It costs more today to go to Natal or Recife [in the Northeast] than to Miami or New York. And even people who are relatively poor are often able to save up enough for at least a package tour. To travel abroad for New Year's or *Carnaval* has become viable and fashionable, especially for homosexuals. And for many of these men who travel abroad, they come in contact with North American or European gay life in a completely new way—not just their fantasy of what it must be like, but the reality of life in the major gay centers. At least partially, this changes the way they think about being homosexual even in Brazil. (Jorge)

On the basis of the reports from men who we have interviewed, the impact of travel abroad and of time spent in the gay centers of the Anglo-European world has been even more influential to Brazilian perceptions and the reorganization of gay life in Brazil than the travel of gay Europeans or North Americans to Brazil. Travel abroad is characterized as an eye-opening experience in which many of the meanings and values associated with gay life in Anglo-Saxon and Western European societies may contribute to a reframing of Brazilian experience:

For many people, the chance to travel to New York or San Francisco changes the way they think about what it is to be gay. Here in Brazil, you have an idea of what gay life is outside of Brazil—but it is very fragmentary. It isn't the same thing as when you see it with your own eyes. The complexity of the gay community is so much greater. To see a place like New York, where there are gay neighborhoods, restaurants, everything. Or to see the Gay Parade in San Francisco. The mixture of culture and politics. It is impossible to imagine anything that extensive in Brazil, but it still serves as a kind of model that is very attractive for many people. Many of the recent developments in Brazil, with gay publications, a much wider range of gay businesses—the model for all of this comes from spending time in places like New York and San Francisco, and adapting some of the gay world there to our Brazilian reality. (Antônio)

The impact of travel and tourism on the part of Brazilians traveling to North America and Western Europe must also be understood as part of a broader pattern involving migration, immigration, and sometimes remigration (moving in both directions), which has also become increasingly frequent in recent years. Like patterns of migration within Brazil, migration and immigration to and from Brazil are complex and diverse, and the potential role of sexuality is difficult to determine—and in all likelihood highly varied. Three major patterns have come to the fore in the last decade: (1) the highly specific, international movement of transvestite prostitutes back and forth between Brazil and southern Europe; (2) the equally complex movement of male hustlers between Brazil and parts of Western Europe, between Brazil and the United States, and between Brazil and other neighboring South American countries such as Argentina and Uruguay; and (3) the long-term residence and/or immigration of gay Brazilians abroad in Western Europe, the United States, and Japan.

While each of these three patterns of migration and/or immigration is complex, all would seem to have increased significantly in importance over the course of the past decade. Among the most longstanding patterns of sexual movement from Brazil to the exterior and back again are closely associated with transvestite prostitution and the complex migration of *travestis* from Brazil to many of the major European capitals (see map 6.3). Just as the larger Brazilian cities attract *travestis* from a range of smaller regional capitals, the possibilities of life abroad also help establish a migratory pattern connecting Brazil to the major urban centers in southern Europe:

> In the case of the *travestis*, the primary destination in the exterior is rarely the United States. On the contrary, Europe is the major destination. Life in Paris is probably the dream of most *travestis*. The major routes of travel are from Rio and São Paulo to Paris, and to the major cities in Italy—Rome, Milan. . . . In recent years, Zurich, in Switzerland, has also become important. They say that most of the *travestis* in Italy and France come from Brazil, or from other South American countries like Argentina. But it has been becoming more difficult for Brazilian *travestis* to get into many of these countries. The police have been cracking down, because they say that the *travestis* are involved in crime or injecting drug use. And there is a big problem with AIDS in some places, and the police often blame this on the *travestis*. So it has gotten much harder for the *travestis* to gain entry. Because of this, there is also a large flow of *travestis* to Portugal, where they get in more easily because they are Brazilian citizens. From there, they cross over

Map 6.3. Migration of Transvestite Prostitutes

more easily into Spain, France, and Italy. Traveling by train or bus and crossing the border over land is much easier than getting in at the international airports. (Antônio)

This flow of transvestite prostitutes from Brazil to Europe is also seasonal, with an important pattern of annual remigration, as well as an eventual return after the possibilities of the foreign market have largely been exhausted:

> At least some of the *travestis* who go to Europe also come back to Brazil on a regular basis. You can see this just by going to the beach in Copacabana. During the summer, from a little before Christmas through the end of *Carnaval*, the *Bolsa* becomes full of *travestis* who have come back from Italy or other parts of Europe. I guess that it is part coming home for Christmas, part vacation during *Carnaval*. But they also say that business is better here during this period. There are so many Italian and French tourists, that they can earn better turning tricks (*fazendo programas*) with foreigners in Brazil than they would in Milan or Paris. And I think that most of them finally wind up coming back for good when they get older. The older they get, the more difficult it is to earn a living, and to put up with the hard life that they have to live—it isn't easy working on the streets in Rome or Paris in the middle of winter. Sooner or later, if they live that long, most of the *travestis* wind up coming back to Brazil. (João)

This movement between Brazil and southern Europe has become a principal population flow—as well as a source of concern for police and immigration control authorities in countries such as France and Italy. It plugs the Brazilian gay world into a wider international universe, and has been an important part of the increasing globalization of Brazilian homosexualities in recent years.[7]

A slightly different pattern of international movement is found among the *michês*. At least three major routes seem to have emerged over the course of the past decade: (1) between Brazil and Western Europe; (2) between Brazil and the United States; (3) increasingly, as other Latin American gay communities have emerged, between Brazil and neighboring countries such as Argentina and Uruguay (see map 6.4).

In the case of the first of these patterns, migration takes young male hustlers from Rio and São Paulo to a number of key European centers such as Amsterdam and London:

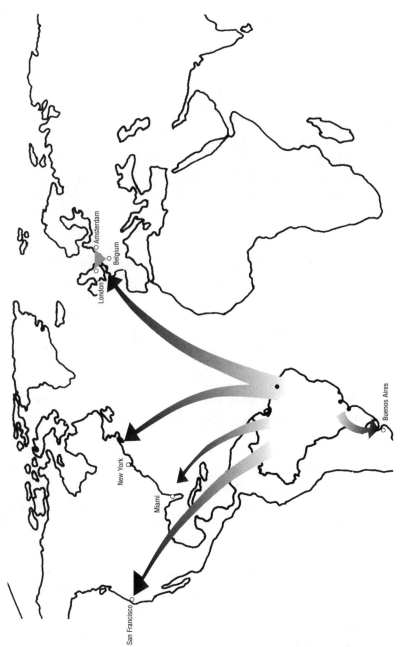

Map 6.4. Migration of Male Hustlers

I know of guys who have hustled in almost all of the major cities in Europe. But it is a lot more common for Brazilians to have success in the northern countries. In the South—in Portugal, Spain or Italy—there isn't much that distinguishes Brazilian *michês* from the locals. Physically and culturally, a *michê* from Portugal or Italy is pretty much like one from Brazil. In the North, on the contrary, a Brazilian stands out. There is more of a myth about Brazilians being really hot—being good in bed. And the lighter-skined Europeans like the dark-skinned Brazilians. So Brazilian *michês* who go to Europe are much more likely to be a success in Berlin or Amsterdam than in Rome or Madrid. There is even an organized network of male prostitution—a kind of triangle that links Amsterdam, London, and Brussels. A friend who works with AIDS in Holland told us about it. . . . They do outreach work with boys in houses of male prostitution in Amsterdam, and they wanted to get some of our educational materials in Portuguese for men who have sex with men, because a lot of the guys who hustle are Brazilian. But he told me that one of the big problems is that they have trouble maintaining contact with the boys. There is a kind of triangle connecting Amsterdam and London and Brussels. The same people run houses or out-call services in all three cities, and they constantly move the boys from one city to another—they keep them on the move to avoid troubles with the police, but also to avoid their making local contacts and building social networks. It is a way of controlling them more easily. And according to Rob [the Dutch AIDS prevention worker], it makes it a lot harder to do outreach. (Rafael)

The movement of *michês* from Brazil to Western Europe, and in particular between a number of specific locations in Western Europe such as Amsterdam, London, and Brussels, seems to be part of a relatively well-organized system, but the migration of *michês* to the United States appears to be far more individual and asystematic:

The *michês* who go to Europe are a lot more likely to go specifically to hustle. They are usually already working as *michês*, and they go because they think that they will do better [financially] in Europe. Sometimes European men even pay their way as part of a business deal—or even a personal relationship. In the United States, I think that it is more informal. It may even be more common for young gay men to go to the United States without the intention of hustling but to wind up turning tricks because it pays better than cleaning houses. But I don't think that street prostitution is very common. Most Brazilians who work as prostitutes in New York or even Miami use the telephone—they put announcements in the gay newspapers and work independently out of their apartments. Look at the adds for "Massage" or "Models" in the local gay papers, and you will always find a few for Brazilian men. (Marcos)

In this case, sexual migration may be less clearly motivated by sex work, per se. Young men migrate to the exterior in search of a better life, whether in terms of work or of living more openly in the gay communities of major North American cities. But the reality of the economy that they encounter in such settings may make sex work more attractive than other options, with a good deal of autonomy and a potential for income far beyond the other forms of employment that are typically open to undocumented aliens in the United States.

A third, newly emerging pattern has also begun to open up between Brazil and a number of neighboring countries in South America. Particularly in the case of Southern Cone countries such as Argentina and Uruguay, where growing gay communities can also be found and where economic and political affairs are increasingly integrated with those of Brazil through the *Mercosul*, increasing gay tourism to Brazil has also tended to stimulate Brazilian movement to cities such as Asunción and Buenos Aires. The case of Otávio, a twenty-six-year-old informant who works as a *michê* in Rio de Janeiro, is in many ways symptomatic of this new pattern:

I had tried for a couple of years to get into the United States. . . . You know, I would meet *gringos* from New York or California in my work at the *massagem* (massage parlor), and would wind up having an affair (*caso*) with them. When time would come for them to go home, they would invite me to go to spend time with them. Some would even offer to pay for my ticket. But every time I tried to get a visa to go to the United States, I was turned down. Every time I felt like I was going to die of shame (*morrer de vergonha*)— because they are cracking down on Brazilians trying to stay illegally in the United States, they have made it very difficult to get a visa. Even for a tourist visa, if they don't like your looks, they ask you to show bank statements, or to prove that you own a home— you know, so that they will be convinced that you have something to come back to, that you won't stay in the United States. But because of my kind of work, I don't have any of those things. I don't earn a paycheck that I can show them, and I certainly don't own a house! So when I tried to get a visa, they turned me down.

God knows that I had no interest in staying in the United States—
I just wanted to visit my friend. But they kept turning me down,
and it made me feel really bad—it feels like racism, like when you
can't get seated at a restaurant or get into a club because of the
color of your skin. I hated it. But when I started to have an affair
with a guy who was here from Argentina, and who offered for me
to go stay with him there, I realized that I wouldn't have the same
problem, because travel between the two countries has become so
easy—you just need your Brazilian ID card in order to cross the
border.... You don't even need a visa anymore. But when I got
there, everything was different then I had imagined. The *argentino*
wanted to dominate my life completely—I guess that he thought
that he had paid my way, so he had a right to dominate my every
move as if he owned me, or something like that. So I split. I
decided to take off on my own. I didn't stay there that long—just
a few months. But I had to eat, to pay for a place to stay. So I
started to turn tricks (*fazer michê*), working the streets in the hustling areas in Buenos Aires. (Otávio)

Although these other Latin American countries are probably less attractive
than the countries of Europe or North America (they share many of the
same economic problems that Brazil currently confronts, with few of its
perceived virtues), the relative facility of movement has thus made them
another important option in recent years for young men seeking to escape
for cities such as Rio or São Paulo.

Like many, if not most, Brazilians living abroad, chances are good that
a high percentage of these men will return to Brazil—perhaps less on a seasonal basis than in the case of the *travestis*, but ultimately, after a more or
less extended period abroad, the desire to return home seems strong. They
see that the gay communities in Brazil have themselves become more visible and organized in recent years, and perhaps view returning as more
attractive and as less of a sacrifice than before. And the flow of men back
to Brazil again contributes to a kind of synergy in which the interface
between the local and the foreign becomes increasingly complicated, the
distinctions between one and the other difficult to identify.

Although this synergy is already evident in the subcultures of transvestite prostitution and male hustling, it is even more apparent in the
broader phenomenon of migration (and sometimes immigration) of gay
men from Brazil to the exterior as well as from the exterior to Brazil.
Throughout the prolonged economic recession of the 1980s, significant
numbers of Brazilians migrated to Western Europe, the United States, and
Japan in search of jobs and better living conditions. Indeed one of the

popular jokes circulating in Brazil during this period suggested that a *saída* or "way out" of the Brazilian economic crisis had finally been found—at the international airport (see also Margolis 1994).

There are few accurate statistics available about the exact number of migrants over the course of the 1980s and the early '90s, but the effect can be seen in often semi-clandestine networks of Brazilians formed in most major cities in the developed world (see, for example, Margolis 1994; see also Page 1995; Portes and Bach 1985). In 1989, for example, the *Folha de São Paulo* reported that as many as 2,000 Japanese-Brazilians were leaving Brazil each month bound for Japan. Formal immigration from Brazil to the United States grew from 2,272 in 1985 to 8,133 in 1991, and tourist visas for Brazilians to visit the United States climbed from 128,000 in 1984 to 390,000 in 1991; estimates are that as many as 600,000 Brazilians may currently be living, whether legally or illegally, in the United States. According to official government estimates, between 1986 and 1990, approximately 1.4 million Brazilians are believed to have left the country to migrate or immigrate abroad, independent of their exact destination (see Margolis 1994).

Gay and bisexual men may well have formed an unusually large percentage of this migratory group, being in general unencumbered by children or extensive family responsibilities. How many of these men may have moved for specifically sexual, as opposed to purely economic reasons, is impossible to know, but our interviews in Brazil suggest that there was a mixture of the two. In some cases, movement might be facilitated by connections already established in Brazil as the result of interactions with travelers or tourists from abroad:

> I spent seven years in all living in New York. I had met Carlos here in Rio. . . . He is Portuguese by birth, but had been living in New York for many years. He came to Brazil fairly regularly because of his work. We had met at a club originally, and had spent more and more time together during two or three different periods when Carlos was in Rio. At the time, I was working in a variety of different part-time jobs, but nothing steady, so when he suggested that I come back to New York for a while, I decided to risk it (*decidi jogar*). I didn't really have anything to lose—and I liked him a lot. Our relationship was really crazy, really intense. New York was like a whole different world. My relationship with Carlos only lasted a couple of years, but by the time it ended I had decided to stay longer anyway. I worked for most of the time in restaurants, as a waiter, mostly in the gay community in the Village. . . . I'm not sure really why I finally came back to Rio—I guess I got homesick.

But I still miss the life style in New York. Maybe I'll move back there someday. (Paulo César, a forty-one-year-old informant from the lower-middle class in Rio de Janeiro)

The case of Campos, a thirty-six-year-old informant from the lower class, is not atypical. Originally from the interior of Minas Gerais, he had already moved twice, first from his home town in the interior to the state capital of Belo Horizonte, and then from Belo Horizonte to Rio, where he had worked in a variety of jobs such as hotel elevator operator or supermarket stock clerk. He had met a gay couple on the beach in Copacabana, and during a number of weeks he had both had sex with the couple himself and had also arranged for contacts between them and a number of other sexual partners:

> INTERVIEWER: How did you wind up going to Italy?
> CAMPOS: Before the Italians left for Italy, they invited me to come. They owned a hotel, in a city a few hours from Rome, and they offered me a job working at the hotel.
> INTERVIEWER: A job at the hotel? Were you expected to have sex with them?
> CAMPOS: No, by this time we weren't even having sex any more. I was setting them up with other guys, so it wasn't to have sex [with them]. It was really the job that interested me. And they offered to pay for my ticket
> INTERVIEWER: Did you like the work?
> CAMPOS: No! I hated it. And I hated Italy. I only stayed for about six months in all. But it was really interesting to see the exterior [i.e., the world beyond Brazil]—the things that are different from here. I learned a lot. And even in a short time I was able to save a little bit of money to bring back to Brazil with me.

For many prospective migrants, the *aposta* (bet or chance) of a better life in one or another of the gay meccas in the developing world has been sufficient motivation to move. For example, Cacá, a twenty-eight-year-old informant from the lower-middle class in Rio, worked intermittently in Rio as a dancer, in both modern dance companies as well as more popular shows aimed at tourist audiences; after a long and difficult period during which he cared for his mother, who had a long-term illness, as well as for his closest friend until his death from AIDS, Cacá decided to try his luck abroad, moving to Amsterdam to look for work and to build a new life:

INTERVIEWER: Do you know anyone in Amsterdam? Do you have any contacts to help you get settled?

CACÁ: I have a few contacts, people I met here in Rio, from dance troupes that performed here. But nobody who I know really well. But my friend José has been dancing in Europe for a couple of years, and has told me a lot about it. That is really the main reason why I want to go to Amsterdam—because of what he told me. The city sounds incredible. I don't know if it will work out, but it is worth a try. I want to live someplace where things are more open—to have a different kind of life than what I have here.

Just as the motives and mechanisms for movement can be varied, so too are the destinations (see map 6.5). Although the United States (particularly the key cities of New York, San Francisco, and Miami) has perhaps been the most common destination for gay men from Brazil going abroad, migration has also taken gay Brazilians to a range of European cities (London, Paris, Amsterdam, Berlin, Rome, and Milan, to name just a few) as well as to Japan (primarily Tokyo):

WALTER: The major gay centers in the United States and Europe are the most important.

INTERVIEWER: Which ones? New York and San Francisco?

WALTER: And Miami too, especially in the past few years. And in Europe, probably Amsterdam, London, Paris for sure . . . Berlin and a number of smaller German cities.

INTERVIEWER: What about Italy? Rome?

WALTER: Not so much, but maybe Rome and Milan for models, or people working with fashion. Japan is important also.

INTERVIEWER: Japan? Where—in Tokyo?

WALTER: Yeah, people always forget that the largest Japanese population anywhere in the world outside of Japan lives in Brazil. Many Japanese Brazilians have returned to Japan to look for work.

INTERVIEWER: I see, for work—but not because of gay life in Japan?

WALTER: No, nobody goes to Japan specifically because of this, but there winds up being a connection. Many Japanese people from Brazil who are gay go back to Japan for work. Daisuke, that Japanese AIDS worker who lived in Brazil for a couple of years in the early 1990s, was here recently and was telling me that a large

Map 6.5. Gay Migration and Immigration from Brazil

percentage of the Japanese AIDS cases are among homosexual
men who have migrated from Brazil.

Even HIV and AIDS have become part of the matrix of influence, as treatment options available in the United States and in Western Europe
become a concern:

> Access to AIDS treatment has also been important for some people.
> It isn't so much the quality of care, since there are fantastic clini-
> cians in Brazil, but the technological part—the new medications
> that are being tested and that you can only get your hands on if
> you are in the United States, or the tests that they have for moni-
> toring viral load or your CD4 count. In Brazil, this still costs a for-
> tune—or it hasn't even been available, or if it is available you can
> only get it by traveling to São Paulo and standing in line at the one
> hospital that has it. Sure, we have been able to overcome some of
> these problems. There are excellent networks to get medications
> from the United States to Brazil, and even the people at the airlines
> and in the customs have helped, facilitating importation or look-
> ing the other way. And we have used contacts to break the rules—
> getting people into protocols that they never should be allowed to
> enter. But it is difficult from here, and there are lots of people who
> prefer to go to live abroad in order to have access. You always give
> up something in terms of your support network here, but other
> things compensate. And there are enough Brazilians in places like
> New York that some services exist. GMHC has had a group work-
> ing on Brazil, and some of the social workers at major AIDS hospi-
> tals are specifically designated to attend the Brazilians. But I think
> that it is really almost exclusively the gay men who go, not the
> women or the straight men, since the gay community is the major
> source of support in those kinds of settings, and it is hard for any-
> one who isn't gay to tap into this. (Antônio)

Even in relatively unexpected settings, such as Japan, and for less than
obvious reasons, such as access to HIV/AIDS treatment, gay and bisexual
men have thus been part of a more extensive pattern of movement of
Brazilians seeking to build better lives for themselves in the closing
decades of the twentieth century.[8] And this movement of gay Brazilians—
whether in search of love or in search of work—has in turn created a network interweaving gay life in Brazil and the outside world. Indeed, some
sense of the quite remarkable complexity of these interconnections can be
seen in the urban networks that are formed simply by plotting the move-

ments that we have documented among our own informants in what is obviously a relatively small sample of the much larger universe of men who have sex with men in Brazil (see map 6.6). These movements open up worlds that only a relatively short time ago were hardly imaginable. And contact with these worlds, in turn, has made it possible to imagine the construction of a gay world in Brazil that, even if distinct from the gay world(s) found abroad, nonetheless resembles them more than would otherwise have been the case.

Ethnoscapes/Homoscapes

Although he certainly did not have either gay life or queer cultures in mind, in his influential work on political economy of cultural processes, Arjun Appadurai has argued for the need to focus attention on the global cultural economy as a complex, disjunctive order that can no longer be understood in terms of simple center-periphery models (see Appadurai 1996). Recognizing the importance of multiple, overlapping centers and peripheries characterized by fundamental disjunctures between economy, culture, and politics, Appadurai has pointed to the relationship between at least five dimensions of the global cultural flow, which he describes as ethnoscapes, mediascapes, technoscapes, finanscapes, and ideoscapes (Appadurai 1996:33). Without going into all of the details of Appadurai's formulation, it is worth stressing that he has adopted the suffix "scape" in order to call attention to the fact that each of these dimensions must be understood as "deeply perspectival": constituted by the historical situatedness or positionality of different sorts of actors, ranging from nation-states to neighborhoods, communities, and even families (Appadurai 1996:33). He defines ethnoscape as "the landscape of persons who constitute the shifting world in which we live: tourists, immigrants, refugees, exiles, guest workers and other moving groups and individuals constitute an essential feature of the world and appear to affect the politics of (and between) nations to an unprecedented degree" (Appadurai 1996:33). By "mediascape," he means the "distribution of electronic capabilities to produce and disseminate information (newspapers, magazines, television stations, and film-production studios), which are now available to a growing number of private and public interests throughout the world, and to the images of the world created by these media" (Appadurai 1996:35). In Appadurai's formulation, such landscapes become the building blocks for what, extending Benedict Anderson (1983), are not merely "imagined communities" but "imagined worlds": worlds constituted by the historically situated imaginations of people, and groups of people, around the globe (imaginations that now depend not so much on print as on electronic media).

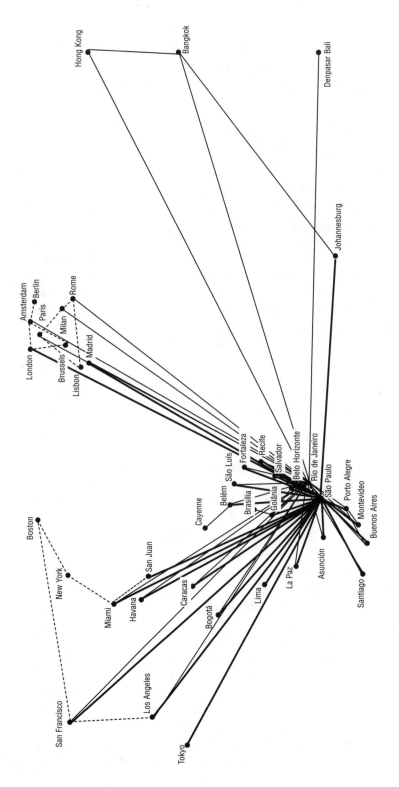

Map 6.6. Urban Networks

Within this framework, Appadurai has thus called attention to the global flow not only of capital but also of people, of images and ideas, that formulate intersocietal relations and processes of social change both locally and globally in the contemporary world. Although his concern is the consequences of this flow primarily in relation to ethnicity and modern ethnic diasporas, his argument is in many ways applicable to homosexuality and the changes in the gay world as well. As we have already seen, the evolving structures of dependent capitalist development have been strong influences on the emerging gay communities found in cities around Brazil, conditioning possibilities not only for investment on the part of both foreign and indigenous entrepreneurs but also for employment in industry, construction work, services, and so on, that motivate the movement of migrants and immigrants within an urban system that has increasingly escaped the limits of national borders—and in which gay social spaces have become increasingly important and increasingly interconnected. But an equally strong influence comes from the electronic capabilities to produce and disseminate information, together with image-centered accounts of reality from which possible scripts can be formed for imagined lives—gay as well as any other. Ultimately, even complex configurations of ideas, terms, and images (including notions such as "freedom," "rights," and "democracy") have become central—in Brazil certainly, but also globally—to the imagination of a world in which sexuality is part of a broader reconfiguration of life in the late twentieth century.

The implications of these changes for the lives of specific individuals, situated in any number of different ways within this complex system, are of course diverse and often contradictory. The options that they open up to a sex worker who happens to come from a middle-class background and a relatively high degree of education in the Zona Sul of Rio de Janeiro are in no way the same as those for a lower-class factory worker in Fortaleza or a semiliterate subsistence farmer in the interior of Ceará, and the ways in which the "imagined worlds" of late twentieth century gay life may play themselves out for individuals from such diverse backgrounds are often very different. Yet at the same time, while recognizing that social and cultural differences—and, perhaps above all, economic inequality and injustice—structure the range of possibilities open to any particular individual, one cannot deny that the profound transformations that have taken place in the global cultural economy throughout the 1980s and '90s have simultaneously ushered in a no less profound set of changes in the ways in which same-sex relations, and the lives organized around such relations, can be imagined and constituted. While it is probably futile to even try to predict the ways in which these worlds may develop and continue to change in the future, if we are to accompany or even begin to comprehend such changes as they occur, we must surely recognize that a radical break has clearly already taken place with the past—that, as Appadurai has suggested, "modernity is decisively at large, irregularly self-conscious, and unevenly experienced" (1996:3), and that the implications of this are today felt not just in London or New York, but in the farthest reaches of the globe.

7

Epilogue

Globalization, Sexuality, and Identity

The arguments that I have tried to develop in this book are inevitably incomplete—limited not only by the horizons of my own interpretive position (situated as it is) but also by the conventions of ethnographic description (the frozen frames of the ethnographic present) as well as by the continual transformation of the moving target that has been the object of analysis (which itself poses the problem not only of ethnographic, but also of historical representation).

Still, I have highlighted the multiple frames of reference, the diverse systems of thought and action, that have shaped the experience of sexuality in general, and homosexuality in particular, over the course of recent decades in Brazil. In particular, I have tried to capture a number of the key contexts in which homosexual experience has taken shape—elements of the increasingly complex and diverse gay subcultures and communities that have begun to emerge in Brazil—and to link these to broader processes of historical change in which they are necessarily situated. Through this lens one can begin to see the kaleidoscope of meanings, images, representations, desires, and practices that make up the gay world in Brazil today, and to suggest some of the implications they have for individuals seeking to make their way in it and to change its boundaries.

Ultimately, the changing shape of homosexuality and gay life in contemporary Brazil must be understood as a complex interplay between individual biographies, local social structures, and broader global processes. As distant and distinct as the experience of homosexuality may seem to be from the organization of economic production or the structures of political power, it is impossible to fully understand the developments of recent decades without some reference to the nature of dependent development as it has shaped processes of industrialization and urbanization, or the evolving history of authoritarian politics, redemocratization, and the consolidation of civil society that have occurred since the late 1970s. These developments, in turn, have themselves been formulated by processes and events taking place on a global level and impacting upon Brazilian life in what may well seem to be even more distant ways—the international debt crisis, the consequences of structural adjustment, and so on. While at first such issues might seem to have little to do with the lived experience of homosexual life, it is the contention of this book that they are not nearly as removed from it as they may at first appear to be. On the contrary, these forces have influenced the emergence of sexual styles, identities, and communities in Brazil in quite tangible ways, and it is ultimately impossible to fully understand these changing realities without reference to this broader context. As much in Brazil as in any other part of the world, capitalism and gay life have been intimately linked yet have evolved distinctly from a more Anglo-European model.

It is in large part as the result of this interaction between local social and cultural systems and generalized economic and political forces over the closing decades of the twentieth century that increasingly complex and diverse homoerotic subcultures and gay communities have been established in large urban centers such as Rio de Janeiro and Fortaleza, as well as in Belo Horizonte, Porto Alegre, Recife, Salvador, São Paulo, and a range of other major Brazilian cities. These cultures and communities, in turn, have increasingly come to provide the focus for social interaction between men who have sex with men (and, to a lesser extent, women who have sex with women) of diverse types and styles. This is not to say that nothing in the way of a gay world existed in Brazil prior to this time. On the contrary, as work by writers such as Trevisan (1986) and Green (1996) has shown, in major Brazilian cities as much as in the New York described by George Chauncey (1994), complex subcultures organized around homoerotic desire have long been present. But these subcultures have clearly been transformed in important ways over the course of recent years, as the result of a range of economic, demographic, and social changes that have simultaneously restructured the nature of Brazilian life as well as the character of Brazil's interaction with the broader global system. The urban enclaves and communities that have emerged in Brazil have been unavoidably altered by outside forces—by the ever-present structures of social inequality and the divisions of class that have characterized Brazilian life more generally, as well as by the growing insertion of local elites, with their particular powers and interests, into the broader structures of the global capitalist economy in the late twentieth century. It is within this interplay that the incorporation and indigenization of external social and cultural influences have responded to local structures and needs—that the symbols and meanings associated with gay life outside of Brazil have been appropriated and reworked within the organization of contemporary Brazilian life. It is within this interplay that the appropriation of local meanings as part of a global cultural economy has also taken place—that a variety of images about Brazilian life and Brazilian homosexualities have taken shape in such far-off places as New York, Paris, or Sydney. It is the kind of interaction that is clearly characteristic of a range of cultural forms in the late twentieth century and that is perhaps especially evident in the changing shape of homosexuality and gay life.

In many ways this adoption, and adaptation, of international gay forms has enabled many Brazilian men to imagine themselves as part of an alternative gay or homoerotic culture that extends beyond national frontiers, and that offers possibilities for realigning the contours of sexual experience both locally as well as globally. In much the same way, it is this complex give and take, this crossing of cultural and well as political borders, that makes the Brazilian *travesti* a desired commodity on the streets of Paris or Milan, that invests the advertisements for a "Brazilian Stud" or a "Muscular Brazilian" in the gay newspapers of New York or San Francisco with a given set of exotic/erotic meanings, or constructs Rio de Janeiro as a destination of choice for North American gay tourist agencies. While there is much about this that should clearly give reason for concern, it would be a mistake, I think, to assume that it is necessarily unthinking or unaware. On the contrary, the importation of international gay styles and symbols (whether of commercial discos, baseball caps and 501 jeans, or rainbow symbols, pink triangles, or red ribbons) within the Brazilian gay world is a good deal more than just an unconscious extension of international capitalism or a sign of Anglo-European cultural imperialism. The appropriation of such signs and symbols (like the appropriation of funk or reggae music, of contemporary scientific innovations, or postmodern literary trends) is a far more complex and dialectical interaction than simplistic notions of external imposition would otherwise suggest. In keeping with the Brazilian tradition described long ago by the writers and artists of the modernist movement in the 1920s and '30s, this appropriation of international cultural symbols also involves a kind of cultural *canibalismo* (cannibalism) in which outside influences are digested, absorbed, and incorporated in order to transform them to local purposes and meanings—and in which this very act of incorporation can itself become partially subversive of the structures of cultural domination that it simultaneously proclaims (see Andrade 1967; Haberly 1983:130). Indeed, it is impossible not to be impressed by the extent to which young gay men (and increasingly women) within this world adapt the signs and symbols of international gay life (with much the same creativity and persistence that the *travesti* defends herself from police harassment or the cruising *entendido* insists in seeking out fleeting moments of pleasure in the shadows of the street) to create a repertoire of symbolic resources that build meaning and make sense of the world around them, and to imagine and ultimately manipulate other worlds in other places.

In much the same way, the increasingly marked presence of Brazil and Brazilians within the gay worlds outside of Brazil is itself a far more complicated phenomenon than it might at first glance appear to be. Employment opportunities and economic options are elements in the migratory movement, but so is the search for freedom or excitement, the emotional entanglements of love, the possibilities for access to HIV/AIDS treatment, the demands of political organizing or AIDS prevention work—in short, there are factors that largely escape the most obvious attempts at analysis, that may well change over time or over the life course of any single individual, and that clearly seem to escape the simplistic dichotomies between center and periphery, between the developed and developing worlds. It is also this influx of outside influences (whether the outsiders are in fact foreigners, or simply the diverse ethnic and economic groups that have long been present, but largely excluded, from the dominant patterns and structures of gay life in the so-called First World) that has begun to break down the apparently monolithic character of white, middle-class, gay male life in many parts of the Anglo-European world, replacing it with what some have described as the more open, diverse, multicultural structures of queer or postgay culture at the end of the twentieth century.

Beyond Brazil

Like most anthropologists, I am always hesitant to venture too far afield—too far away from the settings with which I am most familiar, in which I have direct personal experience—since it is in many ways this direct contact and experience that gives one's work whatever ethnographic authority it may have. In spite of this, I must briefly call attention to the ways in which the processes described here for Brazil are similar to those taking place elsewhere in the world. Indeed, it is precisely because of the interconnectedness of the modern world that the vast majority of the transformations described above are ultimately neither entirely unique nor entirely exceptional. On the contrary, comparable forces would seem to be at work, and similar processes can be found taking place in geographically diverse sites as the twentieth century draws to a close. There is now a growing literature, produced not only by social researchers but often by the members of these communities themselves, that documents the richness and diversity not just of "indigenous" homosexualities but also of the myriad hybrid configurations that have begun to take shape in societies around the world (see, for example, Cáceres [1996] on Peru, Carrier [1995] on Mexico, Gevisser and Cameron [1995] on South Africa, Jackson [1997] on Thailand, Kahn [1996] on India, and Tan [1995] on the Philippines; see also the discussion in Lancaster [1997]).

For anyone who has moved around the contemporary world at all in recent years, the rapidity of such changes and the kaleidoscope of images that they have produced are dizzying. As Dennis Altman, one of the keenest (and most widely traveled) observers of such trends, has described it: "Glimpses of young men in baseball caps and Reeboks, on the streets of Budapest or São Paulo; 'lipstick lesbians' flirting on portable telephones in Bangkok or demonstrating in the streets of Tokyo: such images—none of which are fictitious—are part of the construction of a new category, or more accurately the expansion of an existing western category which can be seen as part of the rapid 'globalization' of life style and identity politics, the simultaneous disappearance of old concepts and the invention of new" (Altman 1996:77–78). Indeed, increasingly visible and articulate gay subcultures, communities, and organizations can surely be found today not only in Brazil but also in countries as different as Indonesia and Mexico, South Africa and the Philippines; not only in Rio de Janeiro and São Paulo (or even Fortaleza) but also in Bangkok, Bogotá, Budapest, Buenos Aires, Johannesburg, Lima, Manila, Mexico City, San Juan, or Santiago. In spite of the many important social and cultural differences characterizing these settings (and that must be attended to in any attempt at analysis), the fact remains that all of them have been caught up in the social and economic processes that have been taking place in the closing decades of the twentieth century, and that have linked such disparate locales as part of a broader, interacting system—processes that have transformed the character of sexual life in general, and of homosexual life in particular.

Yet as Altman has been quick to point out, these complex transformations—this invention of the new and dissolution of the old—can hardly be understood as some kind of "linear genealogy" (1996:79). On the contrary, far more typically in the late twentieth century, one finds that "tradition" and "modernity" (or even "modernity" and "postmodernity") tend to coexist—at best, to form what Marshall Berman described as a kind of "paradoxical unity . . . of disunity" marked by ongoing struggles and contradictions, ambiguities and often anguish (Berman 1982:15). The consequences of this paradoxical juxtaposition, the incredible dilemmas that it poses for anyone seeking to make his or her way in this world, are truly striking. They can be found played out, repeatedly, in the unre-

solved tensions that have marked the lives of the men we have interviewed in Brazil—but they are equally present in the reports coming out
of so many other parts of this increasingly interconnected world.

To even begin to map out these tensions, of course, forces us to confront the kinds of existential dilemmas and contradictions that are today
faced by so many gay people in countries around the world—particularly
the young, and particularly in the countries of the developing world. The
tension, for example, between imitation and assimilation, yet with adaptation and accommodation. The tension between a strongly felt need for
identification (and the very real desire to be part of a community) and the
no less strongly experienced push toward migration or nomadism (to
move away from oppression, to flee the effects and experience of poverty,
or even to escape the results of early, unsuccessful attempts at freedom).
The tension between an expectant hope for the future (with its possibilities for adventure, excitement, the unknown) and a lingering nostalgia for
the past (a longing for a simpler time, for a return home that in all likelihood will never occur).[1]

Such tensions, and the dilemmas they structure, have come to the fore
over the past decade—in Brazil, certainly, but equally so in many far-flung
settings throughout the developing world as well as the fully industrialized west, where many similar processes are taking place in the social organization of sexuality. Particularly during the late 1980s and early '90s, as
monolithic notions of gay and lesbian communities in societies such as
the United States have begun to give way to a fuller understanding of
diversity and difference even in very specific, localized social and geographical settings, the stark differences that once seemed to separate life
in the industrialized west from that in other social and cultural settings
appear to have dissolved into a far more diffuse interplay of images and
diversity. The roots of such diversity, as well as the axes of difference, are
multiple—linked, in particular, to the growing visibility of gay and lesbian
subcultures in different ethnic communities as well as to a growing recognition of class differences cross-cutting the once placid portrait of gay life
that has often been produced and reproduced in mainstream culture as
well as in many self-representations of lesbian and gay cultures. Clearly,
the impact of AIDS has been profound, transforming communities, uncov-
ering differences, and demanding the creation of new social institutions
and emotional responses (see, for example, Levine, Nardi, and Gagnon
1997). Yet so too has the influx of migration and the explosion of media
in Brazil and other societies—a kind of gay diaspora in which not only
Brazilians, but also Indians, Colombians, Filipinos, Mexicans, South
Africans, and so many others are today a visible part of multiple gay
worlds. In the wake of such changes, the fragmentation in what was once

perceived as a relatively monolithic gay community has become apparent, as a growing cacophony of diverse, gay, lesbian, bisexual, queer, and transgender voices have loudly announced themselves—and any pretense to a unified gay or lesbian identity has increasingly slipped away. Indeed, as much for the West as for the Rest, the certainty and relative simplicity that apparently characterized gay life only a short time ago has now dissolved. As Marshall Berman has suggested, quoting Marx in a very different context, it is as if "'all that is solid melts into air'" (Berman 1982:15).

From the Politics of Identity to the Politics of Solidarity

In his analysis of the postmodern condition, David Harvey has convincingly argued that over the course of recent decades we have experienced an intense compression of both time and space, linked, in his interpretation, to the shift from the Fordist mass production of the postwar boom (from 1945 to 1973) to a regime of "flexible accumulation" characterized by more flexible labor processes and markets, by heightened geographic mobility and rapid shifts in consumption practices, by the revival of entrepreneurialism and neoconservatism, and by the cultural turn to postmodernism (see Harvey 1990:124). This compression of time is essential to flexible accumulation, since its success depends upon significant reductions in production turnover time, in the lag between the acquisition of components and the delivery of products. This, in turn, has depended upon the compression of time in consumption patterns, which have come to be dominated by taste and fashion: as tastes and fashions change, out-of-fashion products become disposable and demands for new products must be met. Mass-mediated images become perhaps the most instant (and the most disposable) of products, and experience becomes compressed into an extended present. This compression of time is simultaneously linked to a compression of space, as new electronic communications technologies have increasingly made the cost of communication independent of distance. Capital now circulates around the face of the globe with dizzying speed, and satellite images increasingly create a kind of universal experience. Spatial barriers have imploded and the world system has become a single field of play in which consumption is universalized and capital flows freely (see Harvey 1990; see also Waters 1995).

In Harvey's interpretation, the vast majority of the major social, political, and cultural transformations that have taken place in the world over the past twenty years can be linked to this more basic historical-economic transformation—including the worrisome tendency to resist historical-economic interpretation in favor of aesthetics (Harvey 1990:336). Among the most striking aspects of Harvey's analysis, particularly to anyone who views these changes from the perspective of the South rather than the

North, is the degree to which his chronology intersects with many of the major structural forces and factors that have impacted upon life in the developing world in general—and on the shape of gay life in countries such as Brazil. The major shift that Harvey locates in the early 1970s occurred concurrently with the OPEC embargo, the explosion of the international debt crisis, and the series of shocks that these events would unleash upon the international economy. Though Harvey's examples are drawn largely from his own North Atlantic setting, his discussion of the Reagan revolution, of Thatcherism, supply-side economics, the rise of a new brand of conspicuous consumption, and, indeed, even the postmodern cultural turn could easily be substituted with an equally vivid set of examples from other more marginal settings: structural adjustment, neoliberal economic theory, the redemocratization of developing country governments predicated largely on their acceptance of capitalist models of economic development, the rise of secondary financial markets in countries such as Brazil and Thailand, the "hybridization" (see Canclini 1995) of mass and popular culture in settings such as Mexico, Argentina, or India, and so on. Indeed, it is worth remembering that throughout much of the developing world, an important resurgence of democratic possibilities has occurred concurrently with the greatest inequalities in the distribution of wealth that the world has ever known. The notion of individual rights and the legitimacy of civil society have increasingly become realities for populations emerging from the long night of intolerable dictatorships, but significant forms of social and economic inequality have continued to mark the vast majority of the world's societies, north and south, as the twentieth century hurtles to a close.

For better or for worse, the complex transformations taking place in the organization of homosexuality and the experience of gay life (both south and north of the equator) are modulated by these broader historical changes, and our ability to comprehend them, to analyze their consequences, or even to begin to know how to take action ethically and politically within such circumstances is heavily dependent upon our willingness to explore these connections. In this sense, same-sex relations and gay life can in many ways be a prism through which global processes become visible. Yet if gay life can thus offer us a window or a lens through which to explore such processes, we must also examine how they can simultaneously rebound to shape and reshape social life more generally, and even global processes of change, in the late twentieth century. As Robert Connell and Gary Dowsett have argued, a focus on the social construction of the sexual must always be linked to an analysis of the sexual construction of the social (see Connell and Dowsett 1992). It is not merely that one can monitor virtually every major social, cultural, economic, and political change taking place in late twentieth century life through the prism of same-sex relations, but also that gay cultures are themselves engines of larger change affecting everyone: reorganizing family relations and accepted notions of kinship (pretended families or families we choose, domestic partnership legislation, partner benefits, and so on); offering creative strategies for community-based organizing and service delivery (AIDS prevention outreach, buddy systems, support groups for the elderly, new models for hospice care); reshaping urban spaces and economies (the gay gentrification of inner-city areas, the creation of gay neighborhoods or ghettos, identity-based marketing and merchants' associations as central elements in postindustrial, late capitalist economies); reshaping aesthetic conventions, moral values, and accepted standards (denouncing sex panics, breaking the boundaries of acceptable erotic content in artistic creation, and so on). Both north and south, powerful new ideas, new forms of political organizing, and new experiments in living have emerged from the crucible of gay identities, cultures, and communities that have not only resulted from late capitalist modernity but also driven transformations of modernity.[2]

Indeed, the politics of identity generally and of gay identity in particular are among the most powerful forces in contemporary life at the end of the twentieth century. Yet given the magnitude of the dilemmas that we currently confront—as identities fragment and multiply, dissolve and reshape themselves in this irreversibly interconnected world—the question that remains unanswered is whether the politics of identity will be enough to offer us a viable course out of the current century and into the next. Perhaps the key question is whether we will be able to build upon the politics of identity so as to transform it into a politics of solidarity—a politics capable of hearing not only our own pain and suffering, but also the pain and suffering of others, subject to the multiple forms of oppression, exploitation, and injustice that have been produced by the contemporary world system (Parker 1996). Both north and south of the equator, the shape of the future hangs in the balance.

Appendix I

Informants Cited in the Text

All informants directly quoted in the text have been briefly identified at their first mention. Thereafter, any reference to such an informant is made by name only. For reference, and in order to provide additional information without overburdening the text, an alphabetical list of all informants cited in the text is included in this appendix. In order to protect the anonymity of informants, pseudonyms have been used throughout (with the exception of Herbert Daniel, who died in 1992, and who was well known publicly as a collaborator of the author [see Daniel and Parker 1991, 1993]), and some biographical data have been altered or withheld in order to ensure the privacy of informants. Since many informants have been interviewed repeatedly over a number of years, the age cited for each refers to his age at the last interview. References to social class are based on the informants' own classification.

ALESSANDRO: Eighteen years old, from a working-class family in Caxias, a poor suburban neighborhood in the outskirts of Rio de Janeiro. He currently works as an office messenger boy, but dreams of a career in the performing arts and is taking acting classes in the evenings and on weekends.

ALEXANDRE: Twenty-two years old, from a lower-class background in Rio de Janeiro. He worked in a drugstore in downtown Rio de Janeiro until it was closed, and is currently unemployed.

ANDRÉ: Twenty-four years old, from a lower-class background. Born in Belo Horizonte, in the state of Minas Gerais. Migrated to São Paulo at the age of twenty-three.

ÂNGELO: Twenty-three years old, from a working-class family in the outskirts of Rio de Janeiro. He was able to pass the entrance exam for the state university and studied foreign languages. He currently works as a language teacher in a private school.

ANTÔNIO: Twenty-eight years old, from the upper-middle class in Rio de Janeiro. He works as an attorney, and volunteers in an AIDS-service organization.

ANTÔNIO CARLOS: Thirty-seven years old, from a middle-class background in Rio de Janeiro. He currently works as an assistant bank manager.

ARNALDO: Thirty-three years old, from a very poor background in the interior of Pernambuco. Migrated to Rio in the mid-1980s. Stereotypically effeminate. Works as a hairdresser in a women's hair salon in Tijuca, a lower-middle-class neighborhood in the Zona Norte of Rio. Lives in a *favela* in the Zona Norte.

ARTUR: Forty-three years old, from a middle-class background in Fortaleza. Lived for an extended period of time in São Paulo during the late 1970s and early 1980s before returning home to Ceará, where he currently works with AIDS prevention.

CACÁ: Twenty-eight years old, from a lower-middle-class family in Rio de Janeiro. Worked as a dancer in Rio de Janeiro for most of the past decade, before moving to Amsterdam.

CAMPOS: Thirty-six years old, from a lower-class family in the interior of Minas Gerais. As a young adult, he moved from the interior of Minas Gerais to the capital city, Belo Horizonte, and then on to São Paulo and Rio de Janeiro, where he worked in a supermarket. He also spent a short time living and working in Italy before returning again to Rio, where he worked for a number of years at a gas station before losing his job. Currently unemployed.

CARLINHOS: Twenty-six years old, from a lower-class background in Fortaleza, where he does odd jobs for a real-estate development firm.

CARLOS: Thirty-five years old, from a working-class background in São Paulo. He is an administrative assistant in a manufacturing firm.

CHICO: Thirty-five years old, from a lower-middle class background in São Paulo, where he is employed in a downtown office complex.

CLEBER: Twenty-eight years old, from a lower-class family in Minas Gerais. Migrated to Rio de Janeiro at the age of seventeen.

CLÉRIO: Twenty-seven years old, from the lower class in Rio de Janeiro.

Works as a *michê*, sometimes on the street or the beach, but more usually in a sauna in the Zona Sul.

DANIEL: Thirty-six years old, from the upper-middle class in Rio de Janeiro. He currently works as a business manager.

DARCY: Twenty-four years old, from a working-class background. A university student at one of the major public universities in Rio de Janeiro.

DENILSON: Twenty-one years old, from a lower-class family in Fortaleza. He is an office assistant for a health insurance company.

FERNANDO: Thirty-four years old, from the lower-middle class in Rio de Janeiro. He is a theater manager for the State Secretariat of Culture.

FRANCISCO: Twenty-nine years old, from a lower-middle-class background in Fortaleza, where he works in a hotel.

HERBERT DANIEL: Originally born in Minas Gerais, Daniel traveled extensively throughout Brazil as a member of the armed resistance to the dictatorship during the late 1960s and early '70s. He and his partner, Claudio Mesquita, spent most of the '70s in exile in Paris. Following their return to Brazil in the early 1980s, Daniel became a leading gay rights and AIDS activist, and later founded the first organization of people living with HIV/AIDS. He was one of the first openly gay candidates for elected office in Brazil, and was briefly the Green Party candidate for President of the Republic in 1989. He lived in Rio until his death in 1992.

JOÃO: Thirty-nine years old, from a lower-middle-class background in Rio de Janeiro. He has worked sporadically as a designer and a salesman, and has been active in AIDS prevention activities for more than a decade.

JOÃO CARLOS: Twenty-one years old, from a working-class background in Rio de Janeiro. Currently unemployed and studying part-time.

JOAQUIM: Thirty-one years old, from a middle-class background in Fortaleza, were he is a school teacher.

JOEL: Thirty-three years old, from a working-class background in Rio de Janeiro. He works with a construction company.

JOINHA: Perhaps thirty-seven or thirty-eight years old. A transvestite prostitute who lives in a *favela* in the Zona Sul of Rio de Janeiro.

JORGE: Thirty-eight years old, from a middle-class background. Jorge was born in the North of the country, and his family also lived for a brief period in the South before moving to Rio de Janeiro.

JÚLIO: Twenty-one years old, from the lower class. Born in the state of Pernambuco, in the Northeast. Migrated to Rio with his mother at the age of nine. Migrated to São Paulo at the age of twenty.

JÚNIOR: Twenty-one years old, from the lower class in Fortaleza. Originally from a very small city in the interior of Ceará. Migrated to Fortaleza at the age of nineteen. Currently unemployed.

MARCELO: Twenty-six years old, from a very poor lower-class family in the suburbs of Rio de Janeiro. He works as an office assistant and messenger boy, and takes odd jobs on the side to add to his income.

MÁRCIO: Twenty-four years old, from a lower-class background in Belo Horizonte, in the state of Minas Gerais. He is a check-out clerk for a large department store.

MARCOS: Twenty-five years old, from a middle-class background. Originally from Fortaleza, but now living in Rio de Janeiro, where he is a student.

MÁRIO: Thirty-nine years old, from a lower-class background. Born in Teresópolis, in the state of Rio de Janeiro. He migrated to the city of Rio de Janeiro at the age of eighteen, and is employed in a restaurant in Ipanema.

MARQUINHOS: Twenty-four years old, from a working-class background in Rio de Janeiro, where he works in a manufacturing firm.

MILTON: Thirty-six years old, from the middle class in Rio de Janeiro, where he drives a taxi.

OTÁVIO: A twenty-six year old, working as a *michê* in Rio de Janeiro.

PAULO: Forty-three years old, from the lower class in Rio de Janeiro. Heavily involved with one of the major gay rights organizations in the city.

PAULO CÉSAR: Forty-one years old, from the lower-middle class in Rio de Janeiro. He works as a waiter at a restaurant in Botafogo.

RAFAEL: Forty-two years old, from an upper-middle-class family in São Paulo. He has lived in Rio de Janeiro since the late 1970s, when he moved there as a student. He works in a university in Rio de Janeiro, where he has been extensively involved in both gay and AIDS activism.

REINALDO: Twenty-four years old, from a lower-class family in Rio de Janeiro. He is an electronic equipment repairman.

ROBERTO: Forty-three years old, from a working-class background in Rio de Janeiro. He is a carpenter.

ROBSON: Twenty-four-year-old informant from the working class in Rio de Janeiro, where he works as a nurse, and occasionally as a *transformista*.

RODRIGO: Thirty-year-old informant from a lower-class background in Fortaleza, where he is a social worker.

VINÍCIUS: Thirty-nine years old, from the lower-middle class in Fortaleza. Originally born in the Northeast, but moved with his family to the Central-West, where he married and raised a family before separating from his wife and moving to Fortaleza. Self-identifies as *"bissexual,"* although his sexual practice is currently a good deal more with men than with women.

VITOR: Twenty-six years old, from a lower-middle class family in Rio de Janeiro. A university student in Rio.

WALTER: Thirty-six years old, from the middle class in Rio de Janeiro. He studied to be an attorney, but currently works with an AIDS advocacy organization.

WILLIAM: Twenty-four years old, from the lower class in Fortaleza. Currently unemployed, he makes ends meet through a series of odd jobs.

Gay Rights and AIDS-
Service Organizations

The following is a listing of gay and lesbian organizations, as well as AIDS service and advocacy organizations, that develop significant programs or projects activities for men who have sex with men, as of the beginning of 1998. Though every attempt has been made to be as thorough as possible, the list is almost inevitably incomplete, and at least some newer or smaller organizations have probably been missed. It is intended to provide a sense of the growing organizational structure of the gay and lesbian movement in Brazil, as well as of the range of AIDS-service organizations developing activities related to homosexuality. Mailing addresses and, when available, telephone, fax, e-mail, and home page addresses have been included to facilitate readers wishing to contact Brazilian organizations. The Brazilian gay, lesbian, and transgender network can be reached through its secretariats in São Paulo or Curitiba at the addresses listed below for the Associação Brasileira de Gays, Lésbicas e Travestis (ABGLT). For more up-to-date information concerning many of the organizations listed here, or a more complete listing of AIDS-service organizations independent of whether they develop projects related to homosexuality, readers can consult the listing maintained by the Associação Brasileira Interdisciplinar de AIDS (ABIA) on the Internet at:

http://www.ibase.org.br/~abia

Abrigo por Amor à Vida
Rua Oscar Brandão, 241Torrões—Recife—PE—50640–470
Tel: (081) 227–1649
Fax: (081) 326–2580

AMHOR
Caixa Postal 3656—Agência São José—Recife–PE—50022–970

Associação Brasileira de Gays, Lésbicas e Travestis (ABGLT)
São Paulo: Caixa Postal 65092—SP—01390–970
Curitiba: Caixa Postal 1095—PR—80001–970

Associação Brasileira Interdisciplinar de AIDS (ABIA)
Avenida Rio Branco 43, 22º andar—Rio de Janeiro–RJ—20090–003
Tel: (021) 224–1654
Fax: (021) 253–8495
e-mail: abia@ax.apc.org
Internet: http://www.ibase.org.br/~abia

Associação Cidadania Plena
Rua Quinze de Novembro, 401—Paranaguá–PR—83200–000
Caixa Postal 548
Fax: (041) 423–3253 (I Regional de Saúde)

Associação de Gays e Amigos de Nova Iguaçú—AGANI
Rua Marcial, 42—Juscelino—Nova Iguacú–RJ—26225–140
Tel: (021) 796–3328
Fax: (021) 531–1775

Associação de Travestis e Liberados–ASTRAL
Rua Frei Caneca,139—Centro—Rio de Janeiro–RJ—20211–040
Tel: (021) 232–2181
Fax: (021) 232–2181

Associação de Travestis de Salvador (ATRAS)
Caixa Postal 2552–BA—40022–970

Associação dos Direitos Homossexuais do Triângulo Mineiro (ADHOT)
Avenida João Pinheiro, 1797—Uberlândia–MG—384000–016

Associação dos Homossexuais do Estado do Amazonas
Rua 05—casa 10—quandra 2 Nc/27—Conjunto Renato Souza Pinto I
Bairro de Flores—Manaus–AM—69090–040

Associação dos Travestis de Brasília (ASTRAVEB)
QNE–7—lote 10—sala 102—Comercial Norte-Taquatinga–DF—72125–070

Associação Gay de Imperatriz (AGI)
Rua Urbano Santos, 544—Bairro Juçara Imperatriz–MA—59012–060

Associação Gay de Pernambuco—Gay e Cia
Rua Nossa Senhora do Loreto Nº 2424—Piedade—Jaboatão dos
Guararapes–PE—54410–200

Associação Irmãos da Solidariedade
Rua Santo Antônio, 44—Guarus—Campos–RJ—22082–420
Tel: (0247) 22–9979

Associação pela Liberdade Lilás (ALL)
Rua Abel Silva Nº 532—Cruz das Armas—João Pessoa–PB—58000–000
Tel: (083) 241–2644

Atobá—Movimento de Emancipação Homossexual
Rua Prof. Carvalho de Melo, 471—Magalhães Bastos—
    Rio de Janeiro–RJ—21735–040
Tel: (021) 332–0787
Fax: (021) 331–1527
e-mail: atobamehomos@ax.ibase.org.br

Barra Lés
Caixa Postal 3751—Barra da Tijuca—Rio de Janeiro–RJ—22642–970

Casa de Apoio Brenda Lee
Rua Major Diogo, 779—Bela Vista—São Paulo–SP—01324–001
Tel: (011) 239–2500

Centro Acadêmico de Estudos Homoeróticos da USP–CAEHUSP
Caixa Postal 392—São Paulo–SP—01059–970
Tel: (011) 220–5716
Fax: (011) 2205716/220–5657
e-mail: castro@usp.br

Cidadania Gay
Caixa Postal 100241 Nitéroi–RJ—24001–970

Coletivo de Feministas Lésbicas
Caixa Postal 62641—São Paulo–SP—01295–970

Coletivo de Homossexuais Afro-Brasileiros
A/C APTA
Alameda Barros Nº 86—cj. 02 "B"—São Paulo–SP—01232–000

Coletivo de Lésbicas do Rio de Janeiro (COLERJ)
Rua Senador Correia Nº 48—Laranjeiras—Rio de Janeiro–RJ—22231–180

CORSA
Alameda Barros Nº 86 conj 4A—São Paulo–SP—01232–000

Estação Mulher
Caixa Postal 62631—São Paulo–SP—01295–970

Estruturação
Caixa Postal 3636—Brasília–DF—70084–970

Expressão—Grupo de Defesa dos Direitos dos Homossexuais
Caixa Postal 1500—Campinas–SP—13012–970

GIPD—Grupo Iguais Pela Diferença
Rua José Coelho Barbosa Nº 941—Vila Rodrigues—Assis–SP—19800–000

GRUH-MAC
Rua Dr. Pedro Velho Nº 200—Centro—Macaíba–RN—59280–000

Grupo 28 de Junho—Movimento de Emancipação Homossexual
Rua Ataíde Pimenta de Morais, 37—Nova Iguaçú–RJ—26210–210
Caixa Postal 77097–26001–970
Tel: (021) 240–4169
Fax: (021) 533–1748

Grupo Afins
Caixa Postal 716—Santos–SP—11001–970

Grupo Arco-Íris de Concientização Homossexual—GAI
Rua do Bispo, 316/805—Rio de Janeiro–RJ—20261–062
Tel: (021) 254–6546/568–0227
Fax: (021) 254–6546/568–0227
e-mail: lfreitas@ax.apc.org

Grupo Brasileiro de Transexuais
Caixa Postal 1097—Cuabá–MT—78005–970

Grupo Cultural Triângulo Rosa
Rua Abelardo Goulart Nº 136—Bairro Santa
Terezinha—Muriaé–MG—36880–000

Grupo de Apoio à Prevenção à AIDS—GAPA/Bahia
Rua Manoel Dias Morães, 25–Jardim Ipanema–Bairro
Ondina—Salvador–BA—40155–260
Tel: (071) 245–1741/235–1727/2476554
Fax: (071) 245–1587
e-mail: ongapa@quasar.com.br

Grupo de Apoio à Prevenção à AIDS—GAPA/Ceará
Avenida do Imperador, 1.333—Centro–Fortaleza–CE—60015–052
Tel: (085) 253–4159
Fax: (085) 253–4159
e-mail: gapace@br.homeshopping.com.br

Grupo de Apoio à Prevenção à AIDS—GAPA/Minas Gerais
Rua Tamoios, 671—Conjunto 14–Centro—Belo Horizonte–MG—30120–050
Tel: (031) 271–2126
Fax: (031) 271–2126
Internet: http://www.skynet.com.br/gapa

Grupo de Incentivo à Vida—GIV
Rua Capitão Cavalcanti, 145—São Paulo–SP—04017–000
Tel: (011) 5084–0255
Fax: (011) 5084–0255
e-mail: giv@mandic.com.br

Grupo de Resistência Asa Branca–GRAB
Rua Damião Fernandes, 115—Amadeu Furtado—Fortaleza–CE—60455–600
Tel: (085) 281–9081

Grupo Dialogay
Caixa Postal 298—Aracajú–SE—49001–970
Tel: 079 211–2210/232–1737/2511834
Fax: 079 231 6403

Grupo Dignidade—Conscientização e Emancipação Homossexual
Trav. Tobias de Macedo, 53—Curitiba–PR—80020–210
Caixa Postal 1095–80001–970
Tel: (041) 222–3999
Fax: (041) 222–3999
e-mail: tonidavi@avalon.sul.com.br

Grupo Esperança
Caixa Postal 1095—Curitiba–PR—80061–970

Grupo Gay do Amazonas
Caixa Postal 279—Manaus–AM—69011–970

Grupo Gay da Bahia
Rua do Sodré, 45—Centro—Salvador–BA—40060–180
Caixa Postal 2.552—40022–260
Tel: (071) 322–2552/243–4902
Fax: (071) 322–2552/322–3782
e-mail: luizmott@ufba.br

Grupo Gays e Lésbicas do PSTU
Rua Jorge Tibirica Nº 238—Saúde—São Paulo–SP—04126–000

Grupo Habeas Corpus Potiguar
Caixa Postal 576—Natal–RN—59022–970
Tel: (084) 221–5932

Grupo Homossexual Londrinense
Avenida Paraná Nº 49 A/1º Andar—Centro—Londrina–PR—86020–300

Grupo Ipê Rosa (Associação GLS)
Caixa Postal 114—Goiânia–GO—74001–970

Grupo Lésbico da Bahia
Caixa Postal 6430—Salvador–BA—40060–970

Grupo Livremente
Caixa Postal 109—Cuiabá–MT—78005–970

Grupo Pela Valorização e Dignidade do Doente de AIDS—Pela VIDDA/Niterói
Rua Presidente Domiciano, 150—Ingá—Niterói–RJ—24210–271
Tel: (021) 719–3793
Fax: 021 719–5883
e-mail: gpvniterói@internclub.com.br
Internet: http://www.interclub.com.br/gpvniterói

Grupo Pela Valorização e Dignidade do Doente de AIDS—
  Pela VIDDA/Rio de Janeiro
Av. Rio Branco, 135—Rio de Janeiro–RJ
Tel: (021) 518–3993

Grupo Pela Valorização e Dignidade do Doente de AIDS—Pela VIDDA/São Paulo
Rua General Jardim, 556—Vila Buarque—São Paulo–SP—01223–010
Tel: (011) 258 7729
Fax: (011) 258–7729

Grupo Único Homossexual Macaibense–GRUH-MAC
Rua Doutor Pedro Velho, 200—Caxagah—Macaíba–RN—59280–800
Tel: (084) 271–1245

Grupo Unidas do Guaraituba
Rua Genésio Moreschi Nº 575—Guaraituba—Colombo–PR—83410–000

Grupo "Oxente" de Libertação Homossexual—GOLH
Rua Presidente Gonçalves, 1007—Div. Sept. Rosado—Natal–RN

Liga dos Homossexuais Esperantistas
Caixa Postal 120—Campinas–SP—13031–970

Movimento do Espírito Lilás
Caixa Postal 284—João Pessoa–PR—58001–970
Tel: (083) 224–7326

Movimento Homossexual de Belém (MHB)
Caixa Postal 1559—Belém–PA—66017–970
Trav. Apinagés, 212—Batista Campos—Belém–PA—66017–970
Tel: (091) 224–2012

Nuances–Grupo Pela Livre Orientação Sexual
Rua Vieira de Castro, 22—Porto Alegre–RS—90040–320
Tel: (051) 330–7843

Núcleo de Ação Homossexual-Somos
Rua Capitão Cavalcante Nº 145—São Paulo–SP—04001–000

Núcleo de Gays e Lésbicas do Partido dos Trabalhadores
Rua Conselheiro Nébias, 1.052—Campos Eliseos–São Paulo—01203–002
Tel: (011) 223–7999
Fax: (011) 222–9665
e-mail: ptbrasil@ax.apc.org

Núcleo GLS—Pelo Socialismo
Rua General Semeão Nº 53—Boa Vista—Recife–PE—50050–120

Programa Integrado de Marginalidade—PIM
Rua Senador Corrêa Nº 48—Laranjeiras—Rio de Janeiro–RJ—22231–180
Tel: (021) 265–5002/205–0830
Fax: (021) 205–4796
e-mail: CHILDHOPE@ax.apc.org

Projeto Etcétera e Tal
Rua Dronsfield, 358—Lapa—São Paulo–SP—05074–000
Tel: (011) 833–9785
Fax: (011) 966–0617

Prometeus–GAP
Rua Barão do Rio Branco Nº 181—Porecatu–PR—86160–000

Rede de Informação Um Outro Olhar
Caixa Postal 65092—São Paulo–SP—01390–970
Tel/Fax: (011) 284–5610
e-mail: outroolhar@ax.apc.org

Rosa Vermelha
Rua Visconde de Inhaúma Nº 440—Centro—Ribeirão Preto–SP—14010–100

Satyricon—Grupo de Apoio e Defesa da Orientação Sexual
Caixa Postal 115
Avenida Agamenon Magalhães, 1.048—Campina–PE—55810–000

Transformistas Unidos Lutando Incansávelmente Prevenindo AIDS–Tulipa
Rua dos Bandeirantes, 303—Jardim Novo
Bandeirante—Cambé–PR—86187–010

Tulipa
André Magini Nº 225—Vila João Ramilho—Santo André–SP—09170–320
Tel: (011) 717–2424

Turma OK
Rua do Resende Nº 43—Centro—Rio de Janeiro–RJ—20231–090

Notes

Chapter 1

1. Since the publication of Said's study of *Orientalism* (1978), an increasingly large and creative literature has begun to emerge that focuses on both race and sexuality as central to the discursive production of difference within the context of colonialism (see, for example, Hyam 1990; Stoler 1995; Young 1995). Somewhat surprisingly, however, relatively little work seems to have been done on the reproduction of such distinctions as markers of difference in the contemporary world system.

2. While this historical juxtaposition has been especially important during the twentieth century, it nonetheless has a much longer history, which has been examined in detail by Rudi C. Bleys in his book, *The Geography of Perversion: Male-to-Male Sexual Behavior Outside the West and the Ethnographic Imagination, 1750–1918* (Bleys 1996).

3. On the broader context of globalization and the global cultural economy in the late twentieth century, see, in particular, Appadurai 1996; Harvey 1990; Lash and Urry 1994.

4. Roger Lancaster's work on Nicaragua is perhaps especially exemplary in this regard (see Lancaster 1988, 1992, 1995). Although developed in rather different directions, one might also think of Carrier's recent work on Mexico (Carrier 1995), Murray's research in Indonesia (Murray 1991), or Wilson's research in the Yucatan (Wilson 1995). For an overview of lesbian and gay studies in anthropology that provides a useful summary of much of the work thus far conducted outside of Anglo-European settings, see Weston 1993. For a discussion of cross-cultural comparison, see also Herdt 1997.

5. While similar queries have almost surely emerged within a range of different research communities and networks, in my own case such concerns have been most clearly shaped by a small number of colleagues working primarily on HIV/AIDS internationally: Peter Aggleton, Dennis Altman, Carlos Cáceres, Gary Dowsett, Dédé Oetomo, Michael Tan, Veriano Terto Jr., and other colleagues, almost all of whom share the somewhat unusual status of being both researchers and activists concerned with evolving community structures and political practice.

6. Altman's uncanny ability to identify issues at the cutting edge, and to carry out ground-breaking research, has been demonstrated again and again. See, for example, Altman 1971, 1982, 1986, 1994.

7. And I have indeed witnessed such dilemmas, and thought about them intensely. In addition to my research on sexuality and HIV/AIDS, as well as my work with AIDS activism and community mobilization, I spent a short time in 1992 as Chief of the Prevention Unit for the Brazilian Ministry of Health's National AIDS Program, and have served as a member of the Council of Directors for the Commission on Citizenship and Reproduction, a reproductive and sexual rights coalition in São Paulo. In each of these roles, the negotiation of outsider/insider roles and perspectives has obviously been complicated and problematic—symptomatic, I suspect, of a series of broader shifts taking place in the late twentieth century construction of boundaries and frontiers.

8. Similar issues have been explored at some length in a recent edited volume dealing with field research on the part of lesbian and gay anthropologists (see Lewin and Leap 1996). While much attention has been given to the either privileged (see Bolton 1992) or problematic (see Murray, in Lewin and Leap 1996) access to information that is gained through sexual interactions with informants, less attention has been given to the role of affective (as well as sexual) relations in integrating outsiders within local friendship networks, and hence opening up contact with key informants.

9. For an overview and annotated bibliography of research on male homosexuality, bisexuality, and HIV/AIDS, see Guimarães, Terto, and Parker 1992. For a useful overview of contemporary work, see the essays in Part Two of Parker and Barbosa 1996. On the much more restricted study of female homosexuality, see Heilborn 1992, 1995, 1996; and Mott 1987b.

10. Readers interested in following up on this work should also see *Sexualidades Brasileiras* (Parker and Barbosa 1996), *Entre Homens: Homossexualidade e AIDS no Brasil* (Parker and Terto 1998), *Gênero e Sexualidade: Fragmentos de Identidade Masculina nos Tempos da AIDS* (Peixoto da Mota 1996), *Reinventando a Vida: Histórias de AIDS e Homossexualidade no Brasil* (Terto 1997), and *Cabaret Prevenção* (Almeida 1997) as a point of departure. Further references can be found in these publications.

11. Support for the first phase of this work from 1989 through 1992 was provided by FAPERJ, the Foundation for the Support of Research in the State

of Rio de Janeiro, as well as the World Health Organization's Global Programme on AIDS. Both the second and third phases, from 1993 through 1996, were supported by grants from the Ford Foundation, with additional support for a number of specific activities also provided by the Brazilian Ministry of Health through the National STD/AIDS Program and the FHI AIDSCAP Project/Brazil. The survey carried out in São Paulo was supported by the FHI AIDSCAP Project/Brazil (directed by Maria Eugênia Lemos Fernandes), and the survey in Fortaleza was supported by the Ministry of Health's National STD/AIDS Program through a grant to the Federal University of Ceará (Lígia Pontes, Principal Investigator). For a broader discussion of the diverse components of this work, see also Parker and Terto 1998.

12. With too few exceptions, such as Murray's work on female prostitution in Indonesia (Murray 1991) and Heilborn's research on lesbian couples in Brazil, questions related to lesbian experience in non-Anglo-European settings have generally received far less research attention than issues related to male homosexuality (see also Blackwood 1986)—a disparity that has surely been accentuated in the wake of HIV/AIDS, which provided an important stimulus for research on men who have sex with men, but little incentive for work on female homosexuality. The study of lesbian cultures and communities outside of Europe and the United States is one of the most urgent priorities if we hope to build more decentered understandings of sexual life and experience in the contemporary world.

13. Readers interested in following up on the findings of the survey research should see Parker and Terto 1998, where preliminary findings from the surveys in Rio, São Paulo, and Fortaleza are reported. At least two separate volumes looking more specifically at life history material are also currently in preparation.

Chapter 2

1. The importance of gender-based notions of activity and passivity in structuring both gender relations and sexual interactions between men has been extensively documented. In Brazil, it was first noted as early as 1950s in the work of the sociologist, José Fábio Barbosa da Silva (1959). More recently, the importance of activity and passivity have been examined in a range of anthropological and sociological texts (see, for example, Daniel and Parker 1991, 1993; Fry 1982, 1985; Fry and MacRae 1983; Guimarães 1974; MacRae 1990; Parker 1985, 1987, 1989, 1991, 1994; Perlongher 1987; Trevisan 1986; for an overview of this literature, see Guimarães, Terto, and Parker 1992). A different, though very intriguing, reading of the relationship between penetration, gender, and sexuality has also been developed by Kulick in his work on transvestites in Salvador (see Kulick 1997). Variations on the theme of activity/passivity have been amply documented throughout Latin/o America (see, for example, Adam

1989; Almoguer 1991; Alonso and Koreck 1989; Bao 1993; Block, and Ligouri 1992; Cáceres 1996; Carballo-Diéguez 1989, 1995; Carrier 1971, 1985, 1995; Lancaster 1988, 1992, 1995; Ligouri, Block, and Aggleton 1996; Lumsden 1991, 1996; Murray 1992, 1995; Prieur 1996; Taylor 1985; Whitam and Mathy 1986; Wilson 1995), as well as in the Mediterranean (see Brandes 1980; Gilmore 1990) and a range of even more distant culture areas (see, for example, Aggleton 1996).

2. In spite of the general importance of Roman Catholic religion in Brazilian life, religious beliefs would seem to have very little to do with the organization of sexual stigma in this regard. Priests and bishops are themselves the object of gender-based stigma due to their lack of heterosexual activity and their consequent symbolic association with passive femininity. Jokes or comments about the priests' robes as *saias* (skirts) are common in daily life, as are allusions to suspect homosexual behavior.

3. It is perhaps worth noting that references to *troca-troca* extend far beyond the reports of specific informants. Indeed, the notion of *troca-troca* is sufficiently fixed in popular culture that it is the topic of playful jokes among adults, as well as a reference in popular music, such as Chico Buarque de Hollanda's "Ópera do Malandro" (Hollanda 1978).

4. There is some disagreement about the rigidity of active/passive categories in different parts of Latin America (see, in particular, Murray 1995). My own sense is that there is probably some variation from one country to another throughout the region, as well from more rural to more urban areas even in the same country. In general, there seems to be somewhat more flexibility in the organization of active/passive roles in Brazil than in the Hispanic American countries—just as other aspects of Brazilian culture, such as Roman Catholicism, tend to be somewhat less rigid. Statistically nonrepresentative behavioral studies (based on more or less well-constructed convenience samples) in the wake of HIV/AIDS seem to document a fairly high degree of role switching, at least over the course of an individual's entire life, not only in Brazil (see Parker 1994; Parker and Terto 1998) but also in Mexico (Izazola et al. 1991) and Costa Rica (Schifter and Madrigal 1992). In our work in Brazil we have found that, although most informants tend to have fairly strong preferences for one sexual role or the other, room for negotiation and experimentation nonetheless exists for a significant percentage of men. Unfortunately, much of the discussion of this issue has tended to confuse the analysis of cultural systems and representations with the empirical investigation of sexual behavior—as if the two were somehow one and the same thing.

5. To recount the history of this conceptual framework in Brazil would take a full-length book, or perhaps a series of books, in and of itself. From different angles, at least some of this history has already been documented in studies by Costa 1979; Fry 1982; Fry and MacRae 1983; Green 1996; Trevisan 1986. Key primary texts in the history of homosexuality in

Brazil include Pires de Almeida, *Homossexualismo (A Libertinagem no Rio de Janeiro)* (Pires de Almeida 1906); Roberto Santos, *Carácteres Sexuais Neutros e Intersexualidade* (Santos 1931); Estácio Lima, *A Inversão Sexual Feminina* (Lima 1934); Leonídio Ribeiro, *Homossexualismo e Endocrinologia* (Ribeiro 1938); and Iracy Doyle, *Contribuição ao Estudo da Homossexualidade Feminina* (Doyle 1956).

6. Until very recently, Trevisan's *Perverts in Paradise* (1986) stood out as the only full-length study to discuss the historical development of this subculture in detail. An important history focusing on both Rio and São Paulo has recently been completed by James Green (1996). Glimpses of this history can also be found in anthropological studies by MacRae (1990), Perlongher (1987), and Terto (1989). In Brazil, as in many other societies, among the most interesting and compelling portraits of the homosexual subculture can also be found in literature. See, for example, the Brazilian writers reprinted in Winston Leyland's edited volumes, *Now the Volcano* (1979) and *My Deep Dark Pain is Love* (1983). See also works such as Caio Fernando Abreu, *Triângulo das Águas* (1991); Túlio Carela, *Orgia (Diário Primeiro)* (1968); Gasparino Damata, *Os Solteirões* (1976); Herbert Daniel, *Passagem para o Próximo Sonho* (1982) and *Alegres e Irresponsáveis Abacaxis Americanos* (1987); Darcy Penteado, *Teoremambo* (1979) and *Nivaldo e Jerônemo* (1981); Silviano Santiago, *Stella Manhattan* (1994); Leopoldo Serran, *Shirley: A História de um Travesti* (1979); and Aguinaldo Silva, *A República dos Assassinos* (1976).

7. As will become apparent in the following chapters, in Brazil, as elsewhere, the relationship between homosexuality and AIDS has been complex and profound on a number of different levels. In addition to an extensive sociological and anthropological research literature (see, for example, Guimarães, Terto, and Parker 1992; Parker 1994; Parker et al. 1994), significant artistic responses to the epidemic have also emerged in Brazilian fiction and letters. For examples of the literary response to AIDS in Brazil, see, for example, Abreu 1981; Daniel 1982, 1987; Santiago 1993. For an analysis of the literary response to AIDS in Brazil, see Marcelo Secron Bessa, *Histórias Positivas: A Literatura (Des)construindo a AIDS* (Bessa 1997).

8. I am indebted to Roger Lancaster for the image of the kaleidoscope, from the Greek *"kalos"* and *"eidos"* for "beautiful form."

Chapter 3

1. As I have discussed at length elsewhere (see Parker 1991), the popular expression that "Within four walls, anything can happen. . ." is central to an ideology of erotic transgression in Brazilian sexual culture, suggesting the carnivalization of private or intimate interactions. Carnival itself can be read as a kind of eroticization of otherwise normal life and public space (see Parker 1991, 1997b). These deeply rooted ideological structures play a central role in the construction of the gay world in

Brazil—homoerotic desire and gay life take shape through the participants' sense of erotic transgression, as a kind of constant carnivalization
of the interstices in daily life.

2. Discrimination against same-sex couples is commonly reported by informants, as well as in the media. See, for example, *Jornal do Brasil* 1998.

3. Stories of run-ins with the police, of being shaken down for money, and
often of being forced to have sex in order to be let free without any
charges, are found in a remarkable number of the informant interviews
that we have carried out. While we assume that most of these stories are
in fact accurate, they clearly seem to fit into a narrative structure of con-
siderable importance, which mixes the ever-present fear of police
oppression with a notion of transgression in the unexpected (and fundamentally unequal) interaction with the police officer (or officers), who
are almost always represented as active and aggressive in sexual interactions. No informants ever reported actually having been booked on
morals charges, although this too does take place at times and may even
be reported in the press, as in a recent case of a senior army officer who
was arrested while having sex with another man in his parked car (see
Autran and Almeida 1996). According to informants, however, such
interactions proceed to arrest (rather than some other financial/sexual
resolution) only when an individual stopped by the police attempts to
pull rank, leading to an escalating contest for dominance (between the
police officer and the individual under arrest) that may ultimately end
up in the local police station.

4. *Do babado forte* is an especially curious expression. On the one hand, as
a noun, *babados* refer to the ruffles or flounces of a woman's dress. As an
adjective, *babado* refers to being wet with slobber or drool, and collo-
quially can be used to suggest being head-over-heels in love. All of these
meanings are superimposed upon one another in the use of the expression *do babado forte* to describe an *entendido*—i.e., someone who takes
part in the homoerotic subculture or gay world.

5. Indeed, according to many informants, the very notion of risk, of potentially being "caught in the act" by a passerby or an unusually attentive
observer, seems to be crucial to the erotic tension underlying such interactions.

6. For a detailed ethnography of homosexual interaction in cinemas in Rio
de Janeiro, based on fieldwork carried out in the early 1980s, see Veriano
Terto Jr.'s study, *No Escurinho do Cinema* (Terto 1989).

7. The lines of division between gay and straight, between men who have
sex with other men and those who don't, clearly do exist in Brazil as in
other settings—contrary to some misreadings or misinterpretations,
which seem to interpret the relative fluidity of Brazilian sexual cultures
as though sexual boundaries and sexual oppression simply fail to exist.
These divisions, however, seem to be negotiated in rather different ways.
A straight man entering to use a restroom and encountering gay cruis-

ing going on may make an unfriendly grimace and shake his head, but will probably use the toilet and go on his way. A straight man in a porn cinema may be aware of gay sex in the back rows or the balcony, but will simply concentrate on the (straight) film being shown if he isn't interested in joining in the gay sex. The fear and loathing that might be expected in many Anglo-Saxon cultures seems somewhat less pronounced in such settings. This relative tolerance in no way suggests approval, however—nor does it in any way reduce the objective level of sexually-based oppression and violence that frequently occurs during normal daily life.

8. For an important appropriation of many of the ideas of the Chicago school of urban sociology applied to Brazilian data, see Néstor Perlongher's ethnography of male prostitution in São Paulo, *O Negócio do Michê* (1987).

9. It is important to emphasize that this image is all-too-often played out in reality, as has been extensively documented by a number of gay rights organizations such as the Grupo Gay da Bahia (see Mott 1997). This association with violence has led to significant stigma, even within the gay subculture, and many male sex workers therefore prefer to be called *garotos de programa* (literally, boys who turn tricks) rather than *michês*.

10. For a detailed ethnography of the world of the *travestis*, and of transvestite prostitution, see Hélio R.S. Silva's *Travesti: A Invenção do Feminino* (Silva 1993; see also Silva and Florentino 1996). For a briefer, but nonetheless insightful, discussion, see Kulick 1997.

11. On the *travestis'* use of knives and razor blades, see also the detailed discussion in Mott 1987a.

12. Even in the mid-1990s, telephones are still a luxury for the vast majority of Brazilian households, and fewer than 30 percent of the population nationwide has a telephone available at home. Perhaps even more than automobiles, telephones are thus a sign of status and a marker of wealth, and the prices charged for telephone out-call services (whether by female or male sex workers) are proportionally higher than prices charged on the street.

13. There is a complex interrelation between socioeconomic class and the social construction of race in Brazil. The poorer sectors of Brazilian society are also generally darker. As Charles Wagley argued many years ago, one of the key ways in which racial discrimination functions in Brazil is through class oppression (see Wagley 1968). This structure is clearly reproduced in the social organization of male hustling and transvestite prostitution, and sex workers tend to be, in general, both poorer and darker skinned than are their clients.

14. The inclusion of women here is especially important, for it is really only very recently in the context of such commercial spaces that the gay male world in Brazil has begun to intersect with the lesbian world. While women are altogether absent from the orgiastic interactions of public

space, and present only through a series of often distorted representations in the transactions of transvestites and hustlers, they are increasingly present in such commercial spaces, sometimes dividing space with
gay men, and sometimes alternating with set nights for women and others for men.

15. This relative safety of course has its limits. Over the course of the past
decade, in the wake of HIV/AIDS, many men have come to perceive the
sexual interactions of the gay commercial world as potentially risky in
terms of HIV transmission—as if the concentration of gay men (as
opposed to men who have sex with men but who have a more distant
relationship to the gay subculture) necessarily guaranteed increased risk
of infection. More concretely, the incidence of robbery and physical violence at the hand of partners picked up in gay establishments is perceived to have risen. In particular, a phenomenon known as *"boa noite,
Cinderela"* ("good night, Cinderella"), in which thieves secretly place
drugs in their potential victims' drinks in order to then help them home
and gain entry to their houses or apartments, is said to be widespread.

16. Since the early 1980s, a transvestite named Roberta Close has been especially well-known and popular. She was in fact a cover girl for many of
Brazil's most widely circulating publications, as well as the inspiration
for popular songs, and was at one time described (not always with irony)
as *a namoradinha do Brasil* (Brazil's sweetheart—an expression usually
reserved for the newest female sensation on the hugely popular nightly
television soap operas). At the end of the 1980s, Roberta lived for a time
in Europe and underwent a sex-change operation before returning to
Brazil. She continued to make waves, first as a highly publicized center-
fold in the Brazilian *Playboy* magazine, and also through ongoing (thus
far unsuccessful) attempts to have her sex officially reclassified under
Brazilian law (see, for example, Thuswohl 1997; see also the discussion
in Kulick 1997).

17. Indeed, a highly complex subculture has grown up around the *drags* and
transformistas, both in and out of the commercial clubs. *Concursos* (competitions or pageants), much like the "balls" described in New York by
George Chauncey, and documented particularly in the gay black community by William Hawkeswood (1996) and in the film *Paris is Burning*,
have become increasingly common, not only at clubs and discos but
also through friendship networks and gay organizations such as the
Turma OK in Rio de Janeiro.

18. The male strip review, *"A Noite dos Leopardos,"* was directed and com-
manded by Heloína, an older transvestite performer and entrepreneur.
The show was a long-running success at the Teatro Alaska in Rio de
Janeiro from the mid-1980s through the mid-1990s, and also traveled to
various other cities in Brazil, Europe, and North America. At least some
of the male models who performed in this show can also be seen featured in porn films such as *Carnival in Rio* and *Island Fever* by the Scan-

dinavian film maker Kristen Bjorn, as well as in the film *Via Appia* (named after Via Ápia, the popular designation for the center of male street hustling in downtown Rio de Janeiro) by the German director, Jochen Hick, offering some sense of the increasing interconnections between the international gay commercial/cultural world and the recent development of gay life in Brazil.

19. It is impossible to go into adequate detail here on the importance of work on homosexuality in literature, theater, and cinema in Brazil. Writers such as Caio Fernando Abreu, Túlio Carela, Gasparino Damata, Herbert Daniel, Darcy Pentado, Aguinaldo Silva, and João Silvério Trevisan have depicted homosexual or gay life and experience in Brazil. At least some of their work can be found in a number of useful collections on gay literature in Latin America edited by Winston Leyland (1979, 1983), and a discussion of some of this work can also be found in David William Foster (1991, 1994). Like literature, Brazilian theater has also been especially important in stimulating discussion and debate around issues related to homosexuality. As early as the 1950s and '60s, the work of Nelson Rodrigues, who is widely considered to have been Brazil's greatest playwright, frequently raised homoeroticism as part of his extensive catalogue of obsessive sexual passions and family tragedies (see Castro 1992). In the late 1970s and early '80s, with the decline of censorship in the closing years of the military dictatorship, plays such as Chico Buarque de Hollanda's *Ópera do Malandro* (1978), the theatrical version of Manuel Puig's *Beijo da Mulher Aranha* (1980), and Aguinaldo Silva and Doc Comparato's *As Tias* (1981) raised issues related to homosexuality within the context of social change and political opening. More recently, in the late 1980s and the 1990s, theatrical presentations have continued to play a central role, both in exploring changing conceptions of homosexuality in Brazilian society as well as in incorporating external conceptions through the translation both of classic stories, such as "Giovanni," the musical version of James Baldwin's *Giovanni's Room*, or the more recent classic, "Angels in America" (see Ferreira 1997; Oliveira 1997). While it has received relatively little attention, homosexual or gay themes (or subthemes) have also been common in Brazilian cinema, figuring prominently in films as different as *O Beijo no Asfalto* and *Toda Nudez Será Castigado* (based on plays by Nelson Rodrigues); *Anna Libertina, Madame Satã, Pixote, A Ópera do Malandro* (from the Chico Buarque musical); and *Navalha na Carne*. At the same time, given the immense difficulties confronted by Brazilian cinema in recent years (particularly during the Collar government), it is perhaps not surprising that nothing that could really be described as "gay cinema" has emerged in Brazil, and that gay and lesbian film festivals organized in recent years in São Paulo and Rio (see below) tend to place greater emphasis on films imported from abroad than on the fairly limited number of domestic productions.

20. After a long delay following the demise of Brazil's first significant gay publication, *Lampião da Esquina*, in the late 1970s (see MacRae 1990; Trevisan 1986), more gay magazines and newspapers have begun to spring up in the mid-1990s, and *Sui Generis* is only the most glossy and visible of this new wave. Other publications include *A Folha de Parreira, Nós por Exemplo, Ent.*, *O Caso*, and *O Grito*, though many of these recent publications have failed to survive and publish steadily for more than a short period of time.

21. By far the most extended description of early gay organizing in Brazil can be found in Edward MacRae's ethnographic study, *A Construção da Igualdade: Identidade Sexual e Política no Brasil da "Abertura"* (MacRae 1990). For a different perspective, see also João Silvério Trevisan's important historical study, *Devassos no Paraíso* (Trevisan 1986).

22. The question of the legal status of same-sex relationships has become increasingly important in the wake of the AIDS epidemic. A number of high-profile court cases have debated the legal right of male same-sex partners to inheritance following the death of their lovers, and the Brazilian courts have tended to side with the families of the deceased rather than with their partners—though one recent case in Minas Gerais specifically recognized same-sex partnerships. Legislation introduced by Marta Suplicy, a dynamic first-term representative in the House of Deputies from the Worker's Party (PT) in São Paulo, seeks to respond to this issue. For further information on this legislation and its current status, see Suplicy's Home Page at http://www.solar.com.br/~msuplicy.

23. One might also add here that these same processes simultaneously offer a clear example of how bilateral such symbolic flows have increasingly become in the globalized world of the late twentieth century. It is equally true that models and findings developed in AIDS-prevention work in countries like Brazil have fed back to influence and even shape at least some work in countries like the United States. Work with ethnic communities of men who have sex with men, for example, has been strongly influenced by research and practice in countries like Brazil and Mexico. In an interconnected world, the possibilities for exchange and interaction are always more complex than they may at first glance appear, and we should always be wary of oversimplistic assumptions.

Chapter 4

1. Indeed, "dependency theory" (see Cardoso and Faletto 1979) itself is very much a Brazilian creation, linked to the work of the sociologist, Fernando Henrique Cardoso, whose own history in many ways mirrors the history of Brazil over the course of the past thirty years. During this period, Cardoso passed from leftist critic of the military regime in the 1960s and '70s, to a major actor in the redemocratization of Brazilian society in the 1980s, to president of the Republic and a champion of neoliberal economic reforms in the 1990s.

2. This relationship to the North Atlantic was also relatively simple and straightforward. Throughout the late nineteenth and early twentieth centuries, Brazil sold three-fifths to three-quarters of its exports to only three countries: the United States, Great Britain, and Germany. Within this context, the relative importance of the United States as Brazil's key trading partner has continued to grow steadily throughout the twentieth century (see Skidmore and Smith 1997).

3. Much has been made of the high levels of contraceptive use among Brazilian women in recent decades. It is important to note, however, that contraceptive options have remained very limited, focused almost entirely on the use of oral contraceptives and, especially, sterilization (most often performed in association with cesarean section deliveries), the primary methods that seem to have been promoted by the international population control movement (see Berquó 1993).

4. For further discussion of the role of the United States during the authoritarian period in Brazilian politics, see, for example, Stepan 1973; Skidmore and Smith 1997.

5. Brazil was in fact doubly penalized as a result of the OPEC embargo during the 1970s due to its heavy reliance on the importation of petroleum. One of the major (and largely failed) *obras faraónicas* during the second half of the decade was the military's attempt to substitute imported fossil fuels with nationally produced sugar cane alcohol—the *pró-álcool* campaign that was based largely on subsidized production of alcohol-burning automobiles from the mid-1970s through the mid-1980s.

6. The notion of structural adjustment (and related austerity programs) emerged most clearly, in Brazil as elsewhere, in response to the international debt crisis in the 1970s and '80s, with the International Monetary Fund and the World Bank as its major champions and articulators. With the primary goal of converting domestic economic resources to production for export, and opening the domestic economy to transnational corporations, structural-adjustment lending on the part of the World Bank has been predicated on the adoption of policies such as the privatization of government corporations, the promotion of raw material exports and of export industries, import liberalization and elimination of trade barriers, elimination or reduction of subsidies for agriculture, health care, education and related social areas, and the adoption of restrictive monetary policies and high interest rates in order to control inflation. See, for example, George and Sabelli 1994; Green 1995; Mosley, Harrigan, and Toye 1991.

7. Betinho, the nickname for Herbert de Souza, had been a charismatic leader of the student movement and the Brazilian Left in the early 1960s, and had been forced into hiding and ultimately exile following the coup in 1964. After his return to Brazil in the early 1980s, Betinho founded IBASE (the Brazilian Institute for Social and Economic Analysis), one of the largest and most influential nongovernmental organizations

in the country over the next fifteen years. He and his two brothers all suffered from hemophilia, and when all three were diagnosed with HIV infection in the mid-1980s, Betinho went on to found ABIA (the Brazilian Interdisciplinary AIDS Association) in 1986. He served as ABIA's president until his death in 1997. See Souza 1993, 1994.

8. The Southern Market is a trading alliance involving Southern Cone nations such as Argentina, Brazil, Chile, and Uruguay. It emerged as a conscious response to similar alliances such as the European Common Market and NAFTA.

9. There is an extensive literature on the question of race, and, in particular, its link to socioeconomic class, in Brazilian life. See, for example, the seminal discussion in Wagley 1968. More generally, see Degler 1971, Haberly 1983, and Skidmore 1993.

10. In comparison with the other authoritarian regimes found in South America during this period, the Brazilian dictatorship was perhaps relatively tolerant of sexual difference—making cities such as Rio de Janeiro and São Paulo an attractive destination for sexual exiles fleeing neighboring countries such as Argentina and Chile (see chapter 6 in this volume). Still, in spite of a relative tolerance for sexual deviations so long as they remained private, the military rulers in no way accepted public manifestations or political organizing around gay issues, and even during the *abertura* period, when a number of gay organizations and publications began to form, they were subject to the constant threat of persecution and violence (see Green 1996; MacRae 1990; Trevisan 1986).

11. The importance of Somos as what is perceived to be the first important gay liberation organization in Brazil is repeatedly emphasized, both by informants as well as in the scholarly literature. See, for example, Green 1996; MacRae 1990, 1992; Souza 1997; Trevisan 1986.

12. Tancredo Neves, selected through an indirect election in 1985 as a candidate of compromise between factions on both the left and the right, was never able to take office due to his untimely death shortly after the election.

13. The economics of gay and lesbian communities in the Anglo-European world has finally begun to receive greater research attention in recent years, with a number of important parallels to the emerging gay economy in Brazil. See, in particular, Gluckman and Reed 1997.

Chapter 5

1. This does not mean to say that nothing in the way of a gay world existed prior to the past decade; on the contrary, as work by writers as different as José Fábio Barbosa da Silva (1959), João Silvério Trevisan (1986), and James Green (1996) suggests, complex subcultures organized around homoerotic desires and practices have long been present in urban life in Brazil. The point, however, is that over the course of the past ten to fifteen years, as a number of major social and economic transformations

have taken place in Brazilian society more broadly, there have also been major changes in the character and quality of gay life in most major Brazilian cities.

2.   By the early 1990s, both São Paulo and Rio had reached the status of megacities, with populations of 15,416,416 and 9,796,498, respectively (see IBGE 1992; Minayo 1995; United Nations 1991). While they rank behind supranational financial centers such as London and New York, both are considered to be "first order" international financial centers, with much the same status in the global urban system as cities such as Hamburg, Hong Kong, Miami, Rome, San Francisco, Sydney, and Toronto (see Friedmann 1995; see also Clark 1996).

3.   Over the course of the past decade, the economic primacy of São Paulo has continued to grow, not only in relation to Rio de Janeiro but within the country as a whole. Today it is clearly São Paulo that "articulates" the Brazilian national economy in relation to the global economic system (much like Sydney in Australia, or Mexico City in Mexico), and in this sense the economic importance of São Paulo has clearly surpassed that of Rio (see Knox and Taylor 1995). At the same time, because of the continued strength of the communications industry in Rio, particularly through the massively powerful Globo industries (television, radios, newspapers, etc.), Rio continues to play a central role in relation to what might be described as "cultural articulation," and the two cities continue to function in many ways in tandem as part of a broader global urban/economic system (see Clark 1996; see also Staubhaar 1996).

4.   The social organization of spatial relations in Brazilian cities differs in a number of important ways from that found in most major North American or European cities. In general, the symbolic value associated with both "up" and "down" and "in" and "out" are reversed. In Brazil, the well-to-do generally live down (especially close to the beach or city parks) rather than up in the hills, where spectacular views may be available, but where the lack of transportation and basic urban infrastructure makes residence undesirable for anyone but the very poor. The same is true of the relation between central areas and outlying areas. Choice residential space tends to be in or near the center of town, thus requiring only limited travel time to the financial center of the city and guaranteeing a higher quality infrastructure. Outlying or distant areas, which require long and difficult trips, and where basic infrastructure may well be lacking, tend to be abandoned and left for the poor. The North American notion of a well-to-do suburban life style has gradually begun to acquire some followers in recent years, as will be discussed below, but is still largely foreign to Brazilian culture.

5.   The remarkable Americanization of Brazilian life that has taken place in the Zona Sul as a whole, and in Barra da Tijuca in particular, is striking. In Barra, for example, a kind of "California culture" has taken shape, emphasizing surfing, wind surfing, and other similar water sports; dune

buggies and beach parties; the construction of immense shopping malls with what seem like endless parking lots; the opening of convenience stores, like the 7–11 store, Blockbuster video rental outlets, and similar North American innovations. Perhaps nowhere else in the country is the automobile as dominant in the organization of space and commerce as in Barra da Tijuca. And since Rede Globo, the single most important Brazilian television network, is located in the Zona Sul, with its newest and most modern installations in Barra, and a sizable part of its nightly programming filmed in Barra and depicting the life style of the Zona Sul, Barra da Tijuca (like Copacabana and Ipanema before it) has come to symbolize "the Brazilian dream" of prosperity, beauty, and leisure—in short, the dream of modernity and development (even if in the midst of poverty and elbow-to-elbow with *favelas* and *subúrbios*).

6. On the importance of homosexuality in relation to Afro-Brazilian religious cults, see, for example, Barros, Santos, and Teixeira 1985; Birman 1985; Fry 1982, 1985; Wafer 1991.

7. For a further discussion of *Carnaval*, and of its importance for gay culture (and the importance of homoerotic play and gay motifs for the festival), see Green 1996; Parker 1991, 1997b; Trevisan 1986.

Chapter 6

1. Immigration increased rapidly after the demise of slavery, in 1888, and the declaration of the Brazilian Republic, in 1889, as government policies sought to provide incentives for immigration in order to take up the slack in the labor force that had been created with the end of slavery. Such policies continued in the early part of the twentieth century, as Brazil became one of a number of attractive options for Europeans fleeing the economic problems and political turmoil of their countries of origin. See, for example, Burns 1993.

2. Television programming and reporting on homosexuality, as well as HIV/AIDS in relation to homosexuality, has been important over the course of the past decade. Given the far greater impact of television than any other form of media in Brazil, the ways in which it has addressed homosexuality both in news and information programming as well as in entertainment programming has shaped social and cultural debate. Much of the discussion of these issues has taken place on daytime and evening talk shows or news journals, ranging from in-depth stories on famous gay activists to overviews of the gay subcultures in different cities. In 1990, for example, an hour-long program on Herbert Daniel and his partner, Claudio Mesquita, on TV Manchete's *Manchete Urgente*, had a major impact in presenting gay relationships (and living with HIV) as "normal" parts of modern life. Leading gay activists such as Luiz Mott have been featured regularly on talk shows, such as *Espaço Livre* on TVS, directed at adolescent viewers. The most widely viewed nightly *novelas* of TV Globo, the major network in the country, have begun to include

issues related to sexual diversity and difference, ranging from a her-maphrodite character in *Renascer* in the early 1990s, to the extremely high-profile love affair of two young, equally masculine, college students in *A Próxima Vítima* in 1996 (which was especially notable because of its extremely positive treatment, including the same kind of happy ending for the gay lovers as is typical for the heterosexual couples in the for-mulaic resolution of destinies that normally takes place when a *novela* comes to a close). Such events, broadcast nightly, and reaching audi-ences sometimes as large as 80 million viewers, then become a major topic of discussion in normal daily life, being hotly debated, from vari-ous points of view, by families, groups of friends, colleagues and cowork-ers on the job, and so on, providing one of the major stimuli for changing conceptions of gender, sexuality, and social customs more gen-erally.

3. The popularity of Balinese clothing and tourist art, for example, or reg-gae music, meringue, and other Caribbean beats, are good examples of recent trends.

4. This image was reinforced in a major way by much of the early (and some of the more recent) discussion of HIV/AIDS, in which sex tourism by western gay men was associated (in largely sensationalist reports) with the spread of HIV infection in many developing countries.

5. Salvador is widely considered to be the African heart and soul of Brazil-ian culture. The population of the city (like the state of Bahia more gen-erally) has been heavily black since the days of slavery. It is in Salvador that the traditions of African culture are thought to have been more clearly and authentically preserved. Even white Brazilians from the South revere Salvador as the spiritual center of Afro-Brazilian religious traditions, and *Candomblé* cults from Salvador are considered to be the most powerful found anywhere in the country (see Bastide 1978; Verger 1981). African cultural images in religion, as well as in art and popular music, have been exported from Salvador to the rest of Brazil (and the world) as the consumption of Brazilian Afro-Reggae music, which orig-inated in Salvador, has also become increasingly popular internationally.

6. Many gay intellectuals, such as the Argentine novelist and playwright, Manuel Puig, and the poet and anthropologist, Néstor Perlongher, had an especially strong influence on gay life in Brazil during the late 1970s and early '80s. Puig's *O Beijo da Mulher Aranha (Kiss of the Spiderwoman)*, for example, was an important exploration of sexuality and politics under authoritarian regimes in Latin America, and as a play had a long and influential run in both Rio de Janeiro and São Paulo (see Puig 1980). Perlongher's poetry, and his anthropological studies of male prostitution (see, in particular, Perlongher 1987), were also especially important, though in a slightly more closed gay circuit.

7. Although southern Europe is the primary destination of most Brazilian *travestis*, it is not exclusively so. We have reports of *travestis* working in

a range of other European cities, such as Amsterdam and Berlin, as well as in New York and Miami in the United States. One recent Brazilian novel, *Stella Manhattan* by Silviano Santiago, for example, describes the life of a Brazilian transvestite in New York (see Santiago 1994). But the major cities of southern Europe are nonetheless correctly perceived as the most important foreign destinations for the majority of Brazilian *travestis*.

8. It seems likely that AIDS treatment may have become a less impelling reason for moving in recent years, as the Brazilian Ministry of Health, pushed by activist communities, has made important efforts to distribute antiretroviral drugs and combination therapies through the public health system, as well as to make more widely available the necessary tests that must accompany such new therapies. Still, serious logistical problems continue to exist, and it is difficult to predict how this will evolve in the future.

Chapter 7

1. Special thanks to Roger Lancaster for clearly outlining these complex dilemmas for me.
2. Again, thanks to Roger Lancaster for framing this dual movement.

Bibliography

Abelove, Henry, Michèle Aina Barale, and David M. Halperin (eds.) (1993). *The Lesbian and Gay Studies Reader*. New York and London: Routledge.

Abreu, Caio Fernando (1991). *Triângulo das Águas*. 2d ed. São Paulo: Siciliano.

Adam, Barry (1989). "Homosexuality without a Gay World: Pasivos y Activos en Nicaragua." *Out/Look* 1(4):74–82.

——— (1993). "In Nicaragua: Homosexuality without a Gay World." *Journal of Homosexuality* 24:171–81.

Aggleton, Peter (ed.) (1996). *Bisexualities and AIDS: International Perspectives*. London: Taylor and Francis.

Aina, Tade (1991). "Patterns of Bisexuality in Sub-Saharan Africa." In *Bisexuality and HIV/AIDS*, ed. Rob Tielman, Manuel Carballo, Aart Hendriks, pp. 81–90. Buffalo, NY: Prometheus.

Almeida, Vagner (ed.) (1997). *Cabaret Prevenção*. Rio de Janeiro: ABIA.

Almoguer, Tomás (1991). "Chicano Men: A Cartography of Homosexual Identity and Behavior." *Differences: A Journal of Feminist Cultural Studies* 3(2):75–100.

Alonso, Ana Maria, and Maria Teresa Koreck (1989). "Silences: 'Hispanics,' AIDS, and Sexual Practices." *Differences: A Journal of Feminist Cultural Studies* 1:101–24.

Altman, Dennis (1971). *Homosexual: Oppression and Liberation*. New York: Outerbridge and Dienstfrey.

——— (1982). *The Homosexualization of America, the Americanization of the Homosexual*. New York: St. Martin's.

——— (1986). *AIDS in the Mind of America*. New York: Doubleday.

———— (1994). *Power and Community: Organizational and Cultural Responses to AIDS*. London: Taylor and Francis.

———— (1995a). "Globalisation, the State and Identity Politics." *Pacifica Review* 7(1):69–76.

———— (1995b). "Political Sexualities: Meaning and Identities in the Time of AIDS." In *Conceiving Sexuality: Approaches to Sex Research in a Postmodern World*, ed. Richard G. Parker and John H. Gagnon, pp. 97–108. New York and London: Routledge.

———— (1995c). "The New World of Gay Asia." In *Meridian: Asian and Pacific Inscriptions*, ed. Surendrini Perera, pp. 121–38. Melbourne: Meridian.

———— (1996). "Rupture or Continuity? The Internationalization of Gay Identities." *Social Text* 14(3):78–94.

———— (1997a). "Global Gaze/Global Gays." *GLQ: A Journal of Lesbian and Gay Studies* 3:417–36.

———— (1997b). "On Global Queering." *Australian Humanities Review*, No. 2 (e-mail journal: www.lib.latrobe.edu.au).

Altman, Dennis, et al. (1989). *Homosexuality, Which Homosexuality?* Amsterdam: An Dekker/Schorer.

Anderson, Benedict (1983). *Imagined Communities: Reflections on the Origin and Spread of Nationalism*. London: Verso.

Andrade, Oswald de (1967). *Trechos Escolhidos*. Rio de Janeiro: Agir.

Appadurai, Arjun (1996). *Modernity at Large: Cultural Dimensions of Globalization*. Minneapolis and London: University of Minnesota Press.

Autran, Paula, and Raquel Almeida (1996). "Um mundo caiu: A deshonra de um coronel do Exército pego em flagrante ao manter relações homossexuais." *Veja* (October 2), p. 35.

Bacha, Edmar L., and Herbert S. Klein (eds.) (1986). *A Transição Incompleta: Brasil Desde 1945*. São Paulo: Paz e Terra.

Baer, Werner (1995). *The Brazilian Economy: Growth and Development*. 4th ed. Westport, CT: Praeger.

Bao, Daniel (1993). "Invertidos Sexuales, Tortilleras, and Maricas Machos: The Construction of Homosexuality in Buenos Aires, 1900–1950." *Journal of Homosexuality* 24:183–219.

Barbosa, Regina Maria (1997). "Negociação Sexual ou Sexo Negociado? Gênero, Sexualidade e Poder em Tempos de AIDS." Ph.D. diss., Instituto de Medicina Social, Universidade do Estado do Rio de Janeiro.

Barbosa da Silva, José Fábio (1959). "Aspectos Sociológicos do Homossexualismo em São Paulo." *Sociologia* 21(4):350–60.

Barlaeus, Gaspar (1980). *História dos Feitos Recentemente Praticados Durante Oito Anos no Brasil*. Recife: Fundação de Cultura Cidade do Recife.

Barros, Guilherme (1997). "Ceará é exemplo para o país." *Jornal do Brasil* (March 16), p. 14.

Barros, J.F.P., M.L. Santos, and M.L. Teixeira (1985). *O Rodar das Rodas: Dos Orixás e dos Homens*. Rio de Janeiro: Funarte.

Bastide, Roger (1978). *The African Religions of Brazil: Toward a Sociology of the Interpenetration of Civilizations*. Baltimore and London: Johns Hopkins University Press.

Bell, David, and Gill Valentine (eds.) (1995). *Mapping Desire*. London and New York: Routledge.

Bello, Walden, Shea Cunningham, and Bill Rau (1994). *Dark Victory: The United States, Structural Adjustment and Global Poverty*. London: Pluto.

Berman, Marshall (1982). *All That Is Solid Melts into Air: The Experience of Modernity*. London: Verso.

Berquó, Elza (1993). "Brasil, Um Caso Exemplar: Anticoncepção e Parto Cirúgicos—À Espera de uma Ação Exemplar." *Estudos Feministas* 1(2):366–81.

Bessa, Marcelo Secron (1997). *Histórias Positivas: A Literatura (Des)construindo a AIDS*. Rio de Janeiro: Record.

Birman, Patrícia (1985). "Identidade Social e Homossexualismo no Candomblé." *Religião e Sociedade* 12(1):2–21.

Blackwood, Evelyn (ed.) (1986). *Anthropology and Homosexual Behavior*. New York: Haworth.

Bleys, Rudi (1996). *The Geography of Perversion: Male-to-Male Sexual Behavior Outside the West and the Ethnographic Imagination, 1750–1918*. London: Cassell.

Block, Miguel González, and Ana Luisa Ligouri (1992). *El SIDA en los Estratos Socioeconómicas de Mexico*. Cuernavaca: Instituto Nacional de Salud Pública.

Bolton, Ralph (1992). "Mapping Terra Incognita: Sex Research for AIDS Prevention—An Urgent Agenda for the 1990s." In *The Time of AIDS: Social Analysis, Theory, and Method*, ed. Gilbert Herdt and Shirley Lindenbaum, pp. 124–58. Newbury Park, CA: Sage.

Braiterman, Jared (1994). "Beat It: An Anthropology Oddity." Ph.D. diss., Department of Anthropology, Stanford University.

Brandes, Stanley (1980). *Metaphors of Masculinity: Sex and Status in Andalusian Folklore*. Philadelphia: University of Pennsylvania Press.

Buckman, Robert T. (1996). "Current Status of the Mass Media in Latin America." In *Communication in Latin America: Journalism, Mass Media, and Society*, ed. Richard R. Cole, pp. 3–35. Wilmington, DE: Scholarly Resources.

Buell, Frederick (1994). *National Culture and the New Global System*. Baltimore and London: Johns Hopkins University Press.

Burns, E. Bradford (1993). *A History of Brazil*, 3d ed. New York: Columbia University Press.

Cáceres, Carlos (1996). "Male Bisexuality in Peru and the Prevention of AIDS." In *Bisexualities and AIDS: International Perspectives*, ed. Peter Aggleton, pp. 136–47. London: Taylor and Francis.

Câmara da Silva, Cristina Luci (1993). "Triângulo Rosa: A Busca pela Cidadania dos Homossexuais." Master's thesis, Universidade Federal do Rio de Janeiro.

Canclini, Néstor Garcia (1995). *Hybrid Cultures: Strategies for Entering and Leaving Modernity*. Minneapolis: University of Minnesota Press.

Carballo-Diéguez, Alex (1989). "Hispanic Culture, Gay Male Culture, and AIDS." *Journal of Counseling and Development* 68:26–30.

—— (1995). "Sexual HIV-Risk Behavior Among Puerto Rican Men Who Have Sex with Men." In *AIDS and the Gay and Lesbian Community*, ed. G.M. Herek and B. Green. Thousand Oaks, CA: Sage.

Cardoso, Fernando Henrique, and Enzo Faletto (1979). *Dependency and Development in Latin America*. Berkeley: University of California Press.

Carela, Túlio (1968). *Orgia (Diário Primeiro)*. Rio de Janeiro: José Álvaro Editora.

Carrillo-Rosado, Hector Guillermo (1994). "Lifting the Veil of Silence: Sexuality, Social Influence, and the Practice of AIDS Prevention in Modern Mexico." Ph.D. diss., School of Public Health, University of California, Berkeley.

Carrara, Sérgio (1996). "A Luta Antivenérea no Brasil e Seus Modelos." In *Sexualidades Brasileiras*, ed. Richard Parker and Regina Maria Barbosa, pp. 17–37. Rio de Janeiro: Relume-Dumará Editores.

Carrier, Joseph M. (1971). "Participants in Urban Mexican Male Homosexual Encounters." *Archives of Sexual Behavior* 1:279–91.

—— (1985). "Mexican Male Bisexuality." *Journal of Homosexuality* 11:75–85.

—— (1995). *De Los Outros: Intimacy and Homosexuality Among Mexican Men*. New York: Columbia University Press.

Castelo Branco, Adriana, and Sofia Cerqueira (1995). "O dinheiro cor-de-rosa." *Jornal do Brasil (Revista de Domingo)*, Ano 20, Nº 1.016, 22 de outubro, pp. 30–38.

Castro, Ruy (1992). *O Anjo Pornográfico: A Vida de Nelson Rodrigues*. São Paulo: Companhia das Letras.

Chauncey, George (1994). *Gay New York: Gender, Urban Culture, and the Making of the Gay Male World, 1890–1940*. New York: Basic Books.

Clark, David (1996). *Urban World/Global City*. London and New York: Routledge.

Cohen, Barney, and James Trussell (eds.) (1996). *Preventing and Mitigating AIDS in Sub-Saharan Africa: Research and Data Priorities for the Social and Behavioral Sciences*. Washington, DC: National Academy Press.

Connell, R.W., and G.W. Dowsett (1992). "'The Unclean Motion of the Generative Parts': Frameworks in Western Thought on Sexuality." In *Rethinking Sex: Social Theory and Sexuality Research*, ed. R.W. Connell and G.W. Dowsett, pp. 49–75. Philadelphia: Temple University Press.

Costa, Jurandir Freire (1979). *Ordem Médica e Norma Familiar*. Rio de Janeiro: Graal.

—— (1989). *História da Psiquiatria no Brasil*. Rio de Janeiro: Xenon Editora e Produtora Cultural Ltda.

——— (1992). *A Inocência e o Vício: Estudos sobre o Homoerotismo*. Rio de Janeiro: Relume-Dumará Editores.

——— (1995). *A Face e o Verso: Estudos sobre o Homoerotismo, II*. São Paulo: Estuta.

Damata, Gasparino (1976). *Os Solteirões*. Rio de Janeiro: Pallas Editora.

Daniel, Herbert (1982). *Passagem para o Próximo Sonho*. Rio de Janeiro: Editora Codecri.

——— (1987). *Alegres e Irresponsáveis Abacaxis Americanos*. Rio de Janeiro: Editora Espaço e Tempo.

Daniel, Herbert, and Leila Míccolis (1983). *Jacarés e Lobishomens (Dois Ensaios sobre a Homossexualidade)*. Rio de Janeiro: Achiamé.

Daniel, Herbert, and Richard Parker (1991). *AIDS: A Terceira Epidemia*. São Paulo: Iglu Editora.

——— (1993). *Sexuality, Politics and AIDS in Brazil*. London: Falmer.

Degler, Carl N. (1971). *Neither Black Nor White: Slavery and Race Relations in Brazil and the United States*. New York: Macmillan.

de Lauretis, Teresa (1991). "Queer Theory: Lesbian and Gay Sexualities." *Differences* 3 (2).

D'Emilio, John (1983). "Capitalism and Gay Identity." In *Powers of Desire*, ed. Ann Snitow, Christine Stansell, and Sharon Thompson, pp. 100–113. New York: Monthly Review Press.

de Moya, E. Antonio, and Rafael García (1996). "AIDS and the Enigma of Bisexuality in the Dominican Republic." In *Bisexualities and AIDS: International Perspectives*, ed. Peter Aggleton, pp. 121–35. London: Taylor and Francis.

Díaz, Rafael M. (1997). *Latino Men and HIV: Culture, Sexuality and Risk Behavior*. New York and London: Routledge.

Dowsett, Gary W. (1993). "Sustaining Safe Sex: Sexual Practices, HIV and Social Context." *AIDS* 7(suppl 1):S257–62.

Doyle, Iracy (1956). *Contribuição ao Estudo da Homossexualidade Feminina*. Rio de Janeiro: Lux.

Duberman, Martin, Martha Vicinus, and George Chauncey Jr. (eds.) (1989). *Hidden from History: Reclaiming the Gay and Lesbian Past*. New York: Meridian.

Duyves, Matias (1995). "Framing Preferences, Framing Differences: Inventing Amsterdam as a Gay Capital." In *Conceiving Sexuality: Approaches to Sex Research in a Postmodern World*, ed. Richard G. Parker and John H. Gagnon, pp. 51–68. New York and London: Routledge.

Edelman, Lee (1994). *Homographesis: Essays in Gay Literary and Cultural Theory*. New York and London: Routledge.

Escoffier, Jeffrey (1992). "Generations and Paradigms: Mainstreams in Lesbian and Gay Studies." *Journal of Homosexuality* 24(1/2):7–26.

Evans, Peter (1979). *Dependent Development: The Alliance of Multinational, State, and Local Capital in Brazil*. Princeton, NJ: Princeton University Press.

Ferreira, Mauro (1997). "Peça gay 'Giovanni' ganha nova versão musicada." *O Globo* (January 3).

Foster, David William (1991). *Gay and Lesbian Themes in Latin American Writing.* Austin: University of Texas Press.

——— (1994). *Cultural Diversity in Latin American Literature.* Albuquerque: University of New Mexico Press.

Foucault, Michel (1978). *The History of Sexuality, Volume 1: An Introduction.* New York: Pantheon.

——— (1982). "The Subject and Power." In *Michel Foucault: Beyond Structuralism and Hermeneutics*, ed. Hubert Dreyfus and Paul Rabinow. Chicago: University of Chicago Press.

Frasca, Tim (1997). *De Amores y Sombras: Poblaciones y Culturas Homo y Bisexuales en Hombres de Santiago.* Santiago: Corporación Chilena de Prevención de SIDA (CchPS).

Freyre, Gilberto (1963). *The Mansions and the Shanties.* New York: Alfred A. Knopf.

Friedmann, John (1995). "The World City Hypothesis." In *World Cities in a World-System*, ed. Paul L. Knox and Peter J. Taylor, pp. 317–31. Cambridge: Cambridge University Press.

Fry, Peter (1982). *Para Inglês Ver: Identidade e Política na Cultura Brasileira.* Rio de Janeiro: Zahar.

——— (1985). "Male Homosexuality and Spirit Possession in Brazil." *Journal of Homosexuality* 11(3/4):137–53.

Fry, Peter, and Edward MacRae (1983). *O Que É Homossexualidade.* São Paulo: Editora Brasiliense.

Furtado, Celso (1963). *The Economic Growth of Brazil: A Survey from Colonial to Modern Times.* Berkeley and Los Angeles: University of California Press.

Fuss, Diana (1991). *Inside/Out: Lesbian Theories, Gay Theories.* New York and London: Routledge.

Galvão, Jane (1997). "As Respostas das Organizações Não-Governamentais Brasileiras frente à Epidemia de HIV/AIDS." In *Políticas, Instituições e AIDS: Enfrentando a Epidemia no Brasil*, ed. Richard Parker, pp. 69–108. Rio de Janeiro: Jorge Zahar Editor/ABIA.

Gelder, Ken, and Sarah Thornton (eds.) (1997). *The Subcultures Reader.* London and New York and London: Routledge.

George, Susan, and Fabrizio Sabelli (1994). *Faith and Credit: The World Bank's Secular Empire.* London: Penguin.

Gevisser, Mark, and Edwin Cameron (eds.) (1995). *Defiant Desires: Gay and Lesbian Lives in South Africa.* New York and London: Routledge.

Gilmore, David (1990). *Manhood in the Making: Cultural Concepts of Masculinity.* New Haven and London: Yale University Press.

Gluckman, Amy, and Betsey Reed (1997). *Homoeconomics: Capitalism, Community, and Lesbian and Gay Life.* New York and London: Routledge.

Gontijo, Fabiano de Souza (1995). "Quand l'arc-en-ciel s'écroule sur la tribu: homosexualités et SIDAs a Copacabana." Master's thesis, Centre de Lettres et de Sciences Humaines, Université de Provence.

Green, Duncan (1995). *Silent Revolution: The Rise of Market Economics in Latin America*. London: Cassell.

Green, James (1996). *Beyond Carnival: Homosexuality in Twentieth-Century Brazil*. Ph.D. diss., Department of History, University of California, Los Angeles.

Greenberg, David F. (1988). *The Construction of Homosexuality*. Chicago: University of Chicago Press.

Gregor, Thomas (1985). *Anxious Pleasures: The Sexual Lives of an Amazonian People*. Chicago: University of Chicago Press.

Guedes, Cilene (1996). "Iguais . . . para sempre: Sonhos e medos de quem aguarda a aprovação da lei sobre união civil de gays." *Jornal do Brasil (Revista de Domingo)*, June 2, pp. 14–18.

Guimarães, Carmen Dora (1974). "O Homossexual Visto por Entendidos." Master's thesis, Programa de Pós-Graduação em Antropologia Social, Museu Nacional, Universidade Federal do Rio de Janeiro.

Guimarães, Carmen Dora, Veriano Terto Jr., and Richard Parker (1992). "Homossexualidade, Bissexualidade, e HIV/AIDS no Brasil: Uma Bibliografia Anotada das Ciências Sociais e Afins." *Physis* 2(1):151–83.

Haberly, David T. (1983). *Three Sad Races: Racial Identity and National Consciousness in Brazilian Literature*. Cambridge: Cambridge University Press.

Halperin, David (1990). *One Hundred Years of Homosexuality*. New York and London: Routledge.

Harvey, David (1990). *The Condition of Postmodernity*. Cambridge, MA, and Oxford: Blackwell.

Hawkeswood, William G. (1996). *One of the Children: Gay Black Men in Harlem*. Berkeley and Los Angeles: University of California Press.

Heilborn, Maria Luiza (1992). "Dois é Par: Conjugalidade, Gênero e Identidade Sexual em Contexto Igualitário." Ph.D. diss., Programa de Pós-Graduação em Antropologia Social, Museu Nacional, Universidade Federal do Rio de Janeiro.

——— (1995). "Vivendo a Dois: Arranjos Conjugais em Comparação." *Revista Brasileira de Estudos Populacionais*, pp. 143–56. São Paulo: Associação Brasileira de Estudos Populacionais (ABEP).

——— (1996). "Ser ou Estar Homossexual: Dilemas de Construção de Identidade Social." In *Sexualidades Brasileiras*, ed. Richard Parker and Regina Maria Barbosa, pp. 136–48. Rio de Janeiro: Relume-Dumará Editores.

Herdt, Gilbert (1981). *Guardians of the Flutes: Idioms of Masculinity*. New York: McGraw-Hill.

——— (1987). *The Sambia: Ritual and Gender in New Guinea*. New York: Holt, Rinehart, and Winston.

———— (1997). *Same Sex , Different Cultures: Gays and Lesbians Across Cultures*. Boulder, CO, and Oxford: Westview.

———— (ed.) (1984). *Ritualized Homosexuality in Melanesia*. Berkeley and Los Angeles: University of California Press.

———— (ed.) (1992). *Gay Culture in America: Essays from the Field*. Boston: Beacon.

Herdt, Gilbert, and Andrew Boxer (1993). *Children of Horizons: How Gay and Lesbian Youth Are Forging a New Way Out of the Closet*. Boston: Beacon.

Herdt, Gilbert, and Robert Stoller (1990). *Intimate Communications: Erotics and the Study of Culture*. New York: Columbia University Press.

Hollanda, Chico Buarque de (1978). *Ópera do Malandro*. São Paulo: Círculo do Livro.

Hyam, Robert (1990). *Empire and Sexuality: The British Experience*. Manchester: Manchester University Press.

IBGE (1992). *Censo Demográfico de 1991: Análises Preliminares*. Rio de Janeiro: Instituto Brasileiro de Geografia e Estatística.

Izazola, José Antônio (1994). "La Bisexualidad." In *Antologia Sobre Sexualidade Humana*, tomo 1, ed. M.A. Porrua. Mexico City.

Izazola, José Antonio, J.L. Valdespino, S.L. Gortmaker, J. Townsend, J. Becker, M. Palacios, N. Muller, and Jaime Sepulveda (1991). "HIV-1 Seropositivity and Behavioral and Sociological Risks Among Homosexual and Bisexual Men in Six Mexican Cities." *Journal of Acquired Immune Deficiency Syndrome* 4:614–22.

Jackson, Peter A. (1997). "*Kathoey*><Gay><Man: The Historical Emergence of Gay Male Identity in Thailand." In *Sites of Desire, Economies of Pleasure: Sexualities in Asia and the Pacific*, ed. Lenore Manderson and Margaret Jolly, pp. 166–90. Chicago: University of Chicago Press.

Jornal do Brasil (1998). "Cidadania homossexual: Cabeleireiro decide enfrentar motéis que recusam casais gays" (January 8), p. 20.

Kahn, Shivananda (1996). "Under the Blanket: Bisexualities and AIDS in India." In *Bisexualities and AIDS: International Perspectives*, ed. Peter Aggleton, pp. 161–77. London: Taylor and Francis.

Katz, Jonathan Ned (1995). *The Invention of Heterosexuality*. New York: Dutton.

Kelly, Raymond C. (1976). "Witchcraft and Sexual Relations." In *Man and Woman in the New Guinea Highlands*, ed. P. Brown and G. Buchbinder, pp. 35–53. Washington, DC: American Anthropological Association.

Kennedy, Elizabeth, and Madeline Davis (1993). *Boots of Leather, Slippers of Gold: The History of a Lesbian Community*. New York: Penguin.

Klein, Charles H. (1996). "AIDS, Activism and the Social Imagination." Ph.D. diss., Department of Anthropology, University of Michigan.

———— (1998). "Gender, Sexuality and AIDS Prevention in Brazil." *NACLA Report on the Americas* 31(4):27–32.

Knox, Paul L., and Peter J. Taylor (eds.) (1995). *World Cities in a World-System*. Cambridge: Cambridge University Press.

Kulick, Don (1997). "The Gender of Brazilian Transgendered Prostitutes." *American Anthropologist* 99(3):574–85.

Kutsche, Paul (1983). "Situational Homosexuality in Costa Rica." *Anthropology Research Group on Homosexuality Newsletter* 4(4):6–13.

———— (1995). "Two Truths about Costa Rica." In *Latin American Male Homosexualities*, ed. Stephen O. Murray, pp. 111–37. Albuquerque: University of New Mexico Press.

Kutsche, Paul, and J. Bryan Page, (1991). "Male Sexual Identity in Costa Rica." *Latin American Anthropology Review* 3:7–14.

Lancaster, Roger N. (1988). "Subject Honor and Object Shame: The Construction of Male Homosexuality and Stigma in Nicaragua." *Ethnology* 27(2):111–25.

———— (1992). *Life Is Hard: Machismo, Danger, and the Intimacy of Power in Nicaragua*. Berkeley and Los Angeles: University of California Press.

———— (1995). "'That We Should All Turn Queer?' Homosexual Stigma in the Making of Manhood and the Breaking of a Revolution in Nicaragua." In *Conceiving Sexuality: Approaches to Sex Research in a Postmodern World*, ed. Richard G. Parker and John H. Gagnon, pp. 135–56. New York and London: Routledge.

———— (1997). "Sexual Positions: Caveats and Second Thoughts on 'Categories.'" *The Americas* 54 (1 July):1–16.

Lancaster, Roger N., and Micaela di Leonardo (eds.) (1997). *The Gender/Sexuality Reader: Culture, History, Political Economy*. New York and London: Routledge.

Landes, Ruth (1946). *The City of Women*. New York: Macmillan.

Larvie, Patrick (1997). "Homophobia and the Ethnoscape of Sex Work in Rio de Janeiro." In *Sexual Cultures and Migration in the Era of AIDS: Anthropological and Demographic Perspectives*, ed. Gilbert Herdt, pp. 143–64. Oxford: Clarendon.

Lash, Scott, and John Urry (1994). *Economies of Signs and Space*. London: Sage.

Levine, Martin P., Peter M. Nardi, and John H. Gagnon (eds.) (1997). *In Changing Times: Gay Men and Lesbians Encounter AIDS*. Chicago: University of Chicago Press.

Lewin, Ellen (1993). *Lesbian Mothers*. Ithaca, NY: Cornell University Press.

Lewin, Ellen, and William Leap (eds.) (1996). *Out in the Field: Reflections of Lesbian and Gay Anthropologists*. Urbana: University of Illinois Press.

Leyland, Winston (ed.) (1979). *Now the Volcano: An Anthology of Latin American Gay Literature*. San Francisco: Gay Sunshine Press.

———— (ed.) (1983). *My Deep Dark Pain Is Love: A Collection of Latin American Fiction*. San Francisco: Gay Sunshine Press.

Ligouri, Ana Luisa, Miguel González Block, and Peter Aggleton (1996). "Bisexuality and HIV/AIDS in Mexico." In *Bisexualities and AIDS: Inter-*

national Perspectives, ed. Peter Aggleton, pp. 76–98. London: Taylor and Francis.

Lima, Estácio (1934). *A Inversão dos Sexos*. Rio de Janeiro: Editora Guanabara.

Lindenbaum, Shirley (1989). "Anthropology's Perspective on Human Sexual Behavior." In *AIDS, Sexual Behavior and Intravenous Drug Use*, ed. Charles Turner, Heather Miller, and Lincoln Moses, pp. 157–64. Washington, DC: National Research Council.

Lucena, Eliana (1996). "Comissão aprova união homossexual." *Jornal do Brasil* (December 11).

Lumsden, Ian (1991). *Homosexuality and the State in Mexico*. Mexico City: Canadian Gay Archives.

——— (1996). *Machos, Maricones and Gays: Cuba and Homosexuality*. Philadelphia: Temple University Press.

Lurie, Peter, Percy Hintzen, and R.A. Lowe (1995). "Socioeconomic Obstacles to HIV Prevention and Treatment in Developing Countries: The Roles of the International Monetary Fund and the World Bank." *AIDS* 9:539–46.

MacRae, Edward (1983). "Em Defesa do Gueto." *Novos Estudos Cebrap* 2(1):53–60.

——— (1990). *A Construção da Igualdade: Identidade Sexual e Política no Brasil da "Abertura."* Campinas: Editora da Unicamp.

——— (1992). "Homosexual Identities in Transitional Brazilian Politics." In *The Making of Social Movements in Latin America*, ed. Sonia Alvarez and Arturo Escobar, pp. 185–203. Boulder, CO: Westview.

Manderson, Lenore, and Margaret Jolly (eds.) (1997). *Sites of Desire, Economies of Pleasure: Sexualities in Asia and the Pacific*. Chicago: University of Chicago Press.

Margolis, Maxine L. (1994). *Little Brazil: An Ethnography of Brazilian Immigrants in New York City*. Princeton, NJ: Princeton University Press.

Martine, George (1996). "Brazil's Fertility Decline, 1965–1995." *Population Review* 22(1):47–75.

Martine, George et al. (1990). "A Urbanização do Brasil: Retrospectiva, Componentes e Perspectiva." In *Prioridades e Perspectivas de Políticas Públicas na Década de 90*, Vol. 3. Brasília: IPEA/IPLAN.

Mendes-Leite, R. (1993). "The Game of Appearances: The 'Ambiguexuality' in Brazilian Culture of Sexuality." *Journal of Homosexuality* 25(3):35–59.

Minayo, Maria Cecília (ed.) (1995). *Os Muitos Brasis: Saúde e População na Década de 80*. São Paulo and Rio de Janeiro: Hucitec-Abrasco.

Mosley, Paul, Jane Harrigan, and John Toye (1991). *Aid and Power: The World Bank and Policy Based Lending*. 2 volumes. London: Routledge.

Mott, Luiz (1985). "AIDS: Reflexões sobre a Sodomia." *Comunicações do ISER* 4(17):32–41.

——— (1986). "Escravidão e Homossexualidade." In *História da Sexuali-*

dade no Brasil, ed. Ronaldo Vainfas, pp. 19–40. Rio de Janeiro: Graal.

——— (1987a). "Gilete na Carne: Etnografia das Automutilações dos Travestis da Bahia." *Revista do Instituto de Medicina Social de São Paulo* 4(1):41–56.

——— (1987b). *O Lesbianismo no Brasil*. Porto Alegre: Mercado Aberto.

——— (1988). *Escravidão, Homossexualidade e Demonologia*. São Paulo: Ícone Editora.

——— (1995). "The Gay Movement and Human Rights in Brazil." In *Latin American Male Homosexualities*, ed. Stephen O. Murray, pp. 221–30. Albuquerque: University of New Mexico Press.

——— (1997). *Homofobia: A Violação dos Direitos Humanos de Gays, Lésbicas, e Travestis no Brasil*. Salvador and San Francisco: Grupo Gay da Bahia and The International Gay and Lesbian Human Rights Commission.

Murray, Alison (1991). *No Money, No Honey*. Oxford: Oxford University Press.

Murray, Stephan O. (1992). "The 'Underdevelopment' of 'Gay' Homosexuality in Mesoamerica, Peru, and Thailand." In *Modern Homosexualities*, ed. Ken Plummer, pp. 29–38. London and New York and London: Routledge.

——— (ed.) (1995). *Latin American Male Homosexualities*. Albuquerque: University of New Mexico Press.

——— (1996). *American Gay*. Chicago and London: University of Chicago Press.

Newton, Esther (1993). *Cherry Grove, Fire Island: Sixty Years in America's First Gay and Lesbian Town*. Boston: Beacon.

NoMar (1996). "Por Que Não os Gays." No. 652 (November 14), p. 3.

Oliveira, Roberta (1997). "Paulo Autran vive novo homossexual." *Jornal do Brasil* (March 19).

Page, Joseph A. (1995). *The Brazilians*. Reading, MA: Addison-Wesley.

Parker, Richard G. (1985). "Masculinity, Femininity and Homosexuality: On the Anthropological Interpretation of Sexual Meanings in Brazil." *Journal of Homosexuality* 11(3/4):155–63.

——— (1987). "Acquired Immunodeficiency Syndrome in Urban Brazil." *Medical Anthropology Quarterly*, n.s., 1(2):155–75.

——— (1989). "Youth, Identity, and Homosexuality: The Changing Shape of Sexual Life in Brazil." *Journal of Homosexuality* 17(3/4):267–87.

——— (1991). *Bodies, Pleasures and Passions: Sexual Culture in Contemporary Brazil*. Boston: Beacon.

——— (1993). "The Negotiation of Difference: Male Prostitution, Bisexual Behaviour and HIV Transmission." In *Sexuality, Politics and AIDS in Brazil*, ed. Herbert Daniel and Richard Parker, pp. 85–96. London and Washington, DC: The Falmer Press.

——— (1994). *A Construção da Solidariedade: AIDS, Sexualidade e Política no Brasil*. Rio de Janeiro: Relume-Dumará Editores.

——— (1997a) "Migration, Sexual Subcultures, and HIV/AIDS in Brazil." In

Sexual Cultures and Migration in the Era of AIDS: Anthropological and Demographic Perspectives, ed. Gilbert Herdt, pp. 55–69. Oxford: Clarendon Press.

———— (1997b) "The Carnivalization of the World." In *The Gender/Sexuality Reader: Culture, History, Political Economy*, ed. Roger N. Lancaster and Micaela di Leonardo, pp. 361–77. New York and London: Routledge.

Parker, Richard G., and Manuel Carballo (1990). "Qualitative Research on Homosexual and Bisexual Behavior Relevant to HIV/AIDS." *Journal of Sex Research* 27(4):497–525.

Parker, Richard G., et al. (1995). "AIDS Prevention and Gay Community Mobilization in Brazil." *Development* 2:49–53.

Parker, Richard, Cristiana Bastos, Jane Galvão, and José Stalin Pedrosa (eds.) (1994). *A AIDS no Brasil, 1982–1992*. Rio de Janeiro: Relume-Dumará Editores.

Parker, Richard G., and John H. Gagnon (eds.) (1995). *Conceiving Sexuality: Approaches to Sex Research in a Postmodern World*. New York and London: Routledge.

Parker, Richard, and Regina Maria Barbosa (eds.) (1996). *Sexualidades Brasileiras*. Rio de Janeiro: Relume-Dumará Editores.

Parker, Richard, and Veriano Terto Jr. (eds.) (1998). *Entre Homens: Homossexualidade e AIDS no Brasil*. Rio de Janeiro: ABIA.

Peixoto da Mota, Murilo (1996). "Gênero e Sexualidade: Fragmentos de Identidade Masculina nos Tempos da AIDS." Master's thesis, Escola Nacional de Saúde Pública, Rio de Janeiro.

Penteado, Darcy (1979). *Teoremambo*. São Paulo: Livraria Cultura Editora.

———— (1981). *Nivaldo e Jerônimo*. Rio de Janeiro: Codecri.

Pereira, Carlos Alberto Messeder (1979). "Desvio e/ou Reprodução." In *Testemunha Ocular: Textos de Antropologia Social do Cotidiano*, ed. Everardo Rocha et al., pp. 102–107. Rio de Janeiro: Tempo Literário.

———— (1994). "O Direito de Curar: Homossexualidade e Medicina Legal no Brasil nos Anos 30." In *A Invenção do Brasil Moderno*, ed. Micael M. Herschmann and Carlos Alberto Messeder Pereira. Rio de Janeiro: Rocco.

Perlongher, Néstor (1987). *O Negócio do Michê: Prostituição Viril em São Paulo*. São Paulo: Editora Brasiliense.

Pires de Almeida, J.R. (1906). *Homossexualismo (A Libertinagem no Rio de Janeiro)*. Rio de Janeiro: Laemmert and C.

Plummer, Ken (ed.) (1992). *Modern Homosexualities: Fragments of Lesbian and Gay Experience*. London and New York and London: Routledge.

Portela, Anna Paula, Maria Cecília Mello, and Simone Grilo (1998). "Not Like Our Mothers: Reproductive Choice and the Emergence of Citizenship among Brazilian Rural Workers, Domestic Workers and Housewives." In *Negotiating Reproductive Rights: Women's Perspectives Across Countries and Cultures*, ed. Rosalind P. Petchesky and Karen

Judd. London: Zed Books.

Portes, Alejandro, and Robert L. Bach (1985). *Latin Journey: Cuban and Mexican Immigrants in the United States*. Berkeley and Los Angeles: University of California Press.

Prieur, Annick (1996). "Domination and Desire: Male Homosexuality and the Construction of Masculinity in Mexico." In *Machos, Mistresses, Madonnas: Contesting the Power of Latin American Gender Imagery*, ed. Marit Melhuus and Kristi Anne Stølen, pp. 83–107. London and New York: Verso.

Puig, Manuel (1980). *O Beijo da Mulher Aranha*. Rio de Janeiro: Codecri.

Reis, Toni (ed.) (1995). *I Encontro Brasileiro de Gays e Lésbicas que Trabalham com AIDS/I Brazilian Conference of Gays and Lesbians who work with AIDS, VIII Encontro Brasileiro de Gays e Lésbicas/VIII Brazilian Conference of Gays and Lesbians*. Conference Report. Curitiba: Grupo Dignidade.

Ribeiro, Leonídio (1938). *Homossexualismo e Endocrinologia*. Rio de Janeiro: Francisco Alves.

Roscoe, Will (1991). *The Zuni Man-Woman*. Albuquerque: University of New Mexico Press.

Sahato, G.S. (1968). "An Economic Analysis of Migration in Brazil." *Journal of Political Economy* 76(2).

Said, Edward (1978). *Orientalism*. London: Penguin.

Santiago, Silviano (1993). *Uma História de Família*. Rio de Janeiro: Rocco.

——— (1994). *Stella Manhattan*. Durham and London: Duke University Press.

Santos, Roberto (1931). *Caracteres Sexuais Neutros e Intersexualidade*. Rio de Janeiro: Tipografia Artes Gráficas.

Schiefflin, Edward L. (1976). *The Sorrow of the Lonely and the Burning of the Dancers*. New York: St. Martin's.

Schifter, Jacobo, and Johnny Madrigal (1992). *Hombres que Amam Hombres*. San José, Costa Rica: ILEP-SIDA.

Sedgwick, Eve K. (1990). *Epistemology of the Closet*. Berkeley and Los Angeles: University of California Press.

Segal, Danielle, and Marques Casara (1996). "O Drama de um Soldado Homossexual." *Manchete* (October 26), pp. 10–17.

Seffner, Fernando (1995). "AIDS, Estigma e Corpo." In *Corpo e Significado: Ensaios de Antropologia Social*, ed. Ondina Fachel Leal, pp. 391–415. Porto Alegre: Editora da Universidade.

Serran, Leopoldo (1979). *Shirley: A História de um Travesti*. Rio de Janeiro: Editora Codecri Ltda.

Sheperd, Gill (1987). "Rank, Genders and Homosexuality: Mombasa as a Key to Understanding Sexual Options." In *The Cultural Construction of Sexuality*, ed. Pat Caplan. London: Tavistock.

Silva, Aguinaldo (1976). *A República dos Assassinos*. Rio de Janeiro: Civilização Brasileira.

Silva, Aguinaldo, and Doc Comparato (1981). *As Tias*. Rio de Janeiro: Achiamé.

Silva, Hélio (1993). *Travesti: A Invenção do Feminino*. Rio de Janeiro: Relume-Dumará Editores.

Silva, Hélio, and Cristina Florentino (1996). "A Sociedade dos Travestis: Espelhos, Papéis e Interpretações." In *Sexualidades Brasileiras*, ed. Richard Parker and Regina Maria Barbosa, pp. 105–118. Rio de Janeiro: Relume Dumará Editores.

Skidmore, Thomas (1993). *Black into White: Race and Nationality in Brazilian Thought*. Rev. ed. Durham, NC: Duke University Press.

Skidmore, Thomas, and Peter H. Smith (1997). *Modern Latin America*, 4th ed. Oxford: Oxford University Press.

Smart, Barry (1993). *Postmodernity*. London and New York and London: Routledge.

Souza, Herbert de (1993). *Escritos Indignados*. Rio de Janeiro: Rio Fundo Editora/IBASE.

——— (1994). *A Cura da AIDS/The Cure of AIDS*, ed. Richard G. Parker. Rio de Janeiro: Relume-Dumará Editores.

Souza, Pedro de (1997). *Confidências da Carne: O Público e o Privado na Enunciação da Sexualidade*. Campinas: Editora da UNICAMP.

Standing, H., and M.N. Kisekka (1989). *Sexual Behaviour in Sub-Saharan Africa: A Review and Annotated Bibliography*. London: Overseas Development Administration.

Staubhaar, Joseph D. (1996). "The Electronic Media in Brazil." In *Communication in Latin America: Journalism, Mass Media, and Society*, ed. Richard R. Cole, pp. 217–43. Wilmington, DE: Scholarly Resources.

Stein, Edward (ed.) (1992). *Forms of Desire: Sexual Orientation and the Social Constructionist Controversy*. New York and London: Routledge.

Stepan, Alfred (ed.) (1973). *Authoritarian Brazil: Origin, Policy and Future*. New Haven: Yale University Press.

Stoler, Ann Laura (1995). *Race and the Education of Desire: Foucault's History of Sexuality and the Colonial Order of Things*. Durham, NC: Duke University Press.

Tan, Michael (1994). "Recent HIV/AIDS Trends Among Men Who Have Sex with Men." Plenary lecture presented at the Tenth International Conference on AIDS, Yokohama, Japan, August.

——— (1995). "From *Bakla* to Gay: Shifting Gender Identities and Sexual Behaviors in the Philippines." In *Conceiving Sexuality: Approaches to Sex Research in a Postmodern World*, ed. Richard G. Parker and John H. Gagnon, pp. 85–96. New York and London: Routledge.

Taylor, Clark (1978). "El Ambiente: Male Homosexual Social Life in Mexico City." Ph.D. diss., Department of Anthropology, University of California, Berkeley.

——— (1985). "Mexican Male Homosexual Interaction in Public Contexts." *Journal of Homosexuality* 11(3/4):117–36.

Terto Jr., Veriano (1989). "No Escurinho do Cinema: Sociabilidade Orgiástica nas Tardes Cariocas." Master's thesis, Deparamento de Psicologia, Pontífica Universidade Católica, Rio de Janeiro.

——— (1996). "Homossexuais Soropositivos e Soropositivos Homossexuais: Questões da Homossexualidade Masculina em Tempos de AIDS." In *Sexualidades Brasileiras*, ed. Richard Parker and Regina Maria Barbosa, pp. 90–104. Rio de Janeiro: Relume-Dumará Editores.

——— (1997). "Reinventando a Vida: Histórias sobre Homossexualidade e AIDS no Brasil." Ph.D. diss., Instituto de Medicina Social, Universidade do Estado do Rio de Janeiro.

Terto Jr., Veriano, et al. (1994). "AIDS Prevention for Men Who Have Sex with Men in Rio de Janeiro and São Paulo." Paper presented at the Tenth International Conference on AIDS, Yokohama, Japan.

Thuswohl, Maurício (1997). "Roberta Close enfim é mulher, na Suíça." *Jornal do Brasil* (April 24), p. 5.

Trevisan, João Silvério (1986). *Perverts in Paradise*. London: Gay Men's Press.

United Nations (1991). *World Urbanization Prospects*. New York: United Nations.

Vance, Carole S. (1991). "Anthropology Rediscovers Sexuality: A Theoretical Comment." *Social Science and Medicine* 33(8):875–84.

Verger, Pierre (1981). *Orixás: Deuses Iorubás na África e no Novo Mundo*. Salvador: Editora Corrupio.

Wafer, James (1991). *The Taste of Blood: Spirit Possession in Brazilian Candomblé*. Philadelphia: University of Pennsylvania Press.

Wagley, Charles (1968). "The Concept of Social Race in the Americas." In *The Latin American Tradition: Essays on the Unity and the Diversity of Latin American Culture*, ed. Charles Wagley, pp. 155–74. New York: Columbia University Press.

Waters, Malcolm (1995). *Globalization*. London and New York and London: Routledge.

Weeks, Jeffrey (1985). *Sexuality and Its Discontents: Meanings, Myths and Modern Sexualities*. London: Routledge and Kegan Paul.

——— (1991). *Against Nature: Essays on History, Sexuality and Identity*. London: Rivers Oram Press.

Weston, Kath (1991). *Families We Choose: Gays, Lesbians and Kinship*. New York: Columbia University Press.

——— (1993). "Lesbian/Gay Studies in the House of Anthropology." *Annual Review of Anthropology* 22:339–67.

Whitam, Fred (1979). "The Entendidos: Middle Class Gay Life in São Paulo." *Gay Sunshine Press* 38/39:16–17.

Whitam, Fred, and Robin Mathy (1986). *Male Homosexuality in Four Societies*. New York: Praeger.

Whitehead, Harriet (1981). "The Bow and the Burden Strap: A New Look at Institutionalized Homosexuality in Native North America." In *Sex-

ual Meanings: The Cultural Construction of Gender and Sexuality, ed. Sherry B. Ortner and Harriet Whitehead, pp. 80–115. Cambridge: Cambridge University Press.

Whittle, Stephen (1994). *The Margins of the City: Gay Men's Urban Lives*. Brookfield, VT: Ashgate.

Williams, Walter (1986). *The Spirit and the Flesh: Sexual Diversity in American Indian Culture*. Boston: Beacon.

Wilson, Carter (1995). *Hidden in the Blood: A Personal Investigation of AIDS in the Yucatan*. New York: Columbia University Press.

Wright, Timothy (1993). "Male Homosexuality and AIDS in Santa Cruz, Bolivia: Sexual Culture and Public Health Policy." Projeto Contra el SIDA. Report submitted to the United States Agency for International Development.

Wright, Timothy, and Richard Wright (1997). "Developing a Gay Community: Bolivia, Homosexuality and AIDS." In *Sociological Control of Homosexuality: A Multi-Nation Comparison*, ed. Donald J. West and Richard Green. New York: Plenum.

Young, Alan (1972). "Gay Gringo in Brazil." In *The Gay Liberation Book*, ed. L. Richmond and G. Noguera, pp. 60–67. San Francisco: Ramparts.

Young, Robert J.C. (1995). *Colonial Desire: Hybridity in Theory, Culture and Race*. London and New York and London: Routledge.

Index